D0130951

THE
GORILLA
GAME

The
GORILLA GAME

An Investor's Guide to Picking Winners in High Technology

**Geoffrey A. Moore,
Paul Johnson, and Tom Kippola**

HarperBusiness
A Division of HarperCollins*Publishers*

THE GORILLA GAME. Copyright © 1998 by Geoffrey A. Moore, Paul Johnson, and Tom Kippola. All rights reserved. Printed in the United States of America. No part of this book may be used or reproduced in any manner whatsoever without written permission except in the case of brief quotations embodied in critical articles and reviews. For information address HarperCollins Publishers, Inc., 10 East 53rd Street, New York, NY 10022.

HarperCollins books may be purchased for educational, business, or sales promotional use. For information please write: Special Markets Department, HarperCollins Publishers, Inc., 10 East 53rd Street, New York, NY 10022.

FIRST EDITION

Designed by Irving Perkins Associates

Library of Congress Cataloging-in-Publication Data
Moore, Geoffrey A., 1946–
    The gorilla game : an investor's guide to picking winners in high technology / Geoffrey Moore, Paul Johnson, Tom Kippola.
        p.   cm.
    Includes index.
    ISBN 0–88730–887–2
    1. Stocks.   2. High technology industries—Finance.   3. Investment analysis.
    I. Johnson, Paul, 1960–   . II. Kippola, Tom.
    III. Title.
    HG4661.M59   1998   97–50099
    332.63'22—dc21   CIP

---

98 99 00 01 02 ❖/RRD 10 9 8 7 6 5 4 3 2

To Wayne and Mary Ann Kippola, who took a chance in the early 90s on "overvalued" stocks like Oracle, Microsoft, Intel, and Cisco, and by so doing became the first beta testers of the gorilla game.

TK

To my wife, Pamela; she always believed.

PJ

To my children—Margaret, for the gifts of intelligence and humor; Michael, for the gifts of compassion and insight; and Anna, for the gifts of sensitivity and joy. There is not a day that I do not rejoice in your being.

GM

Contents

Part Four: Passing the Baton

Acknowledgments

The Gorilla Game has been a collaboration from the start, beginning with three would-be authors, no two of whom could have written this book. But it quickly scaled beyond the three of us as we went in search of validation, criticism, insight, and just plain help.

In this context, Geoff would like to extend special thanks to those hardy few to whom he sent portions of the manuscript in various states of dress and undress in hopes that they could penetrate what he could not. Early on, this led to a wake-up call from Jeff Tarter at *Softletter*, which sent us all scurrying back to our keyboards, and later on, a round of finer tuning came as a result of thoughtful feedback from Jim Lattin at the Stanford Business School. In between, we got loads of useful and detailed commentary from Bill Meade, a new friend, an ex-professor from the University of Missouri business school, now on his way to Hewlett Packard. And finally, there was a special dialogue with Russell Redenbaugh, a philosopher and businessman in equal portions, which Geoff trusts will extend itself beyond the boundaries of this effort.

Paul would like to extend special thanks to Ara Mizrakjian, who among other things helped us discover the right flow of chapters and content, Roger McNamee, who is as delightful and supportive a critic as one could ever hope for, and Bill Gurley, who helped us tremendously in understanding the implications of our ideas for the Internet market. In addition, he thanks Steven Cheheyl, Bob Dahl, and Terry Eger, all of whom made substantive contributions to the story of Cisco in Chapter 9, as well as Frank Walsh and Craig Benson, who have had a big impact on his thinking. And most of all, he offers a very special thanks to Michael Mauboussin, Managing Director, Credit Suisse First Boston, who taught him everything he knows about CAP—success may breed a thousand fathers, but Michael is the true, and only, father of the CAP theory.

Tom extends special thanks to Yan Ness, President of WorkWell Health & Safety Systems, and George Richmond, President of The Richmond Corporation, both of whom pushed us on the all important marketing strategy question "who is the target reader for this book?" and to Anthony Wooten of Computer Associates for his input on the customer service and sales force automation stocks discussed in Chapter 10. He also is delighted to acknowledge Steve Carnevale, Partner at Talkot Capital, for his input and feedback on the book, for the numerous conversations they have had about high-tech stocks well before *The Gorilla Game* was born, and for his friendship.

Other reviewers who reviewed drafts of the manuscript to add to our thinking, or simply to put in a word of encouragement at a time when it was most needed, include Norm Fogelsong, Richard Furse, Michael Solomon, Sven Hahr, Ken Fox, Doug Alexander, Sean McDonald, Matt Marshall, Keith Benjamin, Cecelia Brancato, Bob Castle, Nick Colas, Tom Eddy, Andre de Baubigny, Bob Heath, Greg Kouvelas, Chris Nawn, Steve Nill, Andy Page, Paul Sherer, Paul Silverstein, Doug Van Dorsten, Marc Weiss, Ed Weller, Irene Yu, Paul Sonkin, Mike Tanner, Paul Wiefels, Philip Lay, and Mark Cavender. We are very grateful for all the patience and thoughtfulness showed to us.

Books that contributed significantly to our thinking include *Computer Wars*, by Charles H. Ferguson and Charles R. Morris, *Complexity*, by M. Mitchell Waldrop, *Out of Control*, by Kevin Kelly, *The Theory of Investment Value*, by John Burr Williams, *Quest for Value*, by G. Bennett Stewart, III, *Creating Shareholder Value*, by Alfred Rappaport, *Competitive Advantage* and *Competitive Strategy*, by Michael Porter, and all the great stuff written by Warren Buffet.

Meanwhile, at the other end of this production process, we were led gently by David Conti at HarperBusiness and Jim Levine, our literary agent. One thing we have learned about ourselves as a collaborative team is that the ability to make deadlines is not our strongest suit. This put David and Jim under continued pressure to press for deliverables while still pushing back to improve quality. They couldn't have been nicer, and given what they had to work with, couldn't have been more effective. Our collective and collaborative thanks.

In a similar vein we'd like to thank the two public relations teams—one at The Horn Group and the other at HarperCollins—for their efforts in launching this book, and in particular Bonnie Harris at the Horn Group for her enthusiastic leadership and support.

Then there was the day-to-day production support provided by three wonderfully supportive colleagues, Claire Le Juez at Banc-America Robertson Stephens, and Angelynn Hanley and Jennifer Collins at The Chasm Group. Together, they helped keep things under control during the entire project, performed heroic feats of cross-platform manuscript management, and lied cheerfully as to our whereabouts on an as-needed basis. Only authors know how much this kind of support means, and we are profoundly grateful for it.

At home—which is where books get written for the most part— huge burdens fall onto spouses and fiancees. Tom is deeply grateful to his fiancee, Elizabeth Plum, for the numerous roles she played in this book project, including reviewer, writer's block doctor, thesaurus, dictionary, and grammar checker. In addition she was his number one fan while writing this book, and proactively provided whatever was required to keep him writing and moving ahead. Whether he needed motivational support after a long weekend of writing and researching, good strong coffee at 2 AM, conversation with someone about an idea, or laughs to lighten things up, she was there.

Geoffrey and Marie have been married for nearly 30 years, and he is deeply aware that he has put her through all this before. He continues to be amazed by the power of her love to overcome the 4 AM alarm clocks, random occurrences of deep distraction, and bouts of cluelessness, vagueness, or just plain weirdness that he imposes upon her. There is no one on the planet whose ideas he is more interested in or who has had a deeper impact on his thinking and on the kind of person he is trying to be. It is her energy passing through him that makes whatever success he enjoys possible.

Paul would also like to thank his family as they have put up with a lot this year. He thanks them for their patience, support and understanding. He is very sorry that he missed all of those days on the beach at Nantucket—he will try to make it up to you next summer. Paul is constantly amazed with Pam's spectacular abilities as a wife and a mother—she seems to get better at each every day. But most of all, he is forever grateful to have her as his best friend. To his children, Charlotte and Henry, you are the greatest. He is tickled pink that they can't wait to read Daddy's new book about monkeys!

Finally, in a bizarre act of reflexive communication, we would each like to thank the other two members of this team for their contribution to the shared experience in writing this book. It could not have turned out the way it did without the intellectual bantering that took place in numerous phone conversations and thousands of e-mails, and each of us has been changed by the collaboration in ways that we deeply value.

Introduction

In the fall of 1997, as we submit this manuscript to HarperBusiness for production, interest in the stock market in general, and in the high-tech sector in particular, has never been higher. In part this is a function of one of the longest bull markets in history which, as one market wag has put it, "makes us all look like geniuses." In part it is because of the market's exceeding volatility which puts all these genius gains at risk. But perhaps most of all, it is because a select few high-tech companies have created unprecedented returns in record time for those investors fortunate enough to hold them.

No company better exemplifies this impact than Microsoft. Starting life as a PC software company at a time when there wasn't really a PC market, it has in less than twenty years catapulted itself into the most powerful company in the computer industry, making Bill Gates the richest man in the world, and making a whole lot of "Microsoft millionaires" along the way. *Hey, I could use a million dollars*, volunteers a voice deep inside each of us—*How do I get in on this action?*

It is the goal of *The Gorilla Game* to answer that question in some detail.

At the same time, there is another trend at work in our society that is driving increasing interest and engagement in stock-market investing. In the last ten years we have all gotten a wake-up call in the form of a decade's worth of downsizing and corporate decommitment from the once-firm offer of lifetime employment and retirement security. This in turn is driving a shift in our society from *institutional trust* to *self-reliance*.

Hey, I know what you mean, offers up that same voice inside us. *I might* need *that million dollars.*

And indeed we might. As our life expectancy increases, and as society's solutions for supporting its aging citizens reveal themselves to be increasingly limited, we face a requirement to create far more wealth for ourselves and our families than what used to be considered sufficient. This need in turn is putting pressure on our financial plans to generate unprecedented rates of return, well in excess of those that traditional investment instruments can provide. And that pressure, in turn, is leading more and more investors to look more seriously at the high-tech sector. *How can I leverage the upside opportunity in high tech and still protect my family's nest egg?*

It is the goal of *The Gorilla Game* to answer that question in some detail as well.

As a pair of goals, these are ambitious to say the least—some would even say presumptuous. At the very least they raise a couple of immediate questions for the authors, which might be put this way:

- *Just who do you think you are?* As in, why would anybody in their right mind pay the slightest bit of attention to what you are saying?

- *Just who do you think I am?* As in, who is this book really written for, and what expectations do you have for me as one of your readers?

In short, as readers and authors, it's time for us to get introduced.

We'll begin with us. We are three professionals who spend every working day either creating or analyzing business strategies for high-tech companies.

Geoff Moore is a business strategist for high-tech companies and author of two best-selling books on the subject, *Crossing the Chasm* and *Inside the Tornado.* He and Tom Kippola are part of The Chasm Group, a consulting practice based on the framework of ideas in these books. The framework itself describes how high-tech markets develop in characteristic ways that set them apart from other markets, all of which can be traced back to the challenges of the Technology Adoption Life Cycle. The way in which the market overcomes these challenges has the side-effect, in many cases, of catapulting a single company into an extraordinarily powerful position that is surprisingly long-lived. These companies are called gorillas, and *The Gorilla Game* is about how to build a complete investment strategy around buying and holding their stocks.

The chasm/tornado framework has gained broad acceptance within the high-tech industry. Both of Moore's books are featured in graduate school curricula at Harvard, MIT, Stanford, and other leading schools of business and engineering. Venture funds such as Institutional Venture Partners, The Mayfield Fund, Atlas Ventures, and Mohr Davidow have made them required reading for every one of their portfolio companies' management teams. They are also standard reading for the executives at Cisco, Hewlett Packard, Microsoft, SAP, and Digital Equipment Corporation. All this, in turn, has led to consulting engagements for The Chasm Group with these and a host of other Fortune 500 technology companies, as well as with numerous start-ups and small-cap companies that intend to become the next generation of high-tech leaders. The end result is a wealth of experience about the dynamics of competitive advantage in high-tech markets which has helped form the basis for this book.

Paul Johnson is a senior technology analyst at BancAmerica Robertson Stephens, a leading investment bank in the high technology industry. He has teamed up with Geoff and Tom to help convert their business strategy framework into a framework for an investment practice. Paul's credentials took a big step forward when in 1990 he was the first analyst on Wall Street to write a BUY report for Cisco Systems. Since then he has been the one who has made the first call to buy Cabletron, Ascend, and Pairgain, and more generally, the one who first outlined the consolidation trend in the networking sector and explained what it meant.

In 1993 he and a colleague, Michael Mauboussin, a Managing Director at Credit Suisse First Boston, developed a model for understanding how the stock market values competitive advantage, and ever since Paul has used this work to explain why gorilla stocks have a valuation that is so far in excess of their competitors. It is called the *Competitive Advantage Period* model, and it is part of the courses Paul teaches as an Adjunct Professor of Finance at the Graduate School of Business, Columbia University. A simplified version of this work, presented in Chapter 4, lies at the core of this book, where combined with the market development models from *Inside the Tornado*, it provides the essential stock market context for the gorilla game.

Meanwhile, while Geoff and Paul were busy teaching and writing, Tom Kippola and various members of his family with whom he co-invests were just quietly amassing wealth. (Geoff and Paul know there is a lesson in this somewhere, but they are still struggling to grasp it.) Tom had intuitively come up with the rudiments of the gorilla game without any of the underlying theory and began practicing it the day in 1990 when he finally convinced his dad to put $7,000 into Oracle. In the following year Tom and various other members of his family acting on his advice put similar amounts of money into Microsoft, Intel, and Novell, and a couple of years after that into Cisco Systems and Bay Networks. More recently they have been focused on customer support and sales force automation software, as Tom will discuss in Chapter 8. But in the space of seven years they have taken nest-eggs totaling less than $100,000 and turned them into the better part of $1 million, and in the process learned many of the hard-won lessons that are shared in this book. In parallel with this, Tom joined The Chasm Group in 1994 and has subsequently become its managing partner.

So that's who we are—a high-tech strategy consultant, an award-winning Wall Street investment analyst, and a private investor with a strong track record for picking high-tech winners. Together we have tried to create a book that will transfer to you a coherent approach to high-tech investing that is easy to understand, straightforward to execute, and rock-solid in its approach to building personal wealth. All of which leads us to your second question: Just who do we think *you* are?

One way to answer is to say we think you are a *potential gorilla-game investor*. Here's how such a person appears to us:

Figure 1.1

Public stock investment knowledge

	Low	Medium	High	
High-tech industry knowledge	High-tech management teams	Venture capitalists	Technology fund managers	**High**
	Business press	**Gorilla-Game investors**	Growth fund managers	**Medium**
	Novice Investors	Retail stock brokers	General fund managers	**Low**
	Low	**Medium**	**High**	

GORILLA-GAME INVESTORS

As a gorilla-game investor, we think you have or can readily acquire "medium" knowledge both of the high-tech industry and of investment principles. That is, on the industry knowledge side, we think you have or can gain a knowledge of the industry that is better than your retail stock broker's but not as good as, say, a venture capitalist's. And on the investment side, we think you can—and if you continue reading this book, will—know more about investing than, say, most writers for the business press, but not as much as a professional fund manager.

Finally, and perhaps most importantly, the *you* that we have uppermost in our minds is a private investor who is turning to the stock market to provide for your family's future. Far from being independently wealthy, we expect you to have modest capital at the outset and to be deeply concerned about not losing it. As a result, we are going to define an investment strategy that has significant upside potential but that is, at its heart, inherently conservative. That is to our mind the real purpose of the gorilla game—to help private investors participate in the rewards of high-tech stock gains while standing clear of the market's unnerving volatility. To the degree that this notion speaks to your deepest concerns and needs, you are directly in our sights.

There are three other audiences in this grid who also have claims to our attention—and they are all from the top row where, like us, they make their living in the high-tech sector. For these readers our wishes are as follows:

HIGH-TECH MANAGEMENT EXECUTIVES

We hope you will rejoice in a coherent framework within which to discuss the stock-price impact of your business strategies. Increasingly, stock options represent the upside of most management compensation programs and in the case of start-ups, the overwhelming bulk of it. Moreover, our culture has moved in recent years to make shareholder value preeminent among management objectives. In light of both these developments, it is more important than ever to have clear interpretations of the impact of business strategy on stock price and vice versa. The models and vocabulary presented in this book are intended to serve that end, and we hope they will help you and your team communicate better with Wall Street, with employees, with customers, and with each other.

VENTURE CAPITAL PARTNERS

We think you too will benefit from better communications with the management teams you fund. In particular, we hope our emphasis on competitive advantage as the basis for valuation will encourage you in your role as board members to use financial and operational metrics as means to gaining that end and not as ends in themselves. In addition, we think this book raises an interesting financial question for those of you lucky enough to have sponsored a gorilla. Normally it is routine to cash out the entire portfolio upon the expiration of a fund for the purposes of distribution. But if the dynamics outlined in this book are true, it is a huge mistake to liquidate gorilla stock holdings, especially at the beginning of a tornado, which is the most likely time for you to be exiting the fund. That is, history has shown that increases in the valuation of a gorilla stock in the years *after* the IPO dwarfs that *of* the IPO. If this is true, why would you want to cut yourself and your investors out of them?

TECHNOLOGY FUND MANAGERS

In many ways, your everyday practices are far more sophisticated than those advocated in this book. Nonetheless, we hope you will find value in its insights, in particular our attempt to build causal connections among management actions, market responses, marketplace status, and stock price. In addition, while we expect you to find our investment rules for the gorilla game far too conservative and limiting, we think you will be quick to spot more subtle variations, opening up the possibility of even better returns by extending the game along lines we deliberately block off. Indeed, we hope to use our Web site to engage you in an ongoing dialogue around some of these alternative games.

So much, then, for introductions. There is, however, one more issue to address before we move on to our first chapter. There is an element of the gorilla game as an investment strategy that will prove extremely frustrating to anyone who spends the bulk of their time in high tech—*the game almost never advocates investment in any stock that you are interested in!* That is, the specific set of rules we ask private investors to follow, the ones we describe in detail in Chapters 6 and 7 of this book, exclude all but a hundred or so of stocks. Ours is deliberately a *hyperselective investment strategy* which calls for investing in as few companies as possible. The number of hoops a stock has to jump through to get into the final set is so great, and the criteria are so restrictive, that perhaps 100 of the 8000 or so public companies— and no private companies—will qualify.

So please let it be understood that this does not mean we think all these other stocks are undeserving of investment. We have enormous enthusiasm for the prospects of several hundred high-tech firms we know, and we think many of them will (may?) generate extremely attractive returns. But for the gorilla game proper, to meet the specific needs of a *risk-averse* and *capital-constrained* investor, we have imposed a much tighter set of constraints than govern the bulk of high-tech investors currently in the market. We ask our more sophisticated readers to respect that game, therefore, even as they go about finding ways to get around it.

Finally, as the previous paragraph can only begin to hint, we expect from time to time to create a bit of controversy. We also expect, from time to time, to say things that are flat out wrong. We have tried very hard to get things right the first time, but our experience as authors and analysts is, nothing is 100% right ever, and certainly not at the first release. In that light, we have made a commitment to maintain a Web site at www.gorillagame.com, where readers can raise challenges, pose questions, share results, and generally pursue further the topics and strategies outlined in this book. We encourage both active gorilla-game investors and all other interested constituencies to use this Web site as a way to learn, as well as to teach, so that we all can become better at the gorilla game.

Part 1

SETTING THE CONTEXT

1

The Private Investor and the High-Tech Sector

You are having one of those dreams when you are back in college taking a final exam for a course you never actually managed to attend. This one is in economics, and there is just one question on the final. It reads as follows:

> In 1996 the "Big Three" automobile manufacturers—General Motors, Ford, and Chrysler—employed 1,147,000 people to create combined revenues of $365 billion and combined earnings of $12.9 billion. The Microsoft Corporation, by contrast, employed a mere 22,232 people to create revenues of $11.4 billion and earnings of $3.4 billion. Nevertheless, the stock market value of Microsoft exceeded that of General Motors, Ford, and Chrysler *combined!*
> Explain.

You look at your watch. *Okay, I've got two hours, I'm smart, I can do this. Think. What's so special about Microsoft? Well, it's a software company, of course. And cars are, well, hardware. That's it!*
But wait, there's a second part to the question. It reads as follows:

> What is so surprising in this comparison, of course, is the *ratio* of Microsoft's market capitalization both to its sales (called the price/sales, or P/S ratio) and to its earnings (called the price/earnings,

or P/E ratio). As you know from your readings and lectures in this class *(How could I have missed all those classes? What was I doing?)*, the higher these ratios are, the more they show that investors are expecting a very bright future for the company. Microsoft, of course, is not an isolated example, as the following table of other leading companies in the high-tech sector, all taken from 1997 reports, will indicate:

Table 1.1

COMPANY	REVENUES	EPS	# SHARES	PRICE	MARKET CAP	P/S RATIO	P/E RATIO
Intel	$23,990	$3.83	1,633	93	$151,053	6.3	24
Cisco	$6,440	$1.52	669	81	$54,154	8.4	53
Oracle	$6,001	$0.72	980	36	$35,642	5.9	51
Ascend	$1,052	$1.14	189	34	$6,445	6.1	30
McAfee	$266	$1.34	51	66	$3,374	12.7	49
Security Dynamics	$106	$0.50	38	41	$1,536	14.5	81

Source: Bloomberg, 10/13/97
Revenues, shares, and market cap are in millions.

Please make ample use of this data in your answer.

Right. Who are these people? Intel I've heard of, but who's Cisco, and is there a Pancho? Oracle? Ascend? Is this a spiritual thing? McAfee—that's a joke, right? Security Dynamics sounds like the villain in a RoboCop movie.

You notice your heart rate is accelerating, and you commence deep breathing exercises. *No need to panic. I can figure this out. It's all high tech, right? High tech wins, low tech loses. That's the answer.*

You turn to the next page of the question, and you are delighted to see the following table of stock price performances outside the high-tech sector, noting that these are some of the best-managed companies in the world:

Table 1.2

Company	Revenues	EPS	# Shares	Price	Market Cap	P/S Ratio	P/E Ratio
General Electric	$86,697	$2.42	3,266	70	$229,239	2.6	29
Exxon	$119,828	$3.29	2,474	65	$160,679	1.3	20
Proctor & Gamble	$35,764	$2.45	1,350	72	$97,814	2.7	30
Walt Disney	$22,244	$2.76	675	84	$56,964	2.6	31
Nordstrom	$4,613	$2.12	77	62	$4,759	1.0	29

Source: Bloomberg, 10/13/97
Revenues, shares, and market cap are in millions.

That's it. That's the answer. Just gimme some of that good old high-tech stuff they're drinkin', and I'll get to writin'.

But wait, there's more! (You have long since realized this is going to be one of those dreams that's going to drag on and on.) You turn the page one final time to one final table for a number of other high-tech companies, along with more instructions from the professor:

Table 1.3

Company	Revenues	EPS	# Shares	Price	Market Cap	P/S Ratio	P/E Ratio
Novell	$1,007	($0.22)	350	$8^3/8$	$2,928	2.2	NMF
Apple	$7,081	($8.30)	128	$15^1/4$	$1,952	0.3	NMF
Informix	$682	($2.44)	152	$5^{13}/16$	$886	1.2	NMF
Sybase	$1992	$0.25	80	$13^3/8$	$1,068	1.0	53
Bay Networks	$2,172	($1.30)	212	$27^9/16$	$5,832	2.6	NMF
Shiva	$156	($0.34)	30	10	$295	1.6	NMF

Source: Bloomberg
NMF = not meaningful
Revenues, shares, and market cap are in millions.

Needless to say, given the data for these other high-tech firms, you will not make the mistake of thinking that high tech equals stock market success. *(Never even considered it.)* Instead, you will make abundantly clear why Microsoft and why not Novell and Apple, why Oracle and why not Informix or Sybase, and why Cisco and why not Bay Networks or Shiva. *(Of course.)*

Okay, I'm hosed. I'll just go up and tell the prof that for one reason or another I missed every one of his classes, read none of the books, and can I get an incomplete?

Oh, and one final requirement. Please write your essay in Arabic using a ninth-century style guide and spelling manual.

And then you wake up. It was the Arabic. *What a relief. Back to the real world. I'm in control.*

Well, yes and no. You can let go of the Arabic, all right, but until you can answer the exam question in your native tongue, you should neither buy nor sell a high-tech stock.

CRASH COURSE

The first objective of *The Gorilla Game* is to help you correctly answer this test question. We don't think it's going to take a semester. In fact, we think we can get you there by the end of Chapter 4. At that point you should have the necessary knowledge to explain in detail why high tech is treated so differently from other market sectors by the stock market, and why some companies end up big winners while others don't. You will have the understanding needed, in other words, to buy and sell high-tech stocks.

After that, we want you to put your newfound knowledge to work to *play* the gorilla game, to build personal wealth for you and your family while following a conservative, not an aggressive, investment strategy. Enabling you to do so is the second objective of this book. We'll teach you the rules of the game in Chapters 5, 6, and 7, and then we will play out three separate case study games—one historical, one recent, and one currently still in play—in Chapters 8, 9, and 10. Finally, we'll close with two chapters, the first focusing on the process and tools you will need to "play along at home," and the second taking a look at the emerging Internet market and what gorilla-game opportunities warrant your immediate attention. We end the book by taking a snapshot in time, September 17, 1997, a point at which we have constructed our recommended gorilla-game portfolio for the Internet. Needless to say, this will not be timely advice by the time you read this book, but it will serve as a test bed for tracking the performance of the strategies we endorse.

So that's where we're headed. Now let's get back to this exam question and see where it is leading us.

WHY *IS* HIGH TECH DIFFERENT?

First of all, it is *not* the bits and bytes that make high tech so special, so you don't have to be technical to understand what is going on. Instead, as we will explain in detail in the next chapter, it is the *discontinuous innovations* that make the difference. *Innovation* is a concept we are all familiar with—new stuff makes us happy, we buy it, sellers sell it, it's called an economy. *Discontinuity* is the new idea. It means *not compatible with the existing systems*. Electric cars, video telephones, and Web TV, for example, all make exciting promises, but none of them can be used without much of the world changing the way they do business. Prospective customers are attracted to the compelling new benefits, but to get them, a whole lot of existing systems will have to change. That creates a battle in the marketplace whose outcome is uncertain.

Sometimes the battle is lost, and the proposed discontinuous innovation simply disappears. The technology lives on, to be sure, finding its way into other products in a later decade, but the products themselves go to that same burial ground wherein lie the eight-track tapes, laser disc stereos, videophones, and pen-based laptops of yesteryear. Other times the battle is won, but only inside a few niche markets. The established vendors retreat grudgingly, giving up to the new paradigm a defined space, but no more. This is how IBM dealt with Apple's Macintosh's innovations in graphics, how Sun treated Silicon Graphics' work in 3D imaging, and how Digital Equipment Corporation responded to Tandem's nonstop fault-tolerant computing. If these niche markets are as far as the innovations get, if the traditional technologies can hold the line, the establishment breathes a sigh of relief. No new market, no major shift in power, just more business as usual. For the establishment, this is good.

But at other times, the technology leaps out of its niche markets and into the mainstream. It becomes a mass market phenomenon the way PCs, local area networks, laser printers, relational databases, cell phones, voice mail, and electronic mail all have since 1985. When this occurs, a massive shift in spending accompanies it, with a whole new set of vendors coming out of nowhere to produce stunning economic returns. That is, it is not just a new market coming into existence but also a whole new system of commerce to support that market. Business schools call these systems *value chains* or *supply chains*—an interdependent collection of companies working together to assemble the various product and service offerings needed by the new market. It is a revolution, and typically it does not favor the establishment, which historically has tried to resist rather than coopt new technologies. Instead, it throws into prominence a whole raft of new companies that suddenly appear on investment analyst charts because they have begun dramatically outperforming the rest of the stock market.

So that is how a high-tech boom gets going. But why a *boom?* Why not just a modest growth gradually displacing the old with the new over time?

The answer has to do with the dynamics of change, specifically the dynamics of the *Technology Adoption Life Cycle*, and more generally the dynamics of evolution and the idea of *punctuated equilibrium*. In dynamic systems—a term that describes both ecologies and marketplaces—change does not happen linearly. Instead, systems plateau and resist change until enough stress builds up to break the old system and bring in the new. The actual changeover happens in very short order as the systems race to a new plateau where they can again stabilize and start the cycle all over again. This period of rapid change is called *hypergrowth*, and it happens only once in the history of any particular species or market.

From an economic point of view, when hypergrowth hits, the market simply explodes. Companies in hypergrowth markets experience revenue and earnings growth that goes through the roof—30% to 40% *quarter-over-quarter* growth is not untypical. Stock prices catapult as the market tries to catch up to what is a seemingly never-end-ing sequence of upside surprises. This catapult effect is the basic attraction of investing in high tech and the beginning of anyone's interest in the gorilla game.

NOT SMOOTH SAILING

The problem for investors, of course, is that this period of change is *chaotic*—literally. Chaos, as it has come to be defined, is a property of dynamic systems. Its central principle is that essentially insignificant differences at the outset create hugely different consequences later on, and there is no way to rationally predict outcomes based on inputs. Why did IBM mainframes win and not Burroughs, or Univac, or NCR, or Control Data, or Honeywell? Why is Microsoft Windows on our desktops and not Unix or Macintosh or OS/2?

These are not academic questions. As the tables shown earlier in this chapter indicate, you can easily lose the bulk of your capital by investing in the losers in these competitions. Indeed, the volatility of high-tech stocks is so dramatic that, in the absence of a framework such as the one this book provides, private investors have typically, and we would argue rightly, shunned the sector. What else can you do in markets where, when a company misses its revenue projections by a few percentage points, it is *routine* for their stocks to lose 30% or 40% of their value *in a single day?* So, once again now, why is it Intel's microprocessors instead of Motorola's or National Semiconductor's or MIPS' or Sun's SPARC or HP's PA RISC? Why is it Oracle and not Ingres or Sybase or Informix?

At one level, there is no good answer to these questions. If there were, we could predict the winners from the outset, and instead of writing this book, the three of us might be sipping Chateau Margaux atop a penthouse on the Via Tornabuoni in Florence, contemplating which continent we should cruise to next. The fact that we are not shows that we have no way of knowing the winner at the outset. But just as the TV news networks covering national elections can declare the winners long before the last votes are in, so there are ways of predicting the outcome of hypergrowth market competitions early in the game. This we believe we do know how to do, and we will share this knowledge in detail in the chapters to come.

The Cliff Notes version of these chapters is that hypergrowth markets, in order to scale up rapidly, will often spontaneously standardize on the products from a single vendor. This simplifies the issues of creating new standards, building compatible systems, and getting a whole new set of product and service providers up to speed quickly on the new solution set. In short, it makes it much easier for the new value chain to form. The vendor on the receiving end of this spontaneous act of standardization enjoys an extraordinary burst in demand. Everyone wants its products because they are setting the new standard. Its competitors, by contrast, must fight an uphill battle just to get considered. It makes for a huge competitive advantage.

This huge competitive advantage, in turn, comes during a period of intense buying activity—something akin to what the purveyors of Cabbage Patch dolls, Tickle-me-Elmos, and Power Rangers experienced in their respective blockbuster Christmas seasons. But whereas the Christmas toy season brings us examples of eye-popping but quick-fading fads, high-tech hypergrowth markets result in long-standing institutions. This means that the big winners in these markets not only profit from immediate spikes of demand, but even as the initial demand gets fulfilled, are creating dominant market shares that will support them for years and years to come.

These big winners are the gorillas of the gorilla game. They represent the most rewarding investments on the planet, and our goal is to help you build a long-term portfolio made up of these stocks.

STOCK MARKET INVESTING—MASTERY OR MYSTERY?

That brings us to the matter of buying and selling stocks. There is a huge amount of lore about the stock market, and there is no lack of people who will explain to you why it is all wrong and why their theory is the right one. This might make for some entertaining comedy if we all were not so dependent on the market for building the personal wealth needed to provide for ourselves and our families. Since we are very much in that state of dependence, however, it is no laughing matter.

We believe that there is a large body of conventional theory about the stock market that is substantially correct, and while our intent in this book is to make an original contribution to it, we are hoping that our ideas are neither controversial nor disturbing. Indeed, when it comes to sophisticated investors reviewing our work, the comment we would be most gratified to hear is, "Well, duuuhhh!"

The fact is, however, many people who need to invest—and indeed are investing today—are not all that sophisticated when it comes to understanding the stock market. Lacking an understanding of its dynamics, they have no formal basis for knowing when to sell or when to buy. We believe this can be extremely dangerous, and our intent is to use Chapter 4 of this book to change all that. It is not an easy chapter to read, and you may have to read it twice, but surely that's a lot better than being thrown back into your nightmare exam, or worse still, setting out to provide for your family's future with an incomplete understanding.

To give you a head start: The stock price of any company is based on the *present value* of all its *anticipated future earnings*. A share in the company is simply a share of its future profits. Any buying or selling of shares requires the buyer and seller to come to an agreement as to that value. The stock market is nothing more than the accumulation of a whole lot of those agreements, and a company's stock price represents the current point of equilibrium between those who would take it higher and those who would take it lower. The company's total value is simply its stock price, or price per share, times the number of shares outstanding, or what is called its market capitalization, or just *market cap* for short.

What will be obvious by the end of Chapter 4 is that the market caps of companies selling into an emerging market that is just entering hypergrowth are going to be much higher in relation to their annual revenues than those of companies selling into more mature marketplaces. That's because there is a brand new pile of money out there just waiting to be spent, and people are in a rush to spend it, and there are only a few companies with whom they can spend it. It will then become obvious that if one of these lucky companies gets the gorilla position, such that the market tries to funnel the bulk of its purchases into that one company, its value is going to be much higher than any of its competitors. Finally, if you were for some reason still hesitant about investing in such a company, that reluctance should vanish when you learn that most economic experts now believe that the earning power of these gorilla companies will actually *increase over time* relative to their competition as the market matures.

In other words, it's a little bit like betting on a chess tournament in which your side of the board is being played by *both* Gary Kasparov *and* IBM's Deep Blue. Can you lose? Well, anything is possible. But wouldn't you have to say it's a pretty good bet?

THE ESSENCE OF THE GAME

Once we have described the background for understanding high-tech market development, the power of the gorilla, and the way in which the stock market values that power, we will then turn to the investment practices needed to capitalize on this understanding. They can be captured in just a few points, as follows:

- *Find markets transitioning into hypergrowth.* This actually sounds harder than it is. The good news about the gorilla game is you can miss the start by three or four quarters, still get into the game, and still do very well. And each quarter the signals get stronger, not weaker, so it gets easier, not harder, to know what to do.

- *Buy a basket of stocks that represent all the companies that have a clear shot at being the gorilla.* This is the hardest part of the game because it takes genuine industry knowledge. But the knowledge is not secret. You will find "gorilla candidate" lists virtually everywhere you look, and there is typically a cluster of companies that show up on every list, and the gorilla is virtually always on that short list. Again, if you miss the buy by a quarter or two, the game still plays out in your favor.

- *As the gorilla emerges, sell off the rest of the basket and consolidate your holdings in the gorilla.* This is the most counterintuitive aspect of the gorilla game. You *consolidate*, not *diversify*, to reduce your risk. We'll spend a lot of time on this notion because it is critical to your success.

▪ *Plan to hold the gorilla for the long term.* Like most successful investment strategies, the gorilla game takes a *"buy-and-hold"* approach to the market. The fewer decisions you have to make, the fewer mistakes you will make. By contrast, *"buy-and-sell"* strategies inevitably force you to guess at timing. You might as well guess at dice—the odds are not any worse.

▪ *Sell the gorilla only when a new category, based on an alternative technology, threatens to eradicate its power.* Nothing lasts forever, and even gorilla advantages can be eradicated—but typically not from within the market category. This means the threats to watch for will be coming from the outside, and they can catch you—and the gorilla—by surprise. Again, however, the game takes place in slow motion. You will hear rumblings about these threats long before they affect the gorilla's revenues or earnings, and you will have plenty of time to get out safely. Indeed, the greater danger probably comes from overreacting to potential threats that never come to pass, and thereby selling a gorilla stock that has years of good growth left.

That's the essence of the gorilla game.

We think it has three key virtues that should endear it to the private investor risking family capital to create much-needed future wealth:

1: *Lots of upside.* We will show examples of the great gorilla successes to date that are mind-boggling in their appreciation. The prime example, maybe for all time, is Microsoft, which went public in 1986 with a market cap of around two-thirds of a billion dollars, and ten years later was worth more than $130 billion. That's not a doubling or a quadrupling of its investors' money; it's not a ten-bagger (a ten-times return on investment) or a twenty-bagger. That is almost a *two-hundred bagger!*

Is there another Microsoft coming? Probably not. But we expect plenty of gorillas, and we'll be surprised if there aren't some fifty-baggers in there for you.

2: *Limited downside.* The gorilla game takes no bet-on-the-come risks. It does not buy into a category unless the market that supports it has demonstrably entered a hypergrowth state. Now, it is very hard for any company to lose money in a hypergrowth market, and thus you can expect not just the gorilla stock, but also the other stocks you buy, to go up, not down, over the period that you hold them.

To be sure, there will be some non-gorilla stocks that take big hits while they are still in your portfolio, and you will lose money on them, and it will hurt. But overall, gorilla portfolios are the most resilient there are.

3: *Lots of forgiveness.* Mistakes are fundamental to any decision-making process whose outcome is unpredictable. You will make mistakes. What is wonderful about the gorilla game is that it does not require you to get the timing exactly right, either for buying or for selling; nor do you have to get the basket of stocks you buy exactly right (although you do have to get the gorilla in there eventually). It is a good game, in other words, for real people leading real lives that take them away from looking after their investments for extended periods of time.

Those are the virtues of the gorilla game that we think are most important. It also has some limitations, of which three are worth noting at the outset:

1: *It takes discipline.* If you like to buy and sell stocks frequently, this is not the game for you. If you like to gamble, if you like to play a hunch, if you like to take the road less traveled, this is not for you. More than anything else, this game requires maintaining a firm grasp on the obvious. You may be surprised to learn how hard that is.

2: *It requires following the high-tech industry.* We said you don't have to be technical, and that's true. But you do have to follow high tech, and that takes work—a lot of work, potentially, if it is not already part of your job. The good news is, you do not have to play a lot of gorilla games to be successful, and the information you need to play the game is readily available. Moreover, as you will see in Chapter 11, there are a number of new tools that will provide shortcuts to help. But at the end of the day, it still requires time spent away from your family.

3: *It leaves money on the table.* There are huge windfalls in high tech that will never come your way if you play the gorilla game. Get used to it. This is not about winning the most money possible. If that is your goal, you are playing another game. This one is about investing a family nest egg in a safe, rewarding way.

In the final analysis, we think the gorilla game is a particularly appropriate approach to investing for private investors who are risk averse but who need to build wealth faster or in greater amounts than conventional alternatives support. This is the agenda that will drive the remainder of this book.

At the same time, we believe we will have a significant number of readers who will not fit this profile. In particular, we hope our colleagues in professional investment and in high-tech management will also take a serious interest in this book. For these readers, the message is, we know you are not playing the gorilla game as an investment strategy, but you are playing a game where stock prices of high-tech companies are critical to your success. We believe *The Gorilla Game* provides a framework and a vocabulary for setting business and investment strategy that goes beyond the boundaries of any specific set of investment rules to capture the dynamics of the sector overall. In that spirit, we invite you to stay with us on our journey.

How Does the Gorilla Game Compare to Other Investment Philosophies?

The gorilla game is unusual in that it confines itself to a type of market opportunity that is relatively rare and takes significant industry understanding to exploit. That being said, from time to time the gorilla game may look like one of the more traditional styles of investing, and investors may be tempted to say, ah well, I know all that because that's what we have always done. This would be dangerous indeed, so we will close this chapter with an attempt to clearly differentiate the gorilla game from other practices.

■ *It is not concept investing.* This philosophy can look a great deal like the gorilla game because it too is based on investing in emerging markets that are often high-tech. It shares with the gorilla game the notion that when new value chains displace old ones, huge amounts of wealth reconcentrate in new locales. Finally, it is the philosophy that is most frequently associated with winning big gains in high-tech stocks immediately after their initial public offerings (IPOs), when stock prices often run up rapidly without underlying financial performances to warrant such escalation. These "successes," however, are all too often short-lived.

The critical distinction between concept investing and the gorilla game is that the latter is driven by proven, not prognosticated, financial performance. The focus is on the same markets, but the point of entry is much later in their development. Gorilla-game investors should never get trapped by false hypergrowth because they invest based on actual revenues, not projections of boom markets to come.

In our view, concept investing is best left to venture capitalists and others who raise funds to invest in a large number of concepts, assuming that only a few will actually bloom into full gorilla games. Private investors who are not professional investors simply should not assume this level of risk.

■ *It is not momentum investing.* This philosophy also can look like the gorilla game because both approaches advocate buying into a category as it enters its hypergrowth phase. Both also recognize that the future value of participating in this market far exceeds anything that the company's current performance statistics would imply, and thus both predict that the stock market, which clings to its "standard" metrics, will undervalue the category for some time to come.

The critical distinction here is that momentum investing does not distinguish between the gorilla and all its competitors and thus is liable to buy indiscriminately into the category of stocks involved. The gorilla game will show that, for private investors with limited capital and a high sensitivity to risk, the gorilla is the only safe buy in the category, that all the other investments incur a much higher risk of eventually disappointing drastically. Further, we will show that there are types of hyper-growth markets that simply do not generate a gorilla, and therefore, for our particular target investor, should not be invested in at all.

Momentum investing is a high-risk, high-reward game. It takes a "follow the herd" approach in a highly volatile marketplace, with the intent of detaching itself from the herd just at the moment that everyone else runs off a cliff. This is dicey work at best. The gorilla game, by contrast, carves out of the momentum idea the one reasonably safe play.

- *It is not theme investing.* This approach combines concept and momentum investing. The idea is to identify a major trend that will reengineer whole sectors of the economy and then buy all the stocks that can participate in that trend. Electronic commerce, for example, looks to be such a trend, and a theme investor might invest in a dozen or more companies with products in transaction processing, advertising, security, database marketing, and the like. Theme investors try to take the best that futurists have to offer and translate it into a winning portfolio.

As with the previous two approaches, theme investing shares a common element with the gorilla game—in this case the expectation of a hypergrowth market of major proportions. The big difference again is that theme investing creates broad portfolios of many stocks, whereas the gorilla game consolidates down to a very few. This means that gorilla gamers can succeed with much less capital and much less breadth of industry knowledge.

- *It is not value investing.* This philosophy is based on the notion that the market undervalues stocks that are out of favor with institutional investors, and that these undervalued stocks can be detected by analyzing the fundamentals of their business. Bolstered with the notion that most things in life regress toward the mean, value investors count on depressed stocks rising back to a more average valuation. By finding the current crop of depressed stocks, buying them cheap, and selling them when they level out, this strategy makes money.

On the surface, value investors are almost the opposite of gorilla-game investors, and typically the portfolios of the two groups will have no stocks in common. This is because gorilla-candidate stocks are virtually never undervalued in the sense that a value investor means. Microsoft is a good example. There has never been a time in its history when it met the profile of a value investor's target.

Nonetheless, the gorilla game shares with value investing the idea that the market is undervaluing the target stock—but not because it is out of favor, or because its fundamentals are being misjudged. Rather, in the gorilla game, it is the fundamental dynamics of high-tech market development that are being misjudged, and the gorilla's exceptional competitive advantages simply are not being priced into its stock.

■ *It is not technical investing.* This philosophy is based on following the changes in stock price as they relate to pricing change theory, not to the market dynamics of the industries involved. It is all about how the stock market reacts, not about the fundamentals of value. As such, it follows a completely different orientation from anything we have discussed, and is not likely to be confused with the gorilla game.

So what *is* the gorilla game?

■ *It is a form of growth investing.* Like growth investors, gorilla gamers value the forward-looking dynamics of a company's market as a better indicator of its future stock performance than its current price/earnings ratio. Two key points distinguish the gorilla game from growth investing in general:

1: It focuses exclusively on high tech, and specifically on product-oriented companies that sell into mass markets undergoing hypergrowth.

2: It uses consolidation, not diversification, as its primary risk-reduction strategy for long-term holds.

The first of these ideas is likely to seem overly restrictive; and the second, counterintuitive at best. To understand either properly, we need to get a better picture of the dynamics of high-tech hypergrowth markets, and for that we need to turn to the next chapter.

2

How High-Tech Markets Develop

The investment strategy outlined in this book is built in part upon a theory of high-tech market development outlined in *Inside the Tornado*. Released in 1995, that book has defined a vocabulary and framework that has achieved widespread use throughout the high-tech sector, by managers, industry analysts, and increasingly by investment analysts.

This chapter will recap "tornado theory" for the private investor. The goal is to identify recognizable milestones in the development of a high-tech market that the private investor can use as signals for buying and selling. The most important of these milestones is the tornado itself.

The tornado is a compressed period of hypergrowth that occurs once in the life of a market, coinciding with the first surge of mass market adoption of any new technology. It creates a unique set of marketplace dynamics that frequently will catapult a single company into a position of overwhelmingly dominant competitive advantage. This company becomes the gorilla, and the dominant competitive advantages it enjoys will allow it to generate exceptional returns to its investors for an unusually extended period. The whole thrust of the gorilla game is to build long-term holdings in these gorillas.

But to understand how we get to that point, we first need to focus on the dynamics of high-tech markets that make such a strategy possible, and that begins with an understanding of *discontinuous innovations*.

DISCONTINUOUS INNOVATIONS

All markets thrive on the introduction of innovations that stimulate purchasing behavior from buyers who were losing interest in the old set of offers. In most industries, for most of the time, these innovations are *continuous*. This means that they build upon the standards and infrastructure already in place. A new car, new TV, new cereal, new book—to enjoy their benefits, customers need only buy them and start using them. Even in high tech, once you own a computer, new software, a new monitor, a new hard drive, all are plug-and-play continuous innovations—or at least they are supposed to be.

But from time to time technology breakthroughs enable an entirely different kind of offer—what is called a *discontinuous innovation*. The first semiconductor, the first PC, the first spreadsheet, the first local area network, the first fax, the first relational database, the first Web browser—and, for that matter, the first automobile, the first television, the first microwave dinner—all these products introduced completely novel benefits that were extremely compelling. To enjoy these benefits, however, users had to adopt new technologies and put in place new infrastructures that were incompatible with what was prevalent at the time. That means, not only did *they* have to go through a whole learning curve on their own, they also had to wait for all the providers of complementary products and services to get their part of the overall system up and running. Who wants a car with no highways, a VCR without movies to rent, a microwave with no microwavable meals or recipes, a new game machine with no new games? Who wants to own a fax if no one else owns one too?

In others words, offers based on discontinuous innovations have a built-in delayed gratification principle. This makes for an ambivalent offer to customers, which in turn generates a range of reactions, modeled by the Technology Adoption Life Cycle.

THE TECHNOLOGY ADOPTION LIFE CYCLE

This model is the foundation for understanding high-tech market development. It is based on work done by Everett Rogers and his colleagues at Harvard as far back as the late 1950s. It is still the basis for research under the category of *diffusion of innovation* and continues to provide insights to high-tech managers every year.

The model predicts that whenever a market is exposed to a discontinuous innovation, customers will self-segregate into five different response profiles:

Figure 2.1 The Technology Adoption Life Cycle

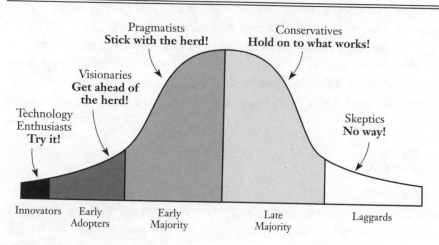

For high-tech markets, these five response profiles have proved remarkably consistent over the years. Each is based on a defining attitude toward discontinuity, as follows:

TECHNOLOGY ENTHUSIASTS

This type of customer believes in the inherent value of technology and is willing to experiment with discontinuous innovations simply to explore their properties in the expectation of finding something of value. In Fortune 500 companies, these people often work in the advanced technology departments, charged with the responsibility of keeping their company abreast of the new technologies. The group also includes legions of hackers and independent developers who are pushing the edges of what's possible on the Internet and elsewhere. And in consumer markets these are the gadget lovers who snap up the latest palmtop organizer or multifunctional peripheral, only to put it down a few months later for some newer, neater toy.

Winning the endorsement of this group is an important step for any new technology in gaining initial market visibility and credibility. The opinions of the technology enthusiasts hold a lot of sway among customers in the early market. That being said, however, these enthusiasts are not representative of the marketplace at large and are not a good predictor of whether a mainstream market will in fact ever develop (as their closets full of old laser disc players, eight-track stereo tapes, and Apple Newtons will confirm).

As a gorilla-game investor, you should not worry about missing out on the latest and greatest when this crew talks up things you have never heard of. We are a long way from any true mass market at this stage, and thus a long way from any investment decision you might make.

VISIONARIES

These customers are typically highly placed executives who are looking to create breakthrough competitive advantages to leapfrog the rest of their industry. They examine discontinuous innovations for opportunities to radically reengineer their company's business processes in ways that might totally preempt a competitive response. When they find one that appeals to them, they champion it in a big way, whether it be the American Airlines SABRE reservations system, Federal Express's use of package tracking systems, or Amazon.com's trailblazing use of the World Wide Web for bookselling. Their goal is to set themselves apart from the herd—by *herd*, they mean the pragmatic majority of people who do not adopt discontinuous innovations until they see other people doing so. Visionaries love doing things that the herd would never do, because if they are successful, they will gain a huge head start over the rest of their competitors.

Visionary customers are incredibly valuable in helping new technologies gain early visibility, particularly via the business press, where they are often celebrated for their forward-thinking approaches to challenging business problems. Like technology enthusiasts, however, their endorsements are not a good predictor of whether a mainstream market will ever actually develop. It often happens that by the time a technology they have sponsored is mature enough to be adoptable by the masses, some other new technology has come along that creates enough uncertainty to stall the market again. This is what happened to massively parallel computers, object-oriented databases, and artificial intelligence.

Gorilla-game investors, therefore, read stories about this type of customer with interest and often start making mental notes to keep an eye on this opportunity, but they refrain from reaching for their checkbook. Instead they wait to see what the mass of customers are going to do.

PRAGMATISTS

These customers *are* the herd. They see new technology as valuable, but only after standards have been set and systems have been thoroughly shaken out. So their strategy is to adopt the new paradigm *if and only if* everybody else does. This is a strategy of *conforming to the herd*, and it is the fundamental underpinning for mass market behavior—I'll do it if you'll do it. This leads to "go as a group" response that has the same effect on market development that block voting has on elections. It makes or breaks the new category.

When the herd does decide to go, it goes all at once, which creates a dramatic spike in growth, or hypergrowth, what we call the tornado. This growth is the fundamental prerequisite for the gorilla game. Therefore, gorilla games cannot start until the pragmatist constituency in the Technology Adoption Life Cycle makes clear that it is adopting.

The opinions and behavior of pragmatist buyers are the critical bellwether for gorilla-game investors. In later chapters we will show you how you can keep abreast of their actions.

CONSERVATIVES

These customers are much happier staying with the systems they have than switching to anything new—regardless of how much better it is supposed to be. Ultimately, when they do buy in, they act as latter-day followers of the pragmatist herd, buying what it bought, only later. Buying late in the life cycle gives them the opportunity to exploit mature competition to negotiate better prices and values. The longer they wait, the better deal they can cut.

By the time this customer gets into the market, the gorilla game has been decided, and changes in the stock prices of the companies in the category will be due less to prospects for future growth than to performance on current earnings. Efficient handling of conservative customers is key to these earnings improvements, but the change in valuation that results is relatively small compared to the previously highly volatile gyrations in market capitalization.

The exception to this rule is the gorilla. Its advantages persist for the life of the product category, and therefore its efforts at execution are rewarded by increasing market share at the expense of the other competitors. Good gorillas, as opposed to lazy, complacent ones, can continue to improve their valuation significantly at this stage in the cycle; and that is why we look to gorillas not just as growth stocks but also as earnings stocks.

SKEPTICS

These are would-be customers who simply never buy from anyone. They see technology investments as overpriced and overpromised, and prefer to spend their money instead on low-cost, nontechnical solutions. These noncustomers are most significant for their ability to block adoption movements from ever really taking off. They reinforce the inertia that high-tech market development strategies must overcome.

As an investor in high tech, you will meet plenty of skeptics, several of whom are likely to be members of your immediate or extended family. Your only defense is, "Hey, I'm not using this stuff, I'm only investing in it."

• • •

Taken all together, these profiles represent the five basic strategies for responding to the opportunity created by a discontinuous innovation. Any one individual might make any one of the five responses, depending on how he or she sees the new technology. That is, real people tend to be early adopters in one area and late adopters in another. In a free market, however, where the mass of people are left to their own devices, these strategies consistently emerge in a self-organizing, highly repeatable pattern of market development. It is this pattern that lies at the heart of the gorilla game, so it behooves the high-tech investor to study it closely.

HIGH-TECH MARKET DEVELOPMENT

The diagram below, read left to right, outlines the progress of a high-tech market's development.

Figure 2.2 High-Tech Market Development

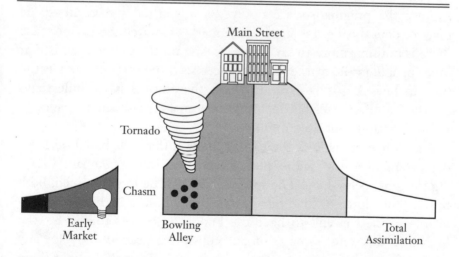

Here's how it plays out.

THE EARLY MARKET

The first commercial activity around a discontinuous innovation is sponsored by visionary customers, supported by technology enthusiasts. Together they seek to use the new technology to enable some radical change that will give them a dramatic competitive advantage over all the other companies in their category. Early market efforts virtually always take place in industrial markets because the amount of high-priced expertise required to bring off such projects is prohibitive to consumer marketing, from the standpoint of both cost and availability.

The most dramatic example of an early-market technology at the time of this writing is electronic commerce over the Internet. Forward-thinking businesses in virtually every sector of the U.S. economy are currently engaged in seeking out competitive advantage by leveraging the World Wide Web to reengineer traditional business transactions. There is a constant stream of articles about Dell Computer, Cisco Systems, Amazon.com, Federal Express, Charles Schwab—each acting as a visionary in its own sector. As yet, however, there is no mainstream market for such systems, as pragmatists still wait and watch.

Since the pragmatists are not yet involved, all the gorilla-game investor does during this stage of the market is watch. So in one sense there is nothing more to say about it. The problem, however, is that other people in the market will say, no, this *is* the tornado, now is the time to buy. A gorilla-game investor, therefore, has to understand clearly the differences between the early market and the tornado, so we will continue our description.

A key characteristic of the early market is that it is based on large deals championed by highly placed executives in the companies buying the new technology. The sponsor needs to be highly placed, both to have the clout to drive through to completion a high-risk reengineering initiative, and to have the budget resources to pay for the high cost of systems integration and consulting needed to deploy any system this early in the life cycle. When you read stories about these deals, expect to hear of bold business actions, of management teams going ahead of the herd. These are early-market signals, not tornado.

Another key characteristic of this phase of market development is that it is built around individual customers, not market segments. Visionary customers do not want to cooperate in helping other companies in their competitive space get current on the new technology. They intend this new technology to be their differentiating advantage. They resist other sales into their sector. They *will* cooperate, on the other hand, with companies outside their competitive space. As a result, the customer list for an early-market company typically features a number of high-profile companies, but frequently there are no two from the same market segment. Use this as another clue to determine where the market is in the life cycle.

The early market is extremely attractive for top-tier service companies like EDS, Andersen Consulting, and Cambridge Technology Partners, which specialize in business process reengineering and systems integration. Customers who want to be first to implement new technologies know they need a host of high-margin services from service institutions that have depth, breadth, and staying power. This creates huge demand for professional services firms, and it is they who garner the lion's share of profits in the early market. By contrast, in a tornado market, product vendors dominate by *minimizing* the service content in an offering in order to proliferate it more rapidly, more broadly, and at lower cost.

All in all, for the company introducing the discontinuous innovation, the early market is a *gestation phase*, a chance to prove out the feasibility of its technology in a few highly customized projects. It is not a source of significant revenue or profit generation, and as soon as the proof-of-concept goal has been met, it behooves these companies to exit the early market and move on to the mainstream market. Unfortunately, between these two markets looms the chasm.

THE CHASM

The chasm is a hiatus in market development during which there is no natural customer for the discontinuous innovation. It is the consequence of the polar opposition between the visionary, who is deliberately going ahead of the herd, and the pragmatist, who is just as intent on staying with the herd. Each strategy wants to keep its distance from the other—hence the chasm between them. Here's how the dynamics play out.

As more and more customers adopt the innovative technology, the time gap between adopting now and adopting with everyone else begins to shrink. At some point visionaries begin to doubt that the gap is large enough to let them preempt a genuine competitive advantage by going ahead of the herd. They fear, in other words, that some fast follower could catch up with them and weaken their first-mover advantage. At this point in the adoption life cycle, therefore, visionaries start losing interest.

At this very same time, however, pragmatists are far from ready to take up the mantle of technology adoption. They are still waiting to see if their fellow pragmatists are adopting, and if so, whether they are having any success. Specifically, they are looking for references within their own community who can testify to surviving the plunge. At this point, however, there aren't any such references—only the odd visionary whose project is too radical to be representative of what a pragmatic person wants to undertake. So the pragmatists bide their time, perhaps by running a small pilot project, but most likely by just going to seminars to keep abreast of events.

On the vendor side, however, while the customers are waffling, the competitors are not. The new technology's success in the early market has attracted the attention of the established vendors, who have a vested interest in maintaining the status quo. They now unite to expel the intruder, sowing seeds of doubt about the new company's financial viability and ridiculing the immaturity of its product and the incompleteness of its integration. If the innovator cannot secure a market position for itself relatively quickly, it will die in the chasm.

This was the fate of expert systems, pen-based computing, desktop videoconferencing, computer-aided software engineering tools, and neural networks. No longer novel enough for the visionaries to find ongoing competitive advantage potential in them, they remained just discontinuous enough to keep the pragmatists at bay. In most cases, the products lingered on for a while, each year generating more costs than revenues, until finally the companies that sponsored them either dissolved or moved on to other things. In such an event, needless to say, all the money invested was lost.

The chasm's ability to take all and return nothing represents the high-tech stock market's volatility at its worst, and it is precisely this kind of risk that the gorilla game deliberately avoids. To be sure, there are successful investors who, at highly discounted prices, buy these stocks at a time when their probability of failure exceeds the probability of success. Venture funds, in particular, have well-developed mechanisms and capital for handling this kind of risk. But private investors normally do not. In any event, no gorilla game ever starts until after the market has demonstrably crossed the chasm.

THE BOWLING ALLEY

The bowling alley represents the *market penetration* phase of the Technology Adoption Life Cycle. It is located at the frontier of the mainstream market, just the other side of the chasm, and represents niches of pragmatist customers who are willing to adopt a new technology ahead of the herd.

But how can this be possible, since pragmatists are by definition herd animals? It is made possible by the fact that subsets of pragmatists, united by a common cause, aggregate into "micro-herds" that move ahead of the main herd. Why? Because they are in pain. They need relief, and the only place they think they can find it is in the new technology.

Specifically, bowling alley market segments typically build up around departmental functions whose managers find themselves saddled with what we call a *broken, mission-critical business process.* These broken processes are jeopardizing the entire enterprise's ability to serve its customers. Top management has put these managers on notice to fix the process, or else. The sense of urgency is great—these are pragmatists who fear they may be about to get fired. As such, they seek out their opposite numbers in similar companies to find out if they have seen the problem, and if so, if they have found a solution. What they discover is that, yes, the problem is rampant, and no, nobody has a solution yet.

This was the situation in the early 1990s, for example, when customer support managers in high-tech firms were overwhelmed with the number of 800-number technical support calls they were getting, and customers were often put on hold for up to forty-five minutes. The existing systems simply could not handle their unusual peak-period demands, in large part because it took so long to answer customers' questions. CEOs would get angry complaints and call the support group onto the carpet. When the support managers talked to their opposite numbers, they found out the whole industry was at fault. It seemed that the complexity of the new systems was so great that no one could manage the load. Thus it was that an entire segment went in search of a solution to a common problem and ended up sponsoring a whole new category of software. And that was how the customer support software market, which we will be discussing later in this book, crossed the chasm and got its first start in the mainstream market.

Examples of other niche markets that have allowed discontinuous technologies to cross the chasm include:

- Graphic artists for the Macintosh (the old methods could not respond to the number of changes and the need for fast turn-around).

- Retail banks for Tandem-computer-based Automatic Teller Machines (banks could not afford to meet their customers' increasing check-cashing demands with more tellers).

- Hollywood film editors for Silicon Graphics digital graphics workstations (it was costing Hollywood tens of millions of dollars to edit and reshoot parts of their films, resulting in huge budget over-runs).

- Wall Street traders for Sun workstations and Sybase databases (traders are always under pressure to find faster and more market-responsive trading systems).

In each case, these segments were stuck with serious business problems that had to be solved immediately but could not be addressed effectively without embracing a discontinuous innovation.

Managers who are under this kind of "broken-process" pressure will sponsor a new technology ahead of the herd, *but only if* the system provider can commit to an end-to-end solution to their problem.

That is, to win over their target segments, each of these product vendors has to commit not just to providing an excellent product, but also to fielding a complete suite of products and services to solve the entire problem for the target segment. This leads them to recruit other companies that have the necessary competencies they lack, thereby forging a whole new value chain where none existed before. Once such a team is formed and the market has rallied around its solution, all other vendors get summarily excluded from the segment (pragmatists like to standardize on a single solution once they find one that works); so these first movers get to enjoy the fruits of market leadership for a long time to come.

It is this capability to support *a new value chain's formation* that makes the bowling alley so strategic to the gorilla-game investor. It is literally a new marketplace coming into being. It is the way that mainstream markets "accommodate" a discontinuous innovation. The reward for every company in this new marketplace's value chain is the opportunity to grow with virtually no competition from well-established incumbent vendors. The bowling alley stage is thus the earliest moment that a high-tech company can truly define itself as a going concern, because for the first time it has committed customers and a protected marketplace to support it in the years to come. As you will see in later chapters, it is also the earliest investable moment in the gorilla game. But we are not yet in a gorilla game proper, because there is not yet a mass market phenomenon. These companies can all look forward to growth, but not yet to hypergrowth. Here's why.

The reason niche markets are called the "bowling alley" is that ongoing market growth will be niche to niche, each entry into a new niche being eased by leveraging the prior niche's solution set and reference base of customers. By this mechanism companies can continue to grow their marketplace in advance of gaining widespread mass market support. Each new niche creates a moment of "micro-hypergrowth," as all the pragmatists in that niche follow the micro-herd to adopt the new technology. But it does not create "macro-hypergrowth"—that is what happens when entire mass markets adopt the stuff from which true gorillas are made. For that to occur the market must transition to the tornado.

This transition is by no means a foregone conclusion. Many markets stabilize in a state we call "bowling alley forever." These markets never transform from niche to mass, but just continue along as a series of niches. This is the pattern that has characterized specialized niche companies like MapInfo and ESRI in geographical information systems, Applied Materials and Lam Research in semiconductor equipment, and Autodesk and Parametric Technology Inc. in mechanical CAD software. Such companies can continue to grow for only so long if they never enter into a true mass market. Sooner or later, they run out of new niches. After that they settle down onto Main Street, typically with good margins, good service revenues, but nothing like gorilla-game market valuations.

In other cases, however, niche markets do lead to later tornado success. The market for Macintosh-based desktop graphics started in graphics departments in Fortune 500 marketing departments, then spread to the ad agencies that created marketing materials for these same departments, then out to the commercial printers who processed these same files. At the same time, by tweaking the application to produce desktop presentations, this market also grew into the other sections of the marketing department, and from there to the sales department, and then to the company at large, as more and more people were using MacDraw, and then Persuasion, and then PowerPoint to create presentations. This transformation from niche to mass market creates the tornado—when the true gorilla game begins, and to which we shall now turn.

THE TORNADO

The tornado is a metaphor for the hypergrowth stage in technology markets caused when the buying resistance of the pragmatist herd finally caves in, and they rush to adopt the new technology *en masse*. This creates a massive updraft in demand, and that sucking sound you hear is every supply chain in the world rushing in to fill the void.

The tornado represents the *proliferation* phase of the life cycle, during which the new paradigm springs up everywhere seemingly at once. It is caused by the same herd dynamics that create the chasm, only now operating in reverse. That is, the same urge to conform that led pragmatist customers to hold back as a group now leads them to jump in as a group. This action creates a mass market overnight—the entire herd in motion—thereby creating a severe inversion of supply and demand. This inversion, in turn, stimulates a tornado, or hyper-growth—not untypically 300% per year in the very early going, "slowing down" to 100% over a longer period—as every supplier in the category seeks to ramp capacity to take advantage of this extraordinary state of affairs.

The tornado is the force behind the exponential customer adoption *S* curves that get drawn over and over again by high-tech market analysts, the ones who track the proliferation of telephones and TVs, faxes and cell phones, e-mail and voice mail, word processors and spreadsheets, relational databases and client/server applications. As of this writing, Internet access for e-mail and the World Wide Web for browsing are both inside the tornado. Traffic is doubling every four months, as are HTML pages and Web sites, and every major network provider has had dramatic outages as it scrambles to keep pace. And this scrambling will continue for as long as it takes the marketplace to catch up to the backlog of demand. Once that happens, once supply again exceeds demand, the marketplace will convert to a more stable, ongoing competition among established players within an established category—what we call Main Street. The hypergrowth era, in other words, will be over.

The key to the tornado from an investor's point of view is the astonishing impact it can have on the relative market share of the vendors competing within it. Typically at the outset, there are a handful of plausible candidates for market leader, all bunched together, each having market share within shouting distance of each other. Sooner or later, however, one of these vendors shoots out of the pack, rapidly distancing itself from the others, taking with it the lion's share of the future sales, and an even greater percentage of the future profits of the sector—*forever!* This is the Microsoft, the Intel, the Cisco, the Oracle—what we call the *gorilla* role.

How is this possible? Why does it happen? It turns out it is *not* a function of having better marketing, or a better product, or any other obvious cause, although all of the above can certainly help. Instead, it is primarily a function of the market itself desperately needing to set technology standards to interface all this proliferation of new products into the existing infrastructure of systems. Unfortunately, because the market is just taking off, there are no such standards, nor in the midst of hypergrowth is there time to deliberate upon them. So the market makes do with de facto standards, basing these on the product architecture of the market-leading vendor.

This is a hugely significant outcome. Whichever vendor is fortunate enough to become the standard-setter in the new market is virtually guaranteed a role in any solution that a complementary partner proposes. If one has the standard database, for example, then every hardware vendor wants it to run on their hardware, every software application vendor wants it to run under their application, and every customer wants it because that way their systems are guaranteed to be compatible with the future releases of all these companies. The power that is thrust upon this vendor, in other words, is awesome.

Vendors, of course, are very much aware of this process, and very much aware of its consequences, so they do all kinds of marketing communications work to try to influence the outcome. It is all a bit like the presidential election primaries in the U.S. As long as the outcome is in doubt, no one has real power, although many will claim it. But as soon as a clear leader emerges, everyone wants to get on their bandwagon, and pretty soon no one else is left in the race. It is this same bandwagon effect that creates the hugely disproportionate demand for the gorilla's products, which drives up their sales volumes and price margins, which makes all the other companies rush to support their offers, which adds even more value to their offers, and which culminates in a market valuation that often outstrips its closest competitor *by an order of magnitude!*

Once achieved, the gorilla position is virtually unassailable. Not only has the company itself become rich and powerful, but also all the other vested interests in the market have a motive to keep it in power. Here's why. A new marketplace has just come into being on a mass market scale. The gorilla architecture is acting something like a reef upon which this new ecosystem has sprung up, and therefore every living thing in the system has a stake in keeping it stable (including the customers).

Once IBM won the mainframe battle, for example, outdistancing the "BUNCH" (Burroughs, Univac, NCR, Control Data, and Honeywell), its position was never again in jeopardy, not just because of IBM itself, but also because so many others had a stake in its ongoing success—all the software companies, all the supporting hardware vendors and the consultants, and all the customers who had committed to the System 360 and 370 architecture. To convert all that code to some other standard was simply not in the cards. One by one the BUNCH dropped back into niches, or faded away altogether, with Unisys (the merger of Burroughs and Univac) the only remaining player, and it on an apparently irreversible decline.

Pragmatist customers adopting during the tornado have instinctively figured out this dynamic. What they used to say to each other was, "Nobody ever got fired for buying IBM." Nowadays they substitute other gorillas for IBM ("Nobody ever got fired for buying Microsoft"), but the philosophy is still the same. The gorilla has the only lasting play and therefore is the only truly safe buy. So inside the tornado, once the gorilla is identified, there is a huge demand for its products, and its sales go through the roof. All the other competitors still do well, but nowhere near as well as the gorilla.

Main Street

The tornado lasts only a few years, perhaps three to five, the time it takes for the initial surge of demand to be absorbed, after which the market reestablishes equilibrium with supply. We call this new state Main Street, and with its arrival one might assume that the power of the gorilla would subside. Surprisingly, if anything, it increases.

Main Street represents the *assimilation and variation* phase of the adoption process. For the first time, high-tech markets begin to behave like other industry sectors. The technology itself is now buried deep inside the product, like a microprocessor inside a BMW, and market attention migrates away from worrying about standards and toward creating minor variations on those standards to enhance particular applications. It means getting a nineteen-inch screen instead of fifteen-inch one, getting 100,001 clip-art images to enhance your presentation software, getting a CD-ROM drive with your laptop. It means finding software tailored specifically for the florist business, or shipping and distribution, or education, instead of just using a standard package. The standards and technology—the operating system, the microprocessor, the database, the network—all are taken for granted; the variations are what now occupy the market's interest.

This has the effect of migrating value from the internal structure of a product, the domain of technological price/performance, to its external interface to the user, the domain of customer satisfaction. The key discipline is no longer engineering but marketing. This is a time when consumer-market opportunities, which may have emerged inside the tornado, can really flourish. It is an era of one-on-one marketing and mass customization, when the introduction of a relatively cosmetic change at the surface of a standard core product creates, for a targeted niche of users, a compelling new value.

Main Street also represents a strategic transition from focusing on acquiring new customers in a hypergrowth market to serving existing customers in a slower-growth market. Hypergrowth, in other words, has had its day. While there are always going to be some more new customers to go out and get, for the first time there is now more money to be made by serving one's installed base of existing customers. New customer acquisition still persists, of course, but the focus of strategy now shifts from winning *market share* to winning *margin share*.

Implicit in this shift is a transition point that the stock market cannot anticipate, the point at which hypergrowth finally does ease off, and the final size of the stabilized marketplace can, for the first time, be accurately projected. At this point it is normal for technology stocks to be marked down, simply because the pricing they had before this point incorporated the possibility of still further hypergrowth, and that is now seen to be no longer in the cards. Stock prices tumble, and investors cringe. But this is not a time of destabilization; rather, it is one of stabilization, and gorilla-game investors should not respond to this repricing as a signal to exit the category. Indeed, they should take it as an opportunity to buy more gorilla stock. Here's why.

Going forward onto Main Street, the competitive advantages of the gorilla, far from subsiding, actually increase relative to its competitors. During the tornado, the market standardized on the gorilla's architecture as a way of simplifying the proliferation of the new paradigm. Now on Main Street every vendor must kowtow to that architecture just to stay in the game. All PC-based software has to be Microsoft- and Intel-compatible—or what is now called "Wintel"-compatible. All networking solutions must be compatible with Cisco's protocols, and all printers must be Hewlett-Packard–compatible. Too many systems are built around these standards—in the sense of both computer systems and supply-chain systems—to make accommodating an incompatible entrant worthwhile. The power of the gorilla standard is thus immense.

In such a light, it does not take a very clever gorilla to figure out that by making minor changes to its architecture, small enough to be absorbable by customers and partners, it can create havoc for its competitors, particularly if these changes are positioned right at the point where the competitor is trying to create a compelling new variation. This is what Microsoft did so effectively to Novell in the early 1990s with Windows NT, and what it is doing to Netscape with its browser strategy at the time of this writing. It is not fair, perhaps, but it is effective.

The reason it is so effective is that the neutral third-party players in the marketplace have plenty of work to do just keeping their systems consistent with the gorilla's; and therefore—somewhat apologetically but nonetheless effectively—they seek to withdraw from supporting any alternatives. Take the case of Microsoft vs. Netscape. Windows PCs are the standard desktop for users of Internet-application software. At present, because Netscape still provides the gorilla share of browsers in the marketplace, they are in a standoff with Microsoft. But once Microsoft has designed its own browser into Windows itself, browsers likely will "dissolve" back into the operating system, thereby positioning Netscape's product as extra software for which there is no compelling need. Simply the fear that this could happen has already reduced the perceived value of the Netscape platform, causing a further shift of customers to the expected gorilla, which will only increase the pressure on Netscape to either redefine the competition or exit the category.

This is gorilla power at work. Microsoft here is not the gorilla on the Internet, but rather the gorilla in PC operating systems who is also threatening to become the gorilla in Internet server operating systems with its NT product. It is using its operating-system-based gorilla power to continually push Netscape off balance. Every time it succeeds, a few of the other members in the marketplace shift their allegiance a little bit, and Microsoft gains a bit of additional market share, which increases its competitive advantage a little bit more.

This sort of attack is extremely difficult to combat. It is part of a larger economic pattern that has been explained by Brian Arthur and others at the Santa Fe Institute as the *law of increasing returns*. Unlike traditional markets, where the power of the market leader is contained at the point of diminishing returns, in technology-based markets there is no diminishing return, and therefore no containment. The powerful simply get more and more powerful. This effect is at the heart of the Department of Justice's heartburn over Microsoft, Intel, and others; for by all preceding rules of competition, the only way one could acquire the kind of power they have is through illegal monopolistic practices. In reality, however, what we are seeing is the essential gorilla advantage, the basis for our claim that, in any technology market, the investor's desired end state is to be 100% invested in the gorilla. Gorilla power may be unfair, but it is not illegal, and it is a stockholder's joy.

TOTAL ASSIMILATION VS. END OF LIFE

Total assimilation represents the end of the Technology Adoption Life Cycle—but not the end of the product category. Indeed, in most industries the bulk of the revenues and profits of the product category are generated long after the technology has been totally assimilated—think of cars, televisions, microwave ovens, and the like. The correct way to visualize this relationship is as follows:

Figure 2.3 Two Life Cycles: Technology Adoption vs. Product Category

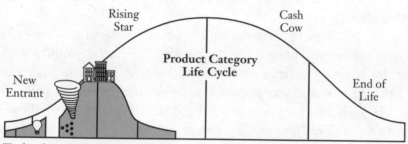

There are three critical lessons to be learned from this diagram. The first is actually a Main Street lesson: *Look how long Main Street is!* Now, understanding the competitive advantages that the gorilla has for the entire duration of the Main Street phase of the market, and understanding the length of Main Street, you can see why the stock market puts such a premium on the price of gorilla stocks.

The second lesson is perhaps the single most profound observation that can be made about technology-based markets:

The power relationships that will govern the category for the entirety of its Main Street market phase are established during the tornado phase—*permanently!*

Marketplace power is fundamentally a function of market share. During the tornado, the mass of customers make their first purchases in the new product category. In so doing, they have to select a vendor. Whichever vendor they select, they will gradually assimilate, meaning that they will make their processes and that vendor's products intertwine. This will create switching costs. Other vendors may subsequently make attractive offers, but the thought of all the work that switching would take will deter the customer from accepting them. This means that whichever vendor the customer starts with is very likely to be the one it stays with. And the same sort of forces operate on business partners. Once one company gets something successful going with another company, there is an inertia that resists further change.

So, market shares get set during the period of hypergrowth—when every customer and business partner makes the initial commitment—then, by virtue of inertia, they last and last and last. The basic business rule here is that you gain or lose a customer in the tornado—for life! The only company whose market-share increases going forward is the gorilla. This happens because as weaker companies fall out of the market, their customers are forced to seek a new vendor, and having been once burned by not going with the market leader, they now intend to rectify that mistake once and for all.

Even when the life of a product category extends decades beyond the tornado that proliferated it, the market-share patterns established during the tornado are the ones that persist. IBM will always be the leader in mainframe computers, just as General Motors has always been the leader in the automotive industry, and Boeing in aerospace, and AT&T in telecommunications. In these cases, to be sure, the outline of the tornado persists faintly, like the geologic residue of some long-ago tectonic shift. Gorilla power has been worn down, and in fact many historic gorillas have grown fat and lazy. But do not let that mislead you as to the reality or intensity of gorilla advantage. Just because some companies have frittered it away does not mean that the power itself is transitory. In Microsoft, Cisco, Intel, and Oracle, the world is meeting a new breed of gorilla whose appetite for growth and power appears to be insatiable. For such companies, extending the life of the product category simply extends the period of their competitive advantage as the gorilla. It is the reason we advocate not just *buying* gorilla stocks, but *holding* them.

The third and final lesson to learn from this last diagram is that, like everything else in life, Main Street ends too. End of life for a product category, however, starts only when an alternative, *displacing* technology enters *its* tornado. In most industries this might happen once or twice a century. In the 1920s the horseless carriage entered its tornado and thereby supplanted the horse and buggy, and perhaps in some future decade the electric car may tornado its way into supplanting today's combustion-driven vehicles. Such displacements have the same effect as what Michael Porter, author of *Competitive Advantage*, has termed a *substitution threat*—they attack the category not from the inside but from the outside. But whereas Porter is typically looking at substitutions of one mature category for another— say, beer for wine or wine for liquor—high tech is characterized by substitutions based on discontinuous innovation. This happens with alarming frequency.

Consider the past twenty years alone:

- Unix servers have displaced proprietary minicomputers, which in turn had previously displaced proprietary mainframes as the dominant server platform.

- PCs have displaced terminals as the dominant desktop device, which in turn had shoved out typewriters.

- Windows has displaced DOS, which had previously displaced CP/M as the leading PC operating system.

- Word has displaced WordPerfect, which had displaced WordStar, which had displaced Wang as the leading word processor.

- Windows NT has displaced Novell as the file and print server of choice going forward, which in turn positions it to challenge Unix for overall server dominance in the coming century.

Substitution threat is a fact of daily life in high tech; and more important, it is the one force that can bring an end to the gorilla game. If the category goes, gorilla power goes with it.

That is why Microsoft totally redefined its business in the mid-1990s in light of the emergence of the World Wide Web. The company saw that the Web browser could well substitute for Windows in the future as the primary desktop operating system. It is why HP merged its Unix and Windows NT server divisions into one, to meet the rising threat that Microsoft's server operating system will eventually erode the position that Unix itself has just recently won. It is why Informix, a relational database company, acquired Illustra, an object-oriented database, in the hopes of attacking Oracle and bringing its relational-database gorilla game to a close. It is why Intel, far and away the leader in CISC microprocessors, has teamed up with HP to incorporate the latter's RISC technology into the next-generation Intel platform—to keep all the other RISC alternatives at bay. Substitution threat is what keeps gorillas up at night and is the reason Andy Grove, the CEO of Intel, says, "Only the paranoid survive."

This concludes our survey of how high-tech markets develop, following patterns deeply imbedded in the Technology Adoption Life Cycle. The model has proved both fruitful and reliable to several generations of high-tech management, and it provides a critical framework within which to understand high-tech investment.

The critical connection between technology markets and financial markets is a mutual interest in *power*. Management strategy seeks to increase power to gain competitive advantage in a marketplace. Investors take an interest in this same goal because companies with competitive advantage provide higher returns to their shareholders. In the next two chapters we are going to explore this linkage in detail, looking first into the structure of the gorilla's competitive advantage, and then into the way that translates into higher stock prices and market capitalization.

Both of these chapters, we must warn you now, require some heavy lifting. Power is a subtle concept all by itself, and when you link it to money, it becomes more slippery still. But this is the linkage that is at the heart of all investing, so we had best get on with understanding it.

3

Understanding Gorilla Power

THE NATURE OF COMPETITIVE ADVANTAGE

To begin with, let us be clear that the power we care about in this book is the power of a given company to provide above-average returns to its investors. To accomplish this goal, companies need to develop unique competitive advantages. These advantages tend to express themselves in four dimensions:

- Getting more customers
- Keeping more customers
- Driving costs down
- Keeping profits up

What we will show in this chapter is that gorillas in the high-tech sector have competitive advantages that not only far outstrip any of their rivals but surpass those of any other type of company in the free market today.

The seminal work on understanding competitive advantage in general is Michael Porter's work, as captured in *Competitive Strategy* and *Competitive Advantage*. Countless managers have studied its principles to frame their analyses of the competitive dynamics in their business sector and the appropriate strategic response their company should make. For the most part, these managers have focused their thinking on actions under their direct control—how to reduce costs, improve methods of production, differentiate products through more targeted marketing, beat competitors to market through faster cycle time, and the like. And all of these are fruitful avenues for acquiring more marketplace power.

In recent years, however, business strategy has shifted from focusing on the company as an autonomous unit to interpreting its performance as part of a larger ecosystem. Nowhere has this shift been more pronounced than in high-tech business strategy, where creating new markets is inherently a cooperative enterprise. These cooperatives are sometimes termed *value chains* because they involve the linking up of numerous entities to fulfill a specific value proposition to a target customer. Like all other human institutions, value chains need clear and stable power structures to sustain themselves going forward. The companies that gain ascendancy within these value chains, however, not only have power *over* the chain, they have the power *of* the chain. That is, they can compete using the chain itself as a weapon, not just their own company's offers.

Gorillas are the preeminent value-chain leaders. As we explained in the previous chapter, for value chains to scale up rapidly the scope and volume of their offers to meet the hypergrowth demands of the tornado, they need standards to ensure that things glue together right. The market creates these protocols on the fly by standardizing on the conventions imbedded in the market-leading products that make up the chain. That was the power behind the phrase "IBM-compatible" in the rise of the PC market. It is the power behind the phrase "Intel Inside" today. Companies that can get their protocols designed into the very standards of the market have enormous influence over the future direction of that market. That is the essence of gorilla power.

THE GORILLA ADVANTAGE

Let's see how value-chain power plays out to create gorilla advantage in each of the four dimensions of business competition:

- *Getting more customers.* This is a market-leader effect. The top company in any market attracts the dominant share of the market's attention. It enjoys better press coverage, more favorable shelf space, and shorter sales cycles just because everyone expects it to be the winner.

But in high tech there is an additional force operating—*business partners actively bring new customer opportunities to gorillas on an unsolicited basis!* In some cases, these partners are currying favor with the gorilla in the expectation that it, in turn, will share some of its bounty with the partner. But in other cases, even when the partner resents the gorilla, it still brings the gorilla into the deal just to ensure that its side has the winning offer. As the de facto standard, in other words, the gorilla sees a lot more deals than any of its competitors. This gives the gorilla the opportunity to sell more, which gains more customers still, which only reinforces its power going forward. It is callled the law of increasing returns.

- *Keeping more customers.* This is a function of two forces—*barriers to entry* and *switching costs*. The former keep competitors out, and the latter keep customers and partners in. It behooves investors to understand both.

Barriers to entry represent work that a competitor must do in order to match another company's offer to the customer. The more work, the higher the barriers to entry. That's true in any market. But in high tech, once again the gorilla has an advantage—*it can make more work for its competitors anytime it wants!* Anytime the gorilla changes any of its interfaces, everyone else in the market has to match it just to stay with the standard. Competitors are faced with two choices, neither of which is particularly attractive. Either don't do this work, and become incompatible with the marketplace standard, or do the work, and forgo whatever value-adding project they were going to put those resources on instead. In either case, the gorilla has a relatively straightforward mechanism for keeping its competitors off balance as often as needed.

Switching costs represent work that a customer or a business partner must do in order to change to another company's offer. The more work, the higher the switching costs. Again, this is true in any market.

But in high tech, switching costs are exceptionally high, for two reasons. First, the interdependency of systems can be so complex that wholesale switching is simply not an option. And second, because high-tech systems become obsolete so fast, taking time to switch from one to another eats into the total time that one could benefit from the new offer, thus reducing its attractiveness. In short, the pain of switching is rarely offset by the gain, and most switches are driven by involuntary forces, such as the Year 2000 problem, rather than any desire to explore greener pastures. So the gorilla, who has the most to gain from the market not switching, has a whole lot of environmental support. This pays off for investors, because if you have the English Channel protecting your island, you don't have to spend a lot of money on building a Great Wall.

■ *Driving costs down.* The fundamental way to drive costs down historically has been economies of scale. The more you buy or make, the more units you can spread your fixed costs over, the less per unit. That's true in any market. But high tech has a way to make that sort of saving look like chicken feed. How about this deal instead: *Want something but it is too expensive? Make somebody else pay for it!* That is routine for a gorilla. Here's how it works.

In a value chain, the cost of the total solution is spread over all the companies participating in the chain, but the relationship between cost and value is not constant. Some parts of the offer have low cost and high value, others just the opposite. All are necessary to the total offer's success, so none can be eliminated. But what if you can confine your offers to just the low-cost, high-value ones? That is precisely what a gorilla can and does do.

Gorillas carve out the sweet spot from the value chains they dominate and leave the scraps to the partners. When the customer demands some high-cost, low-value enhancement, the gorilla makes sure that the burden falls on someone else, not them. They outsource, in other words, the low-value work. If the partner doesn't like it, they are free to leave. There is always someone else to take their place. And if a partner or competitor tries to preempt the gorilla's claim on the high-value stuff, the gorilla can always change the standards on them to throw them off balance.

It is this form of power that causes every other company in the value chain to genuinely hate the gorilla. They don't hate the people, they hate the company, because it is feeding off their work to make its profits higher. And there is nothing, apparently, that anybody can do about it.

- *Keeping profits up.* In one sense, we have already described how this works. If a business can get customers cheaply, keep customers cheaply, and specialize only in high-value, low-cost offers, profits cannot be far away. But once again, the gorilla has an extra competitive advantage in its cache—its products are *worth more.*

Well, not really—not the products, but rather the *whole product* from a gorilla is worth more than its competitors' whole product. A whole product is the complete set of products and services needed by customers to fulfill whatever value proposition motivated their purchase. When companies compete with the gorilla, they lament the fact that their products are better than the gorilla's but they still lose the sale, or gain it only after discounting the price significantly. This is because their whole product is not competitive.

Gorillas have great whole products because every potential business partner gives priority to complementing the market-leading solution before they put resources into complementing some other offer. The reason why is that the gorilla's product has more market share and thus offers a better return on investment. As a result more stuff and better stuff comes out in support of the gorilla's offer than anyone else's. This makes the gorilla's offer more valuable to the customer *at no additional cost to the gorilla!* Pretty sweet, huh?

If all this doesn't seem like magic to you, then you have lost your sense of wonder and need to go see *Peter Pan* again. This really is pixie dust. Gorillas honestly can fly. That's why we want you to invest in them.

But perhaps you are too left-brained for such flights of fancy. So let us drive down to the very core of gorilla advantage and get a fix on it once and for all.

PROPRIETARY OPEN ARCHITECTURES WITH HIGH SWITCHING COSTS _____

The power of the gorilla is based on its control over a value chain. That control, in turn, has its roots in what the high-tech community calls *architecture*, something we'll have more to say about in a moment. An architecture is *proprietary* when it is under the control of a single vendor, in this case the gorilla. It is *open* if its interfaces are published and other vendors are encouraged to integrate their products with the gorilla product to create a whole product for a target customer. Finally, an architecture has *high switching costs* if, once the value chain has formed, the work to swap it out is so costly as to make it unthinkable. The whole combo—a proprietary open architecture with high switching costs—is the formula for gorilla power, assuming the company is successful in assembling the partners needed for a working value chain around this architecture, and the market for that value chain goes into hypergrowth.

This formula owes a great deal to a book entitled *Computer Wars* by Charles Ferguson and Charles Morris. They were the first ones to explicitly call out the importance of *architectural control* to marketplace power. The idea is as straightforward as it is elegant, and we are proud to appropriate it. Here's how it plays out.

Architectures define the way in which various parts of a system hook into one another in order to make the whole thing work. They are incredibly significant because, once an architecture has been agreed to, it is very hard for a competing architecture to gain adoption. For example, once a society agrees on driving on the left or right, it is not likely to entertain the alternative. There is just too much infrastructure already committed. Gaining control over the formative architectural decisions, therefore, is the key battle in any gorilla game.

Architectures can be controlled by a single company or by a group. When they are under the exclusive control of a single company, they are called *proprietary*. The opposite of a proprietary architecture is one that is controlled by some form of committee—a standards body or consortium. Having proprietary control over an architecture at the heart of a tornado market represents the acme of gorilla power. Microsoft has it, Intel has it, and Cisco has it; and all their market caps reflect it.

Architectures can be either *closed* or *open*. If closed, the secrets of the architecture are closely guarded, and only licensed vendors can build products using the architecture. This is how Nintendo entered the market. It is also how Polaroid built its fortune. If an architecture is open, on the other hand, its protocols are published, and any vendor who chooses can build products to its specifications. This is how Intel, Microsoft, and Oracle operate.

In hypergrowth markets, where the first goal of market development strategy is to eliminate bottlenecks to growth, the most rapidly proliferating architectures have proved to be *proprietary* and *open*. The advantage of proprietary control is that the architecture can adapt rapidly and stay coherent. This is the advantage that Microsoft has enjoyed in its competition with the Unix operating system. The advantage of an open architecture is that many vendors can develop products for the market in parallel. The PC tornado provides a good example. IBM insisted that Intel license its 8086 chip architecture to second sources, although Intel resisted the idea; and in the end this proved a boon to Intel's own growth. The market grew incredibly fast, thereby institutionalizing Intel's architecture as a de facto standard.

When proprietary architectures are open, other companies leverage the hypergrowth market of the gorilla, increasing their sales but also increasing the gorilla's value as a standard. Indeed, having a proprietary open architecture, like Windows or Oracle, gives a gorilla the strongest position in a hypergrowth market. Later on, when these markets pass out of hypergrowth, multivendor support is no longer so important. Customers are all locked in to the new architecture, and the amount of new business on Main Street is such that a single vendor can handle all the volume requirements comfortably. Now it becomes more advantageous to the gorilla to restrict licensing. This situation is reflected in Intel's attempts after 1994 to withdraw or limit the right to clone its chips.

The word *open* has become a source of confusion in high tech because vendors in the Unix community have tried to make it the opposite of *proprietary*. When used in this way, *open* really means *committee-controlled*. The attraction of a committee-controlled architecture is the freedom it offers customers and partners to pursue a best-of-breed strategy when it comes to picking component products and thus avoid getting locked into having to buy everything from a single vendor.

Committee-controlled architectures have serious drawbacks, however. First, they lack a single implementation, each vendor being free to create its own interpretation of the standard, and thus the anticipated freedom from switching costs is often an illusion. Second, because these architectures are in the hands of a committee, they are often slow to change, particularly when that committee is made up of warring competitors. Tornadoes reward timely iterative improvements, thereby playing into the hands of proprietary architectures.

This line of thinking helps explain the market power of Microsoft as compared with the consortium of vendors, led by Sun, Netscape, and Oracle, that is battling it. The consortium is promising freedom from Microsoft domination. This promise is compelling to the other vendors in the computer industry since Microsoft, along with Intel, has a history of driving everyone else's profit margins down as theirs go up. These marginalized vendors are therefore attracted to the opportunity to participate in setting future standards, thereby protecting their own interests. The problem is, they can't get to the next step easily, as the storm around Java indicates.

Make no mistake, the goal of the Java consortium is to break free from Microsoft's grasp. At the same time, however, vendors do not want to create a "new Microsoft," so both Sun and Netscape are under constant pressure to stay with the group. Unfortunately, in the customer competition, Microsoft is under no such pressure, so Sun and Netscape are not staying with the group but instead are adding differentiating features at a breakneck pace. This undermines the very promise that was intended to hold together the anti-Microsoft consortium. And Microsoft itself is adding to the confusion by offering to deliver control over one of its key technologies for the Web, Active X, to a committee-controlled consortium. All of which leads to the question: So who is proprietary now?

That all this activity is made up of self-interested machinations is painfully transparent to everyone involved. It is obvious that every player wants proprietary control if they can get it, and if not, wants to block any other player from the same goal. The object lesson for the gorilla-game investor is clear: *Wherever possible, seek out markets where the gorilla candidates have proprietary control of an open architecture.*

NOW ADD IN THE HIGH SWITCHING COSTS

When a company has the power of a proprietary architecture in a product category that imposes high switching costs, it achieves the acme of gorilla power. To capture this lesson for good, consider the following diagram.

Figure 3.1 Power in Hypergrowth Markets

Proprietary Architecture?

	No	Yes
Yes (High Switching Costs?)	■ Fabrication facilities ■ File systems ■ Network cabling	■ Microprocessors ■ Operating systems ■ Routers
No	■ DRAMs ■ Hard disk drives ■ Network Interface Cards	■ ASICs ■ Floptical disk drives ■ Browsers

To make absolutely sure you understand the dynamics of gorilla power, let's walk through the various positions of the companies offering products in each of these four squares.

- *Upper right: Proprietary with high switching costs.*

This is where the gorilla game is played. These companies control not only their own destinies but also those of their partners. We've said enough about them already, so let's move on.

- *Upper left: Nonproprietary but high switching costs.*

As the examples here demonstrate, there are many high-tech buying decisions that result in customers or partners getting locked in without the help of a proprietary architecture. For a chip manufacturer to change a fabrication facility, for example, is to put at risk process characterization lessons that directly affect overall yield. In other cases, changing file systems, or even just upgrading to the next release of your word processor, threatens a lot of downtime with little incremental gain to justify it. And who do you know who would be willing to go back and *restring* all the cables that run through our walls and ceilings?

By virtue of the pain of switching, companies in the upper-left quadrant have an easier time than most *keeping* their *existing customers*. But when they seek to *acquire new customers*, they have no special leverage. As a result, while they have stable and typically long-lived businesses, they tend to earn only a modest premium over commodity margins. This translates into market valuations far lower than the gorilla's.

- *Lower right: Proprietary but low switching costs.*

Products in this category offer added value by virtue of their proprietary nature, but are plugged into larger systems in a way that makes them readily substitutable. ASICs, for example, are the application-specific integrated circuits that give every appliance its own personality. They are changed typically with each new generation of the product. Iomega disk drives and Netscape browsers are two end-user examples of products that can be swapped out relatively easily if future offerings are better from another vendor.

The good news for companies in this quadrant is that their lack of switching costs makes them much easier to try, if for no other reason than customers can see they are not making a long-term commitment. The bad news, of course, is that no one is making a long-term commitment. Because the value is there, these companies usually earn good margins when their products are best in class, but they must continually innovate to keep regaining the right to their customers' business. Their market capitalization, as a result, tends to be bouncy, spiking up when they have a hot product, diving down when they don't. Gorillas, by contrast, have much more stable stock valuations because, even when they do not have the best product, the market is predisposed to buy from them anyway.

- *Lower left: Nonproprietary and low switching costs.*

This is a pure commodity marketplace where execution rules. The good news here is that demand is huge. More and more DRAM is needed for every PC as the software gobbles up memory. And as we create files, that means more and more need for hard disk drives. And as we network more and more, every PC needs a network interface card.

The bad news, of course, is profit margins. In commodity markets, it is almost impossible to consistently generate above-average returns, particularly in a world where some governments are willing to underwrite a large chunk of the operating costs for some of a company's competitors. Regardless of their size, the premiums these companies earn on their stock are minuscule compared to those of even a minor gorilla.

So the key to gorilla power is to be high and to the right—proprietary with high switching costs. Let's see how this power plays out against the gorilla's direct competitors within its own product category.

Gorillas, Chimps, and Monkeys

As we have been discussing throughout this chapter, the marketplace's need for a standard architecture leads it to fixate on the market leader and confer upon it gorilla powers and financial rewards. What then does the marketplace expect from the other companies in the category?

Basically, the marketplace offers these companies the opportunity to play two alternative roles to the gorilla: the *chimp* and the *monkey*. The monkey role emerges later in the history of the market than the chimp's. Because the monkey role is the easier to understand and to play, however, we will look at it first.

Monkeys are simply companies that clone the gorilla architecture and offer products 100%-compatible with the gorilla products at a discount. Their offers are particularly attractive to customers who either cannot afford or cannot get the attention of the gorilla. Advanced Micro Devices (AMD) is a monkey to Intel's PC microprocessor gorilla, Borland with its QuattroPro spreadsheet was a monkey to Lotus 1-2-3, and Amdahl still plays monkey to IBM's mainframe offerings.

The point about monkeys is that they live and die purely based on execution. If one monkey falters, another one will be there to take its place. They do not have permission to change standards, and therefore they cannot create new markets. Moreover, whenever the gorilla makes any change to its de facto standard architecture, monkeys must stop whatever they are doing and reengineer their offers to restore 100% compatibility. As such, they are inherently committed to a "read and react" strategy, never able to plan beyond a horizon that is dictated by the gorilla.

As investments, therefore, monkeys are attractive primarily to opportunistic investors—people who get into and out of the market quickly. The good news about monkeys is that, having no architectural commitments of their own, they can move swiftly to take advantage of the huge markets created by the gorilla. This creates tremendous revenue opportunities for them. The bad news is that monkeys can never create sustainable barriers to entry. That is, their market share is always an illusion, for they have no way to prevent the gorilla from coming in and snatching away their customers whenever it wants. Their market position, therefore, is inherently and permanently unstable.

But for the life of the tornado these companies can generate a lot of revenues and profits. This makes them attractive as short-term investments. For private investors, however, who are best off buying infrequently and holding for the long term, they are a poor choice. They are never part of the gorilla game.

The other primate born in the tornado zoo is the *chimp*. Chimps are companies that tried to become the gorilla but just didn't get picked. As such they have already invested heavily in their own product architecture, one they had hoped would become the gorilla standard, and one that is thoroughly incompatible with the gorilla's.

This fact of incompatibility is the shaping element for their future business strategy, for it gives the chimp the exact opposite marketing problem from the monkey's. Whereas the monkey has market scale but no barriers to entry, the chimp has barriers to entry but no market scale. That is, whatever customers it can win, it can keep, because like the gorilla, it too has proprietary control of an architecture. But since that architecture is incompatible with the gorilla's, and the market is standardizing on the latter, it cannot get all that many customers. Customers are leery of not going with the standard, and business partners do not want the added expense of supporting a second architecture, especially when the market for the leading candidate's is so much bigger.

The chimp is thereby forced to take one of two paths:

1: Continue its attack on the gorilla in an attempt to wrest mass market control away from it.

2: Retreat into one or more niche markets to become a "local gorilla" inside the niche.

We now know from the past decade of high-tech market history that the first of these strategies is simply fatal. Recall that in a tornado, the marketplace must have standards in order to scale up the scope and volume of its offerings. The gorilla's product architecture is the basis for those standards. Anything or anyone who threatens that architecture threatens the marketplace as a whole. So when a chimp attacks the gorilla, everyone in the marketplace—the customers, the service providers, the complementary products providers—all have the same response: *Shoot the chimp!*

This could easily be the title for a movie about the history of IBM's OS/2 operating system for PCs. IBM never realized that it was playing a chimp role. It had spent too much money on OS/2, and by God it had invented the PC, and no upstart West Coast bespectacled little twerp was going to take it away from them. The problem was, they weren't fighting Bill Gates. They were fighting every PC application company that had swung over to Windows, every information systems (IS) director who had finally decided to commit to Windows, every peripheral manufacturer who found in Windows a solution to the escalating cost of writing multiple device drivers for multiple applications—in short, they were fighting the very marketplace they had fostered. It had turned on them, and they, who had always held proprietary control over their customer and partner bases in the past, had no frame of reference to understand the dynamic. As such, they continued up until as recently as the first half of 1996 to launch repeated attacks against Windows, advocating OS/2 as the better choice. To realize how impossible that choice really is, just ask yourself how much money would have to be spent today to reengineer Windows out of the marketplace. (Answer: about as much as it would take to convert to driving on the other side of the road.) There is not that much money on the planet. It is not called the Wintel standard for nothing.

So chimps must never attack gorillas—at least not directly. Instead, their correct response is to take the second alternative noted above— to focus on niche markets whose special needs are being ignored by the gorilla's mass market approach, to enter and dominate those niches as rapidly as possible. Here the liability of a nonstandard architecture is more than overcome by the added value of making special commitments to the niche's unique needs. At the same time, chimps can continue to compete aggressively for new customers in the general mass market, playing the role of a kinder, gentler vendor. There are always mass market prospects who get alienated by the gorilla's high-priced arrogant ways and become angry enough to override their pragmatist bias toward the safe buy.

Overall, in a tornado market the chimp's goal should be to build a respectable market share—ideally a number two position in the mass market anchored by niches of customers within which they are number one. This gives them "local gorilla" powers inside their niche, where they are the market leader and therefore set the architectural standards, and global respectability. Their installed base is eminently defensible inside the niches—indeed, if they execute well, virtually unassailable—plus they have interesting opportunities in the broader market if the gorilla should ever stumble.

This, essentially, is the history of Apple Computer's strategy for the late 1980s and early 1990s. Apple's subsequent problem-filled history emerged only after the PC market moved onto Main Street. At that point two bad things happened from their stockholders' point of view: The gorilla never stumbled, and the company lost patience and focus. It tried to assault the gorilla in its stronghold of corporate IS. Unfortunately, because its chimp architecture required its own dedicated support, Apple's partners could not afford all the software adjustments necessary to make this assault viable. And once Microsoft's Windows 3.1 made a graphical user interface available in a DOS-compatible form, there was no inherent weakness in the gorilla's armor to exploit. Apple got caught outside its own castle, was cut off, lost direction, and as of this writing is having to completely rethink its options in the PC industry.

This kind of problem is inherent in the chimp position on Main Street. It is not that its existing customers defect. It is rather that every new customer coming onto the market, seeing the gorilla as the standard, tends to join the latter's camp, so over time chimp market shares necessarily erode. As this happens, the partners so necessary to fielding a complete solution begin to defect, for although they like their more privileged position in the chimp's value chain, they can no longer get enough new revenue from it to justify the commitment. This in turn further weakens the value of the chimp offer, hastening further erosion in market share, and making for a truly vicious cycle. The correct short-term response for the chimp is to develop new niche markets, but these are often hard to find and not always available. The correct long-term response is to find a new tornado.

It is case studies like Apple's that make us exclude chimps from the gorilla-game target portfolio. It is not that chimps are not "holds"— they can in fact generate decent long-term returns—but as companies they are difficult to manage because their competitive position never really stabilizes. Their best strategy, as noted, is to use their current position to launch an attack in some new area where they can become the gorilla—as HP, which was a chimp in the proprietary minicomputer market, did when the market shifted to Unix. But in such a case, the gorilla game strategy calls for investing in them only after they show up as gorilla candidates in the new tornado market. For the present market, the gorilla game says to sell chimps and put that money into the gorilla.

A ZOOLOGICAL EXCEPTION: GORILLA-LESS TORNADOES

While there is no such thing as a gorilla without a tornado, there are tornadoes without gorillas. These are mass markets that come into existence around nonproprietary standards. Fax machines, monitors, keyboards, disk drives, mice, DRAM memories, scanners, PCMCIA cards, modems—all either began as or developed into markets where no one vendor controls the technical standards. Yet all have gone through mass adoption with tornado-level demands.

When markets develop without the dimension of architectural control, no one vendor gets a permanent lock on the marketplace. Seagate, for example, dominated 5 1/4-inch hard disk drives, but Conner Peripherals dominated 3 1/2-inch hard disk drives; at the end of the day neither had any proprietary advantages, and Seagate bought out Conner in a market that had become completely commoditized. Similarly, Toshiba may dominate one generation of DRAM memory, Samsung the next, and maybe Texas Instruments a third, but none of them can force the other vendors to defer to its standards.

Markets such as these still consolidate behind a strong market leader, but that leader lacks proprietary architectural control over the future of standards. Therefore it cannot force its competitors off balance. Nor, in many cases, can it create high switching costs. The power of a hierarchy will still obtain, of course, but the duration and strength of any one vendor's competitive advantage will be much lower.

The problem for an investor is, at the outset of a market's formation, as it heads into the tornado, it is not always clear whether or not any gorilla candidate will actually achieve the goal of architectural control. As a result, you can end up with investments in two different types of market leaders, both having the same market share, but having very different competitive advantage positions. To describe the difference, a parallel set of terms to gorilla, chimp, and monkey are needed. We have chosen *king, prince*, and *serf.*

KINGS, PRINCES, AND SERFS

These terms, like their zoological cousins, are intended to reflect the status of *leader, challenger*, and *follower*—in this case, in a high-tech market whose development is *not* controlled by any single vendor's proprietary architecture.

- *King.* The market leader, properly with a two-times lead or better over its closest competitor. The market will allow a little leeway here, but if the lead shrinks too far, the king becomes a prince—see below—and we have a kingless market.

Kings enjoy a number of gorilla-like benefits, including economies of scale, favorable distribution terms, enhanced access to customers and partners, and favorable public relations. But because they lack architectural control, and because switching costs are low, they cannot force their competitors onto the defensive the way a Microsoft, Intel, or Cisco can. As such, kings never enjoy a day's rest.

Compaq has been a king in PC servers, having traditionally held a two-times lead over Hewlett-Packard and IBM, although that lead has never been safe. Seagate is a king in hard disk drives, 3COM in Ethernet cards, U.S. Robotics in modems, and Motorola in cell phones and pagers. All of these companies lead their respective markets, but none has the power to manipulate a de facto standard, and none enjoys high switching costs. Thus Motorola, despite its 50% market share in cell phones, is under severe margin pressure from the cellular access providers who threaten to substitute another vendor's product for their free-phone offer to their customers.

In an attempt to reassert architectural control, U.S. Robotics in 1997 has challenged the entire modem industry to a standards war over the future architecture of 56 kbps modems, all in an effort to convert itself from king to gorilla. We will have more to say about this in the final chapter of this book. For now, it is enough to note that everyone else in the market is shocked and appalled that U.S. Robotics would even consider such a thing—which normally means they wish they had thought of the idea first.

- *Prince.* A market challenger, or potentially a coleader of a market that has no definable king. Typically this company has around 10% to 15% market share. Hewlett-Packard is a good example of a prince in the PC market overall. It was able to attack Compaq's 33% market share in the server market and come into a tie for second with IBM at 19% each. It then attacked the PC desktop market, leveraging its printer divisions' clout with the resellers, and accelerated from nowhere into the top five. But again, if next year they were to fall out of the top ten, the only people who would really notice would be HP shareholders and employees.

Dell Computer, which arguably is the most exciting player in the PC market in 1997, is also a prince. It is using distribution excellence to change the dynamics of competition, but it has no opportunity to put in place architectural barriers to entry or to create high switching costs. It is thus forever engaged in an execution-based competition.

Princes make an interesting contrast to chimps: On the downside, they have no proprietary barriers to entry to keep competitors at bay; on the upside, their competitors, even if they are kings, have no barriers to prevent the princes from attacking them. Additionally, unlike the category of chimp, the category of prince permits aggressive merging. Chimps do not merge well because their mutually incompatible architectures undermine the synergy intended by the merger. HP and Apollo's Unix workstation merger, for example, was unable to unseat Sun. But princes who operate under the same architecture standards can aggregate far more effectively. We have yet to see a prince-to-prince merger of any substance in the PC industry—the Packard Bell to NEC merger appears to have been an abortive try—but the king/prince/serf model predicts that we ought to.

■ *Serf.* A market also-ran. This company often has 1% or less market share and is living hand-to-mouth off of opportunistic sales. Individually these companies are insignificant, but taken collectively they serve a key role in the tornado, filling out the low end of the market, meeting the needs of those customers who cannot qualify for the attentions of a king or prince.

There is one arena where serfs can dominate, and that is in commodity markets where there is insufficient revenue or volume to attract a prince or a king to compete. Screen savers, clip art, and free-space pointers are all examples. The typical future of such products is that within a generation or two they simply get integrated into the systems they have been augmenting. The best outcome for a serf at that point is to get acquired as the vehicle for this integration. Worst case is, it's back to the mines in search of the next commodity market.

Markets that have the "royalty structure" of king/prince/serf, as opposed to the "primate structure" of gorilla/chimp/monkey, pose an ambiguous challenge to the gorilla-game investor. In the purest sense they are not part of the game. The problem is, life is not all that pure, and sooner or later it is likely you will fall into one of these markets. The key thing to remember when you do is that a king's power is neither as dramatic nor as persistent as a gorilla's, so you have to play much more cautiously and watch more closely for erosions in the king's position. These issues will be highlighted in our case study on the network hardware tornado, and also play a role in our discussion of investing in the Internet.

FROM COMPETITIVE POSITION TO INDUSTRY POSITION

So much for our discussion of the role of proprietary architectures and high switching costs in the gorilla game. They represent the core forces that keep the gorilla in position *relative to its competitors*. As such, they are the essence of its *local market power*. Now we will turn our attention to a surrounding set of forces that establish a gorilla's position *relative to the industry as whole*. These forces determine the gorilla's standing *relative to other gorillas*, and are at the core of its *global industry power*.

The industry position of a gorilla, its status and therefore its power relative to other gorillas, is directly proportional to the number of other purchases it can influence. The more purchases it influences, the more power it has. The more power it has, the greater its valuation, and the more likely it is to win out in a competition against another gorilla. Gorilla-game investing is all about putting your money behind the power.

The first principle of understanding one gorilla's power relative to another's is to analyze what role each of them plays in bringing together a whole product. The diagram below illustrates the fundamental layering that is incorporated in any high-tech offer.

Figure 3.2 Layers of Technology

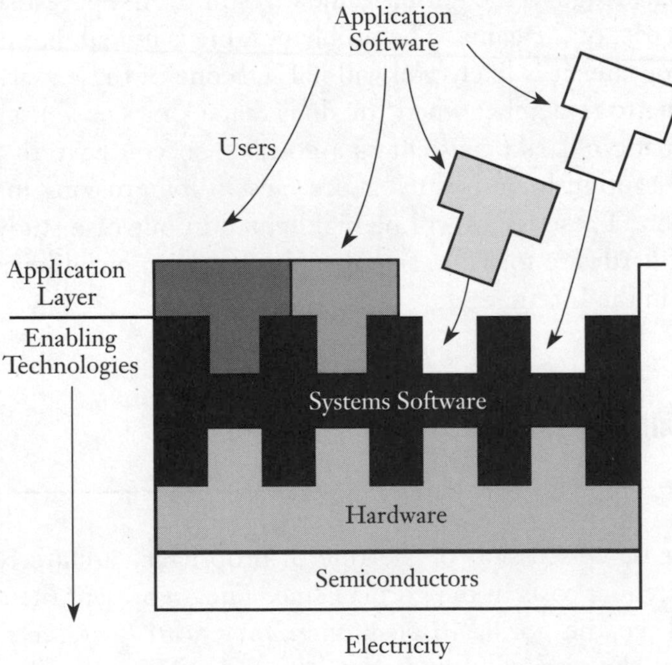

At the base of any of the high-tech offers we consider in this book is electricity. At the top are end users, some set of human beings who are going to benefit from the system whether they touch it or not. To transform electricity into useful value to people, the computer industry funnels it through the four layers diagrammed: semiconductor, hardware, system software, and application software. Here's the value each layer adds:

- *Semiconductors.* These are the engines of high-tech growth and the ultimate source of all the wealth the sector is generating. In and of themselves, they transform electric pulses into ones and zeroes. But their real significance to investors is that every eighteen months these chips *double in price/performance.* This is the famous Moore's Law, named for Gordon Moore, the cofounder of Intel. The reason it is possible is that the cost of any single chip is primarily a function of the number of chips a factory can produce, and that number, in turn, is largely a function of the size of the chip. The smaller the chip, the more chips per factory, the lower the cost. The industry keeps shrinking their chips and passing the savings on to the rest of us. This ultimately is the fuel that high-tech burns.

- *Hardware.* To make the semiconductors usable they have to be strung together with a lot of other stuff to make hardware systems, be they computers, telephones, factory equipment, or the like. Hardware used to be the big-ticket item in high tech; the software was thrown in for free. The 1990s has seen a reversal of this relationship, however, so that nowadays it is the hardware folks who are straining against commoditization and low margins. To push back against this force, hardware companies are internalizing more and more software in their products (sometimes calling it firmware, if they ship it inside a chip).

- *System Software.* Software in general contains the instructions that tell hardware what to do. System software specifically takes responsibility for running a computing environment. It coordinates the functions on the computer it is on—moving files back and forth, sharing memory, allocating resources, keeping the time and date, and the like—as well as that computer's interactions with other computers on the same network. Indeed, networks themselves can be thought of as made up entirely of system software and the hardware needed to run it. In the past ten years, much of the power that used to reside with hardware vendors has migrated to the system software folks, especially those who have leading computer and network operating systems.

- *Application Software.* These are the programs that actually interact with end users, presenting to them letters and spreadsheets and order transactions and graphs and reports. They translate what has heretofore been nothing more than an inert system of signals into meaningful, valuable information or entertainment. As such, they are what the customer sees, and the degree to which they prove valuable is a driver for the success or failure of any potential tornado market. When a piece of application is extremely successful, such that it drives a tornado market, it is called a *killer app*.

We will have a lot more to say in a later chapter about the taxonomy of companies that fill in the layers of this computer industry diagram. For now, the point we want to make has to do with distinguishing between the *enabling technologies*—semiconductor, hardware, and system software—and *application software*. Gorilla games among the former tend toward a much more winner-takes-all outcome than competitions in the latter. It has to do with the relative power of each layer to affect the businesses operating in other layers. Here's what's going on.

APPLICATIONS VS. ENABLING TECHNOLOGIES

The plug-in structure of layered technology makes it critical for standards to emerge in the enabling technology layers, but not as critical for this same process to occur in the software application layers. That is, while all software applications must interact with a common set of underlying enabling technologies, they do not necessarily need to interact with each other. As a result, application-based standards do not have as broad an impact as infrastructure-based standards.

Consider the following comparison of gorilla market share positions:

Figure 3.3 How the Big Get Bigger: The Impact of Network Effects

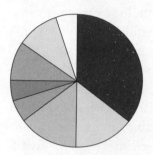

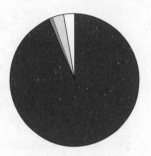

Application software   Enabling technologies

In the pie chart to the left representing application software, the complexity of the offering is such that it does not commoditize easily, and thus cannot proliferate as broadly or interoperate with other systems as intimately. As such, these vendors have network effects only with entities immediately adjacent to their market space—the database vendors, hardware vendors, and systems integrators.

By contrast, in the pie chart on the right, showing the pattern in enabling technologies, products commoditize extremely well, allowing them to proliferate into markets far afield from the original starting points and generate a high degree of network effects. These, in turn, put pressure on the overall marketplace to standardize exclusively on a single set of components, driving market shares to the extraordinary levels that companies like Intel and Microsoft enjoy.

Combining these observations with the principle that gorilla power is partially a function of being able to manipulate standards to one's own advantage, we come to two conclusions:

1: The power of a software applications gorilla is less than that of an enabling technology gorilla.

2: The core enabling-technology gorillas have the highest form of power in the gorilla game.

A curious but important consequence of the first statement is that chimps in an application software market have much less to fear from the gorilla than chimps in an enabling technology market. Indeed, this is proved out. Whereas enabling technology categories shake out severely, there are any number of successful second-tier application companies that thrive in and around the presence of a gorilla. In the overall market for client/server financial systems, for example, where SAP is the gorilla, PeopleSoft, Oracle Financials, J.D. Edwards, Lawson Software, SSA, Hyperion, Platinum Software, Dun & Bradstreet, and Software 2000 all have viable, and in many cases fast-growing, businesses. This means that investors are more free to take "chimp risk" in the applications sector than they would be with enabling technologies. The significance of this observation will become clear in a later chapter, where we argue that investment in application categories should start during the bowling alley phase of market development, while those in enabling technologies must wait for the start of the tornado.

The significance of the second statement, that enabling-technology gorillas are the most powerful animal in the high-tech jungle, can be summarized very simply: *Pay attention to them!* Viewed positively, these gorillas support the entire industry, and all higher-layer vendors benefit from their investments. Without them the remainder of your high-tech portfolio would be valueless. Viewed negatively, however, they threaten every other species on the planet, including a host of vendors whose stocks you will want to hold, for at any time they may be able to leverage their low-level architectural control to privilege a higher-level offer of their own that competes with companies who used to be among their partners. Because all other vendors in the marketplace are ultimately both dependent upon and vulnerable to these gorillas, their behavior must be scrutinized on a daily basis, even if one were not invested in them.

The main takeaway from these observations, however, is that one should be invested in these companies. The manifesto for investing in enabling-technology gorillas reads as follows:

- Because their power is so large,

- Because that power can increase dramatically with the right strategic moves, and

- Because you have to track these vendors closely regardless,

- *Enabling-technology gorillas should be at the heart of every gorilla-game portfolio.*

The gorilla-game investor will note with pleasure that the domain of enabling technologies thickens with every passing year. That is, between the bottom of the enabling software layer, which is the operating system, and the surface, which is the interface to the software application, there can exist any number of other enabling technology layers. Database software lives here, as does messaging software, and a whole variety of other services so arcane they are often just called "middleware." But arcane though they may be, they are being called into existence by the increasing complexity of distributed computing, a trend that shows no signs of abating anytime soon. These intermediate layers appear likely to evolve in a manner akin to the deeper enabling software layers, privileging a single, dominant gorilla blessed with ever-increasing market share.

At the same time, however, gorilla-game investors should not be blind to some attractive advantages held uniquely by application software. Unlike their enabling-technology cousins, applications are the only products that the end-user customer ever actually sees. *Therefore, whereas enabling products have the most industry power, application products have the most customer power.*

Customer power is particularly important in markets that have not quite made it into the tornado. At this phase, the ability to go straight to the customer and stimulate demand is a huge competitive advantage, and even big established enabling-technology gorillas will come courting to gain a foothold in the new marketplace. So when markets are in the bowling alley, application vendors actually have greater power than enabling-technology vendors. It is only after markets and infrastructures get swept up into the tornado, and customer demand can be increasingly taken for granted, that the power seeps down into the underlying layers.

For this reason, we think there is a companion manifesto for investing in application-software gorillas. It goes like this:

- Because they lead much of the new market development,

- Because they participate in all the benefits of gorilla dynamics (albeit on a more modest level than their enabling-technology cousins), and

- Because the risk of buying and holding them is lower than with enabling technology companies (since the power of an application gorilla to wipe out the rest of the category is less fearsome than that of an enabling-technology gorilla),

- *Software application gorillas should be a part of—indeed, probably the major part of—every gorilla-game portfolio.*

The reason we say "probably the major part of" is that a relatively large number of these companies will do reasonably well, whereas proportionately fewer will do well in the enabling-technologies space. In the interests of portfolio diversity, therefore, we think they play a sound, risk-reducing role.

COMPETITION AMONG THE LAYERS

Another key point to be made about the four layers of technology is that each layer competes with the others for the opportunity to add value to the end user. In any given market, one or more layers get the upper hand and use that power to take the lion's share of the profits. Here is how it has played out in several markets to date:

- In the mainframe computer market, from the outset, the hardware layer vendors dominated, with IBM taking the lion's share of the market. Probably the second most successful company has been Computer Associates, who started in system software and then expanded into application software. In general, however, applications were late in coming to this party and never gained real ascendancy, and semiconductors were for the most part captive functions within the hardware organizations.

- In the minicomputer market, by contrast, the database vendors, members of the systems software layer, took over the reins of power, led by Oracle with its strategy of porting the database to every hardware company's computer. This made that software a natural layer to standardize upon, relegating the underlying hardware and operating system to more of a commodity status. This phenomenon became even more pronounced when minicomputer vendors migrated their platforms all to the same operating system, Unix. We will have more to say about the history of the database tornado in the first of our case studies. Application vendors began to come into prominence with this common platform beneath them. Semiconductors were still captive functions.

- With the rise of global networking, the choice of computer hardware becomes increasingly arbitrary, even at the mainframe level, and the focus has shifted to networking hardware, another element of the enabling hardware layer, instead. Cofueled by the simultaneous rise of the Internet, and the general conversion to electronic mail (the killer app), this category has spawned a series of tornadoes, as we shall have occasion to discuss in the second of our case studies. Oddly, while e-mail, the application software, is the killer app, it has been, almost since birth, a commodity. Semiconductors, on the other hand, now come into prominence, as more and more of the network hardware is assembled from merchant chips.

- In the client/server tornado, application software vendors have come to the fore, having successfully commoditized the database layer beneath them. Today for business systems, the first choice one makes is no longer the hardware or the database, but rather the application. That gives those vendors the top-dog position, at least with the customer. SAP is a gorilla in this space for enterprise-wide business software, but there are a whole slew of new tornadoes coming, one of which, customer service software, we take on in the third of our case studies.

- In addition, the Internet has given rise to a whole new category of offer that consists essentially of services, or content. This category is competing for investment capital with the traditional product-centric offers of high tech. Where will its power shake out? Does it warrant adding another layer model, or is it another form of application software? We'll discuss this in our final chapter, where we take up investing in the Internet space.

- Finally, in the personal computer market, where Microsoft and Intel rule, it is the hardware layer that has been most commoditized. The industry is totally dependent on Intel to continue its price/performance generosity, and therefore semiconductors have an exceptionally strong seat at the table. Microsoft's ongoing power comes from its operating system position in the enabling software layer. Application software, which dominated in the 1980s, has become increasingly commoditized, with Microsoft dominating through a wonderful Main Street strategic coup of consolidating the commodities into its Office suite.

The significance of these competitions between layers is that they affect a gorilla's overall competitive advantage and thus its overall market capitalization. When the competitions are at arm's length, the consequences are relatively modest. They intensify, however, as we drill down a level into the competition between "adjacent gorillas," each intent on expanding into the other's turf. Here the consequences of a shift in power can have a major impact on the value of your holdings.

COMPETITION BETWEEN GORILLAS

When any company emerges as a gorilla, it always gets the full suite of competitive advantages we have been discussing *local to its marketplace*. As long as that market is isolated from other markets, these advantages result in dramatic competitive advantage, raising the valuation of that company far above the others in its category. If the local market is sufficient to allow the leading companies to go public, then gorilla-game investing strategy can be applied to the category, with gorilla-game returns.

The only issue that remains is one of longevity. These gorilla advantages are secure only as long as the gorilla's marketplace remains distinct from other gorillas' marketplaces. This puts two elements in conflict with each other: *scalability*, the ability of the market to expand in scope and volume, and *barriers to entry*, the ability to maintain its separation from other markets. Both are required to sustain ongoing gorilla-like valuations. However, the more scalable a market is, the more likely it is to intersect with another gorilla's turf, and the more challenging it is to keep other companies out. Conversely, the higher the barriers to entry protecting a market, usually the more complex the solution is to replicate, and therefore the harder it is to scale the market. There is a trade-off, then, between scalability and barriers to entry.

Whenever this trade-off condition occurs, the barriers-to-entry play is safer in the short term, and the scalability play is safer in the long term. Here's why. Strong barriers to entry will always protect the competitive advantage of a company from being taken away but may limit its ability to grow through entry into new markets. As a result, the scope for exercising that advantage will reach a limit as the market saturates, and after that the company's market capitalization will gradually erode, there being no new growth areas in which to exploit its competitive advantage.

Stocks in this situation enter a curious limbo state. If their category remains isolated and distinct from the rest of the market, their returns will continue to justify holding them. Cadence in Electrical CAD and Autodesk in Mechanical CAD are examples of such companies. But they are now essentially stationary targets for any expansion-minded gorilla who can come up with a way to bring its commodity-based power into what has heretofore been a high-value niche. This is the threat, for example, that Silicon Graphics, a gorilla in high-end 3-D visualization systems, finds itself under from Intel, driving PCs to higher and higher graphic performance levels.

Conversely, a company in a highly scalable market with low barriers to entry will quickly attract any number of dangerous competitors, some far better established than itself, forcing the company to engage in a footrace against them. At the outset of this race, any mis-step could be fatal, and their gorilla status is greatly at risk. But the longer they keep ahead, the more the marketplace forms itself around their standards, the more gorilla advantages they enjoy, the greater the barriers to entry become. Thus their risk decreases over time, and with lots of market room to grow into, their market capitalization continues to expand. These are stocks one does not want to exit from early; they are your long-term holds.

Marimba may become an example of one such company, entering the Internet market with a leading offering for "push" technology, and Progressive Audio another, with its "data streaming" technology. (It's hard to tell because neither's market has yet crossed the chasm.) In either case, if these companies can get out ahead of the pack fast enough, and stay out there, they win. But they are just as likely to get subsumed by larger players as these steamrolling giants finally catch up to their space. Often their safest strategy is to sell out at the height of their value, as Vermeer did to Microsoft for its FrontPage Web-authoring technology. Timed optimally, these acquisitions can be extremely profitable for the gorilla-game investor.

When Gorillas Fight

When a smaller gorilla is subsumed by a larger gorilla, assuming it is for good strategic reasons, the shareholders of both companies bene-fit. Indeed, this is the reward for the smaller company's successful execution of a focused strategy targeted on a hypergrowth market. That's a good outcome from a "gorilla collision."

There are also bad ones. When two gorillas, each in the process of imperialistically expanding its territory, encounter each other and decide they must fight to the death, three things can happen, and two of them are bad:

1: *Your gorilla loses out to the other gorilla.* This will have the effect of submarining your gorilla's stock as it gets redefined as a chimp in a larger gorilla game. It is what happened to 3COM in the LAN switching market in 1996, when its share fell from 50% to 17% as Cisco's rose from zero to 38%—all in the space of a year. It is what happened to Shiva when its remote access devices market got redefined by Ascend, and its stock went from $80 per share to $8.

2: *The two gorillas fight to a standstill.* This leads the stock market to cut back on the market value of both companies as it becomes clear that neither will be able to extend its market growth into the other's territory. Alternatively, if they persist in fighting, the competition can lead to severe price erosion, reducing their earnings and eroding their market valuation. Overall, undecided collisions normally do not have a cataclysmic downside effect on gorilla stocks, but they do start to put a limit on future upside potential. This has been the apparent outcome in Autodesk's undecided collision with Parametric Technology Inc. in the Mechanical CAD market. It is something to watch for in the coming collisions between Ascend and Cisco over the future of the remote access market, between Hewlett-Packard and Xerox over the future of the print/copy marketplace, and on a grander scale, between Microsoft and Intel over the "beyond the PC" movement.

On the other hand, in a gorilla fight there is one very good possible outcome:

3: *Your gorilla wins,* which leads to a dramatic uptick in the value of your portfolio, as the added value of ruling a new market supplements the already highly valued market cap of your gorilla's stock. When Cisco, the gorilla in routers, confronted Bay Networks, the gorilla in hubs, and won, both stocks were readjusted dramatically, to Cisco's glee and Bay's chagrin.

Overall, gorilla collisions pose the single toughest challenge in the gorilla game. They do not have a probable outcome. It is more like a chaos function whose output swings wildly one way or the other based on seemingly insignificant changes in input. Sometimes the safest course is to own both gorillas, take the loss and the gain, and average their impact. Sometimes it is better to get out of one gorilla and keep the other. Sometimes it is best to get out of both gorillas. But we are getting ahead of ourselves, for buying and selling is the focus of a later chapter. For now, just be alerted to the phenomenon, and know to watch out for it carefully.

GORILLA POWER AT WORK: THE EXAMPLE OF INTEL

Gorilla power, as we have discussed in depth, is a function of a company's competitive position in its own market and its industry position relative to other gorillas. Industry position has power in a static situation just based on clout with the current set of partners and customers. But the strongest of all industry positions is when a company has strategic advantage not only in its current markets but also for entering new markets. That is the position of the major enabling-technology gorillas today.

Intel offers a prime example. Founded in the 1960s, it has become one of the most profitable companies in the world, with some of the highest annual profits for any company in history. All of this has stemmed from its initial "design wins" in the early 1980s, when its microprocessor was chosen by IBM to be the centerpiece of its new PC. Their 8088 and 8086 CPUs quickly became the de facto standard for most PC vendors around the world (a notable exception being the Japanese market, where NEC's CPU became the de facto standard).

Intel's de facto standard architecture has an astronomical switching cost. Consider how much infrastructure would have to be pulled up and then redeployed just to get back to where we are today. Most enabling software, including Microsoft's operating systems, is written specifically for the Intel CPU. To be sure, Digital has secured Microsoft support for its Alpha chip, something Motorola could not do for the Power PC. But Digital's position is no more secure for future releases of the operating system than Apple's is for future releases of Microsoft Office. At the end of the day, market share will have its way.

The market position of Intel's architecture ensures that the competitive advantage within category is long-lived. This frees Intel from the pressures of chimp competition. It does not free it, however, from the pressure of monkey competition. AMD and National Semiconductor, with its acquisition of Cyrix, both have successful cloning efforts under way. These challenge Intel's margins and force it to compete more like a king and less like a gorilla than it would like to. However, it is all a matter of degree. The company still has massive market share advantage and still secures premium margins for its latest products.

What has been so miraculous about Intel has been its ability to *extend* its de facto standard advantage. Intel has leveraged its original 8088/8086 CPU line into a series of very successful generations of CPUs, starting with the 80286 in the mid-1980s and continuing with the 80386, 80486, Pentium, Pentium Pro, and Pentium II. Each of these generations has gone through its own tornado, one after another in a carefully managed sequence, so that just as one was nearing the end of its tornado, the next was just beginning. This "scheduling of tornadoes" has enabled Intel to stay in what seems like a perpetual tornado, a recurrent and seemingly stable condition of perpetual hypergrowth. And before the end of the century, its next-generation microprocessor, codeveloped with Hewlett-Packard, is expected to continue Intel's streak.

Intel's leverage, however, does not just extend into successive generations of higher performance CPUs. It also extends into subsuming the functionality of other kinds of chips. The motherboard of a PC—the main circuit board—is made up of the Intel CPU plus dozens of other supporting chips designed and manufactured by various other chip manufacturers. Each successive generation of Intel CPU, however, has eliminated the need for some of those supporting chips by including their functionality right into the CPU. In the move from the 80386 to the 80486, for example, Intel incorporated floating point processing into the main CPU, thereby taking those dollars away from competitors' offerings. And more recently, it has made the same sort of assault on graphics coprocessors.

Intel's ability to leverage itself into some of the other supporting chipsets has caused many to call the Intel CPU the "black hole" of the PC motherboard. Today a number of other supporting chips in a

PC are potential candidates to wind up in future versions of the Intel CPU, including ones for sound, multimedia, communications, and videoconferencing. Vendors who provide these chips today are, in the words of one wag, "picking up dimes in front of steam rollers." It is easy pickings, but sooner or later you have to give these markets up to the big guy.

As if owning the "black hole" of the motherboard were not enough, Intel has also leveraged itself into the PC motherboard manufacturing business, such that it is now the number one manufacturer of PC motherboards in the world. When Intel runs TV ads claiming to be "the computer inside," they're not kidding. Most PC manufacturers have been relegated to the position of final assemblers—packaging Intel's motherboard (the computer inside), together with Microsoft's operating systems and whatever added value they can come up with for themselves. Scott McNealy, CEO of Sun Microsystems, has often joked that his company is not interested in entering the PC business because the PC manufacturers are "merely resellers for Intel and Microsoft."

As a gorilla-game investor would expect, over the years Intel's profits have soared, and so has its stock price. In the seven years beginning in 1990 through the end of 1996, Intel stock appreciated 1200%, for a 44.3% compounded average annual rate of return. Over the same period, Intel's chief competitor, Advanced Micro Devices, a monkey who has done very well selling clones of Intel's CPUs, has appreciated 212%, for a 17.7% compounded average annual rate of return. AMD's return is not bad, except when you compare it to Intel's. Only gorillas deliver gorilla returns.

GORILLAS UNDER ATTACK, AND COUNTERATTACKING

At this point you might imagine that gorillas are the irresistible force, the immovable object, and immortal to boot. Instead of investing in indexed funds, let's just invest everything we have in known gorillas, and then we can all go home. That would work if it weren't for one more force that has to be factored into the gorilla game: *substitution threat from a future discontinuous innovation.*

Lotus 1-2-3 was the gorilla in spreadsheets—until the discontinuous innovation of Windows came along and created the opening for Microsoft Excel. Digital was the gorilla in minicomputers—until the discontinuous innovation of Unix came along and created an opening for Sun and Hewlett-Packard. Dun & Bradstreet was the gorilla in corporate financials on the IBM mainframe—until the discontinuous innovation of client/server computing came along and created an opening for SAP. When any layer of technology shifts, all the gorilla-game power positions potentially go back up for grabs. When this happens, as often as not it is the incumbent who is operating at a disadvantage because everyone else has nothing to lose.

In the old days, when gorilla companies were more sedate, they clung to their traditional markets and privileged margins as long as they could. This meant each year they gave up market share and marketplace power to the new generation of gorillas attacking their franchise. There was, if you will, a changing of the guard. But now companies have seen the impact of that strategy and no longer "go gentle into that good night."

To hold on to their gorilla advantages, successful high-tech companies now realize they must confront the onslaughts of discontinuous innovation aggressively and eliminate them by whatever means possible—typically by throwing overboard one or more principles that had been core to their business heretofore. Below are recaps of three successful gorilla counterattacks against such substitution threats:

1: In the mid-1980s a gang of vendors, including Sun with SPARC, HP with PA RISC, and MIPS with its R3000, attacked Intel's microprocessor hegemony, with the proposition that RISC (reduced instruction set computing) architecture offered a ten-times improvement in price/performance over traditional CISC (complex instruction set computing) chips, including Intel's. The company was able to fend them off, however, by

A. Immediately fielding some very skillful public relations to create FUD (fear, uncertainty, and doubt) around the new category.

B. Subsequently incorporating an increasing number of RISC features into its CISC chips.

C. Finally coopting the RISC paradigm entirely via an alliance with Hewlett-Packard to codevelop Intel's seventh-generation CPU, based in part on HP's PA RISC architecture.

This is gorilla competitiveness at its finest.

2: When local area networking switches threatened to replace the need for routers, Cisco bought Crescendo to protect itself in the LAN switching space, and then bought Stratacom to protect it in the telephony WAN (wide area networking) space—the latter at a cost of $4.7 billion. As noted earlier, 3COM, the early leader in LAN switches, got shunted aside by the combined might of Crescendo's more modern technology and Cisco's gorilla marketing muscle. If a gorilla can get to the fire before it burns out of control—i.e., before it generates a stable gorilla alternative—it can usually save its ranch. The market is simply too dependent on the gorilla not to give it every chance to succeed.

3: When Netscape's browser threatened to become the first thing users saw on their computer when they turned it on, Microsoft recognized that its fundamental control of the desktop was in jeopardy. It reorganized its entire company in order to adapt, and has been gaining significant market share in the browser wars ever since. With each new release of the Windows desktop, the company goes further and further toward its promise to embed the browser in the operating system, thereby dissolving the very category that to this day still threatens its rule. Once again, this is gorilla power at work, guarding the plantation against a standard that does not even exist yet.

As these examples show, even when they are attacked by a substitution threat, gorillas have strategic advantages that can let them counterattack effectively. In the old days, gorillas used to be too enamored of their high margins and cushy market positions to field a really aggressive response, and new classes of competitors could get in and eventually displace them. But this latest generation of gorillas, having learned from the past, does not share this weakness, and it is becoming increasingly challenging for new technologies to break through.

THE SIGNIFICANCE OF THE GORILLA FOR INVESTORS

As we have seen, by virtue of the dynamics of technology markets, gorilla companies enjoy persistent competitive advantages far in excess of the other companies in their category. This means they can be expected to generate financial returns far in excess of their category, and for that reason we can expect them to enjoy premium valuations as equities.

While gorillas have spawned some of the great executives of our time, the primary force behind ongoing gorilla success is not brilliant management but rather the tacit support of the marketplace at large. Indeed, numerous later-stage gorillas have had some pretty awful management at times and still come through successfully. The market simply does not want them to fail because if they did, everyone dependent on their architecture would have to reengineer a whole layer of technology just to get back to where they were. That would be a bad deal all around. So the gorilla *must* stay.

That is the essence of gorilla power. It is what makes gorillas such good investments. Now that we have developed this argument at length in the context of the high-tech marketplace, it is time to look at these same issues in light of the financial marketplace. So from Main Street we will now head over to Wall Street.

4

Understanding the Stock Market

THE VALUATION OF COMPETITIVE ADVANTAGE

In the previous two chapters we have explained how and why technology markets during the tornado give a single company, the gorilla, a disproportionate amount of industry power in a very short amount of time. This phenomenon is not lost on the stock market, which in turn accords a disproportionate amount of market capitalization to this same company. In the stock market's most basic terms, a gorilla looks like a very hot company in a very hot category, and its price gets bid up.

Nevertheless, we are going to suggest that the market undervalues just how hot this gorilla is. That is why we are going to buy the gorilla's stock. But we have to say at the outset that the stock will not look undervalued—it would certainly not attract a value investor—so we need to have a framework for understanding just what is going on.

In this chapter we offer a simple and straightforward model for this purpose. It says that the primary determining factor for any company's stock market value is its perceived competitive advantage, or lack thereof, in its major markets. We are going to use this model to explain the stock market dynamics of the high-tech sector in general and of the gorilla game in particular. In part our goal here is to show how the gorilla game fits into conventional investment theory. At the same time, however, we hope to steer investors away from a whole slew of complicated issues that, in our view, add little value to the investment decision process and make investing itself far too daunting a task.

But first we interrupt this chapter with a special bulletin for the reader (from Geoffrey):

Sometime in the 1980s, a book came out called *DOS for Dummies*. It was such a hit that pretty soon other "dummies" books followed, even one called *Sex for Dummies* by Dr. Ruth (I know because she gave me two of them, sensing perhaps a remedial student). Well, this chapter could just as easily be titled *The Stock Market for Dummies*.

To write a good "dummies" book you need three things: a domain expert (that's Paul), a real-world practitioner (that's Tom), and a designated dummy (that's me). For the rest of this chapter I will be the one writing, and I offer you my personal guarantee that I am putting nothing down on the page that has not first been explained to my satisfaction.

So if you are, like me, a trifle intimidated by this topic, take it from the dummy—it's not *that* hard. It may take a second read—it took me more than that, for sure—but this stuff does make sense, and you really do need to understand it if you are going to be comfortable with any investment strategy.

We now return you to our regular programming.

First Principles

The first principle of investing is that if you buy shares in a company, they must be worth something. Why?

Well, okay, there is a market for them, be it the NASDAQ or the New York Stock Exchange or whatever, and there are people who will buy your shares back, and so you could say they are worth whatever those people will pay for them. But why are they worth anything to those people? What's going on here?

The answer is, to buy a share in a company is to buy a share of all its future profits after taxes. It doesn't matter whether those profits are distributed in the form of a dividend, or held back as retained earnings to use for future investment. They are what you bought a share of. And the value of that share is based on the stock market's expectations of the amount and the timing of the profits to be generated.

So the first lesson of the market is that stock prices are based on expectations about future operating profits. Both the word *expectations* and the word *future* have significant ramifications that need further attention. Let's begin with *future*.

WHAT'S THE FUTURE WORTH?

Today you have a dollar. Suppose I say, give me the dollar today, and ten years from now I will give you back two dollars. Good deal or bad deal? How would you know?

Essentially this is the offer that every investment transaction is based on, so it behooves us all to have some basis for thinking through the question. The accounting profession has actually come up with a formal methodology for attacking the problem, called *discounted cash flow analysis*. It sounds "accounting-ish," and it is, but at its heart it is based on a simple idea—a future dollar is not worth as much as a present dollar, and you can actually quantify by how much.

That future dollar is worth less for two reasons:

1: There is some risk that you might lose the dollar or some portion of it.

2: There is a certain amount of money you could have made over the same period simply by putting the dollar into a risk-free investment.

To overcome the risk factor, investors must be promised a rate of return that is attractive enough to warrant the chance of losing some or all of their money. Additionally, that rate has to be over and above the amount of money they could have made by just buying a bond— essentially a risk-free investment. That is, if I can make 5% from Uncle Sam, and someone wants me instead to invest in a private company, they have to make the return better than 5%. The greater the risk, the greater the difference needs to be. These two factors—the risk-free rate of return plus the risk adjustment—make up the total offer to the investor.

Let's suppose the promise is for a 15% return, and that I accept the offer. An accountant would say, Aha, if it takes $1.15 worth of future dollars to get one of today's dollars, then a future dollar is worth 100/115 of a present dollar, or 87 cents. That's the formula for the first year—discount the future dollar's value as 87% of a present dollar's value.

Okay, what about the following year? Well, that's another year Geoffrey has to go without his money—a year when he could have invested it elsewhere. Furthermore, the more time that money is in someone else's hands, the greater the risk that something could go wrong. So the returns promised for Year Two cannot be worth as much as those for Year One. The accounting method says, we can model that. Tell you what, keep the discount rate the same, but make it cumulative. Year Two's money is worth 87% times 87% of the promised amount, Year Three's 87% of that, and so on.

Here's what it looks like in the form of a chart:

Figure 4.1 Face Value vs. Net Present Value

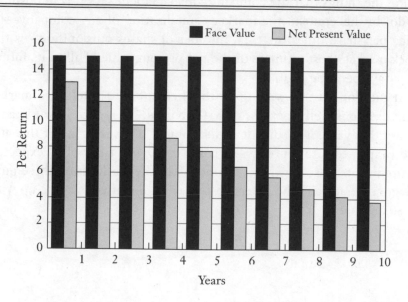

The left-hand column for each year is the promised rate of return—in this case, 15% per year for ten years. That is the face value of the offer to the investor. The right-hand column for each is the net present value of that same 15% promise to the investor today. What the graph says is that, for a $100 loan, the $15 promised in the first year is worth $13.04, the $15 promised for the next year is worth $11.34, for the following $9.86, and so forth. The further into the future you go, the more you have to discount the promise in order to calculate its present value. Thus the promise of returning $15 per year for ten years, or $150 all told, is worth $75.28 today. In sum, money promised in the future (a bird in the bush) is not worth as much as I own today (a bird in the hand), but it is always worth something, and using this kind of methodology people can actually put a specific value on how much.

The stock market operates to the same end. A share of stock is a share of a company's future returns. The price of that stock is based on the market's expectations of the net present value of these future returns. Some of those returns may come from one-time transactions—money invested in CDs or derivatives or real estate—but the stock market does its best to ignore this kind of performance. It is interested primarily in returns from operations, money made from doing the things that the company's management says it is in business to do. In this context, the market capitalization of any company—its price per share times the total number of shares outstanding—is the stock market's best estimate of the net present value of all of its future after-tax operating profits.

At the time of this writing, both Microsoft and Intel have market capitalizations well in excess of $100 billion. To realize how extraordinary that value is, realize it is discounted! That is, it is not the sum of all expected future profits—it is the *net present value* of all expected future profits. Just how much money does the world think these guys are going to make? And where in the world did anyone come up with these numbers?

INCORPORATING EXPECTATIONS

The bar chart we used to describe net present value was in one sense very simple. The promise each year was both specific and unvarying: I'll give you another $15 if I get to hold on to your $100 for another year. That works for a loan or a bond, but not for a company. Its promise is much less specific and much more variable. The truth is, management does not know how much they are going to return. All they can do is forecast to the best of their ability and make that forecast available to investors as input. They can, in other words, *set expectations.*

Investors, in turn, look at the material produced by management—the discussions of operations in each quarterly report is a good place to start—and then factor in their own information and ideas to come up with their own set of expectations. Based on these expectations, they may decide to bid for a share of this management team's future operating profits. The amount of that bid is a direct reflection of their estimate of the net present value of the share they would get of those future profits (whether they know it or not).

To actually buy a share, of course, there must be a seller as well as a buyer. If the bid is accepted, that means that someone else thinks the net present value is less than or equal to the price offered. The seller in other words has a different set of expectations. On an individual basis, the seller's motive could be almost anything. Maybe they "know" the company is going to tank. Maybe they just want to get their money out to buy a house. Who knows? But on an aggregate basis, in a market where there are many buyers and many sellers, individual motives cancel out. The system instead operates more like the laws of chemistry and physics—it seeks an equilibrium point where the expectations of buyers and sellers converge.

The stock market simply acts as a broker among investors, letting them buy and sell from each other. Each transaction represents a moment of equilibrium when, for at least one buyer and one seller, a mutually satisfactory valuation has been reached. That price is posted and becomes the reference point for the next transaction. In a market with broad dissemination of information, low costs of transaction, and an enforced legal system, prices tend to stabilize relatively quickly and then, going forward, change only on changes in expectations.

Visualizing Expectations

Diagramming these ideas helps to understand what is going on. Here is a chart reflecting how investors might view a company they expect to grow steadily over an indefinite period of time:

Figure 4.2 Valuing a Growth Company

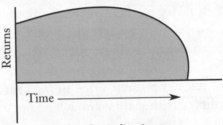

Market Capitalization

The vertical axis in Fig. 4.2 represents returns—profits or earnings divided by the amount invested; the horizontal axis, time. The curved line represents the changing present value of these earnings as they get projected further and further out in time. Because of growth, the curve goes up in the early years—earnings will increase because revenues will increase. That growth is not projected to cease, but the confidence of the investor in it happening decreases the further out in time you go. This causes the curve to flatten and then decline. Eventually that confidence drops to zero—where the curve falls back to hit the baseline—not because of any doubts about the team or the strategy or the market, but just because beyond a certain point in time the investor thinks any further projection is simply too speculative.

The shaded area under this curve represents the present value of all the future returns the stock market is willing to include in the projection. That area equals the market capitalization of the company. Buying shares in the company means buying shares of that area. The bigger the area, the more valuable the company, the more the stock price goes up. This particular chart could stand for any number of reasonably successful, non-gorilla companies operating in markets that are not in hypergrowth.

Continuing with our exercise in visualization, sometimes a management team will argue it not only takes money to make money, it takes time to make money. For a while, they say, they expect to lose money as they develop the market and build up production capacity. But then the market will take off, and the investors who bought in early will make a bundle. This creates expectation curves that look like this:

Figure 4.3 Starting Under Water

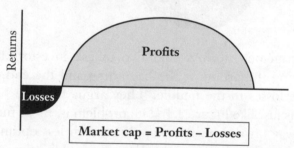

The area in Fig. 4.3 below the horizontal line represents losses, or negative returns. These must get subtracted from future profits or gains above the line to calculate the *net* present value of the company to investors. Thus the company's market capitalization equals the area above the horizontal line minus the area under it (the line itself standing for zero).

This chart is typical of start-ups and venture-capital-backed companies. The big challenge in this type of investing is how much confidence to place in the projections. Venture capitalists worry about four major risk factors—technology risk (can it work?), market risk (will the customers buy it?), financial risk (will we have or make enough money to cover our expenses, including the period of losses?), and people risk (are these the people who can do it?). Gorilla-game investors, by contrast, never take the first two risks—they buy only proven technologies that are already in hypergrowth markets.

Finally, sometimes a good company falls on bad times. In high tech, for example, it might be that its technology is being displaced with some new discontinuous innovation and thereby becoming obsolete. That creates an expectation curve that looks like Fig. 4.4:

Figure 4.4 Headed for a Fall: Management's View

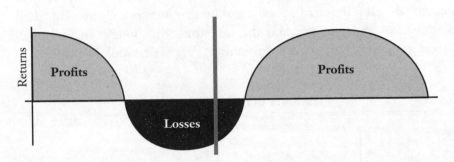

This management team would like to ask investors to stay the course, getting the profits at the beginning and the end, and living through the losses in the middle. They argue that the back half of their curve is just like Figure 4.3. The problem is, those future profits are a long way off and investors apply a much less optimistic confidence factor to those projections. Factoring in the time element of risk, the actual net present value of those future profits would look more like Fig. 4.5:

Figure 4.5 Headed for a Fall: An Investor's View

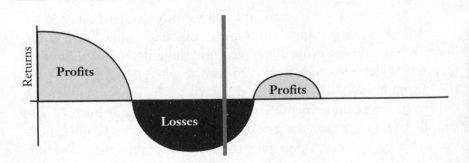

Looking at the future this way, rational investors would prefer instead to sell now. Even if management's view is correct, they reason, the right thing to do is sell now and then buy back at the time represented by the bold vertical line. At that point, if the management forecast is true, the profits on the right in Fig. 4.5 will have swollen back up to their original size, and the new curve going forward really will look a lot like Fig. 4.3.

Fig. 4.5 represents the way that Novell and Apple look to investors in the middle of 1997. The problem for these management teams is that, if everybody agrees to sell now and buy back in later, where is the funding for getting through the period of losses? The answer is, there isn't any funding, at least not any at a valuation that management can accept. This explains why when companies get in real trouble, they must not turn to some radical discontinuous innovation as the answer. Even if they had the stuff to bring this technology across the chasm and create a tornado market, they don't have the money or the time.

VISUALIZING THE GORILLA

Each of the diagrams above represents a different set of expectations for the future operating profits of a company. The easiest way to understand the power of the gorilla game is to overlay the market capitalization chart of an average company onto that of a gorilla. Here's what it looks like:

Figure 4.6 Gorilla vs. Normal Company

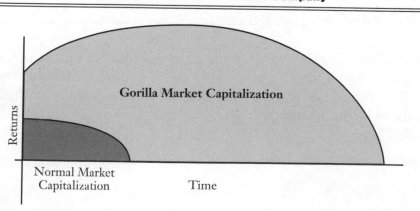

Where is all the increase in area coming from? Primarily from three sources:

1: The gorilla's curve is starting out higher on the vertical axis than a normal company. That is because, given its extraordinary advantage in power, it is expected to have far higher revenues and far better earnings from the outset.

2: Because it is in a hypergrowth market, its growth rate is far higher than normal, causing its curve to rise more steeply than otherwise would be possible. This makes for a *fatter* area under the curve.

3: Because it is going to be the *permanent* leader of this new market that is currently in hypergrowth—that is, the leader not just during the tornado but for the full duration of Main Street as well—investors have much higher confidence in its earnings projections. Indeed, they are willing to project these earnings as far into the future as they are willing to project the market itself. This makes for a much *longer* area under the curve.

If you put all these factors together, they equate to the competitive advantages of the gorilla, and the length of their duration we call the *Competitive Advantage Period*, or CAP. Strong companies have long CAPs; weaker ones have shorter ones. The chart that follows is intended to show exactly how CAP fits into stock market valuation.

CAP CHARTS

We are now ready to introduce a more comprehensive version of the diagram we have been building all along. It is called a CAP chart, and it takes all the ideas we have been discussing and overlays onto them some additional information for a financial context. Here's what it looks like:

Figure 4.7 Competitive Advantage Period Chart

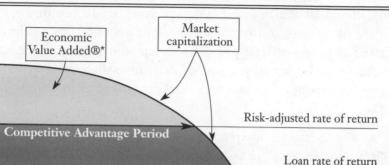

Dummy Alert: This is by far the most technical chart in the book. It is probably more technical than you want, but you must do your best with it. We are going to use it as the frame of reference for explaining a whole lot of things you may have never understood before, but you have to get this one to get those explanations.

Expert Alert: This chart is highly simplified from your point of view. If you like to really get underneath the covers on this stuff, go to our Web site at www.gorillagame.com and talk to the real experts (I'm the dummy, remember).

The theme of this chart is "earning the right to an investor's capital." It looks at the various reference points an investor would use to determine if putting money in a given company is a good investment or not. Let's go over each of these reference points one by one:

- The horizontal line at the bottom of the chart represents a zero level of return on investment. This might come from putting money under the mattress. You don't lose the money—that's the good

*EVA is a registered trademark of Stern Stewart & Co.

news—but you do lose out to inflation, and you certainly don't create any additional wealth to help you and your family in future years. In a world of robbers and terrorists, a zero rate of return might be perceived as good—at least you get to keep your money. In a protection racket, you are actually asked to do worse than that—pay a fee to keep your money. But in a free market, zero is rock bottom for most of us.

■ The next line up represents the return you could earn from putting money in a "risk-free" investment such as a treasury bond or CD. The idea here is that the investment is equally as safe as putting your money under the mattress, but at least makes you some money for the future. For most investors, this return is not sufficient to meet their financial goals. But it does set a benchmark, in that any *risk-bearing investment* must exceed this number to be worthy of consideration.

■ The next line up represents the return that a lender such as a bank requires from a company in order to loan it money to help fund its operations. This has higher risk than a bond because the company may default on the loan. But it has lower risk than stock investment because it is secured by collateral. Since investors get no collateral, the returns promised to them have to exceed this number as well to be viable.

■ The next line represents the minimum risk-adjusted return at which it makes sense for an investor to put money into this company. Below this line they get a bad deal. Above this line they get a good deal. This is the real baseline against which company performance is measured. In other words, investors give a company no credit for achieving returns until after they exceed this level. If the company does exceed this number, its stock price starts to get bid up. If it falls below, or looks like it will in the future, its stock price gets bid down. That's why we use this line as the baseline for the CAP chart proper.

One final note on this line. Unlike every other line on this chart, you can't look up the figures for this line. They do not exist in any report, nor can they be calculated directly from any reported numbers. Instead, the line represents a consensus in the investment community that can only be inferred through indirect means.

■ The curved line, as we have been noting all along, is calculated by projecting future earnings and then discounting them over time to accommodate two effects:

A. The net present value effect, which says that future dollars on paper are not worth as much as present dollars in hand.

B. The future uncertainty effect, which says that the further into the future a claim is made, the less confidence you can have in it coming to pass.

By the operation of these two effects alone, sooner or later a company's projected earnings will be valued at less than the risk-adjusted return rate. At that point, additional investment ceases to be attractive.

■ The point at which the curved line intersects the risk-adjusted return line equates to some future date beyond which no further projections of competitive advantage are valued. The time interval between now and that date is the Competitive Advantage Period. During this interval the company is expected to have a competitive advantage over other companies in its category that will permit it to generate returns in excess of those required to offset the risk of investment.

■ The shaded area under the curve represents the net present value of the company's anticipated future ability to create profits in excess of the minimum risk-adjusted rate of return. This is called the Economic Value Added (EVA®)*, and the size of this area represents the size of the "good deal" for owning the stock. We believe that changes in the size of this area, and this area alone, account for the overwhelming bulk of changes in a company's stock market valuation, and hence its stock price.

To sum up all the foregoing, the critical takeaways from CAP theory are two:

1: The premium any company earns in stock market valuation is a function of how much it can be expected to outperform its risk-adjusted rate of return.

*EVA is a registered trademark of Stern Stewart & Co.

2: The ability to outperform the risk-adjusted rate of return is a function of the company's competitive advantage in its primary markets.

Investing, therefore, is all about understanding competitive advantage. That is the underlying thesis of the gorilla game.

Stated this way, the gorilla game might seem more than a bit daunting. The high-tech marketplace, after all, is extremely complex, and few private investors have the industry background to sort out subtle differences in competitive advantage. That's when you need to go back to Figure 4.6, the chart that contrasts the gorilla with a normal company. We are not talking about subtle effects. Cisco's stock is worth an *order of magnitude* more than Bay Networks'. Intel's is worth an *order of magnitude* more than AMD's. You do not need a microscope to play this game. As we have already said, all you really need is a firm grasp on the obvious.

USING CAP CHARTS TO DEMYSTIFY THE MARKET

Later on in this chapter we are going to use CAP charts to gain a better understanding of how the market values all high-tech stocks—gorillas, chimps, and monkeys. But before we do, to get you more familiar with this approach, we will first show how these charts shed light on some familiar valuation changes that affect the entire stock market.

THE INTEREST RATE EFFECT

To begin with, here is how a CAP chart represents the effect of interest rates.

Figure 4.8 Impact of Lower Interest Rates

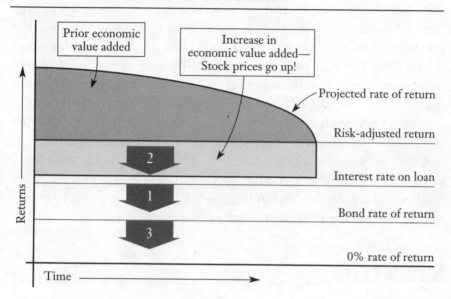

The impact of changing interest rates affects only the vertical axis (returns) and not the horizontal one (Competitive Advantage Period). So changes in interest rates affect all stocks the same. If rates go down, the value of a stock goes up because the company's risk-adjusted rate of return gets lowered. Here's why.

The distance between the interest rate on a loan and the risk-adjusted rate of return is a measure of the incremental risk entailed by an unsecured investment. If that risk has not changed, the distance between the two rates should not change. Therefore, if interest rates go down (the arrow marked "1"), then the risk-adjusted rate of return should as well (the arrow marked "2"). But lowering that rate has the impact of increasing the shaded area between the projected rate of return—which has not changed—and the baseline. The additional area equates to more economic value added, which means higher market capitalization—hence the stock price goes up.

Lower interest rates also cause bond prices to go up by a similar line of reasoning. Again, the gap between a secured loan and a bond represents the added level of risk that the lender is taking over and above the bond investor. If the interest rate on the loan goes down (the arrow marked "1"), and the difference in risk is unchanged, then the interest on a bond should be lowered as well (the arrow marked "3"). But since the promised return on a bond is fixed by contract and cannot be lowered, the equivalent effect is created by raising the price of the bond. Here's an example. Say a $1,000 bond is committed to return $100 per year by contract, or a 10% rate of return. If it now only has to earn 9% to be competitive as a risk-free investment, it only has to return $90. If that is the case, then the $100-per-year income it is contractually committed to return is actually worth $1,111, and the market instantaneously reprices the bond to reflect this new figure.

That's why, when interest rates go down, stock prices and bond prices go up. Now that we understand that, going forward we are going to disregard the lines related to interest rate, bond rate, and zero rate of return, and just use the risk-adjusted rate of return as our baseline.

HIGHER TAXES

So much for the impact of lower interest rates. Now let's turn our attention to higher taxes on business profits, another factor that affects the stock market as a whole. When such taxes are raised, CAP charts change like this:

Figure 4.9 The Impact of Higher Taxes

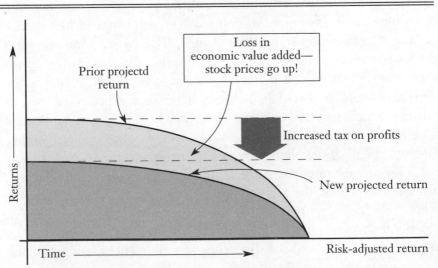

Once again, the impact is felt on the vertical axis (returns) only—the issue of competitive advantage is moot because the impact on all companies is the same. In this case, it is bad. The government is taking away profits that otherwise would have gone to shareholders. This decreases the net present value of future operating profits by the amount inside the diagonally shaded portion of the curve. A decrease in future profits creates less area under the curve—less economic value added. The market cap is therefore lowered, and the stock's price goes down.

BETTER EXECUTION

There are a whole host of business people who have little patience for strategy and who would put the weight of business success instead on execution. In stable markets, where variations in strategy have limited impact, this is not a bad idea. Here's how better execution shows up in a CAP chart:

Figure 4.10 The Impact of Better Execution

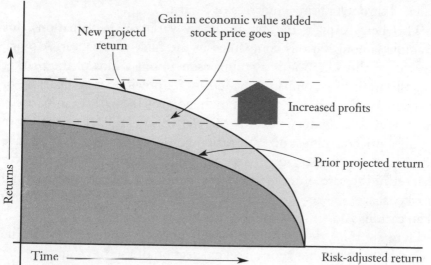

Basically, this is the same chart as in the tax example, except now the shaded area is being added on in the form of additional profits to the shareholders. Better execution gives a better rate of return over the same Competitive Advantage Period. It does not change CAP itself.

This observation helps explain how the stock market reacts to a positive earnings surprise from a high-tech company. In the absence of any perceived change in the competitive dynamics of the sector, the stock price goes up, reflecting an adjusted estimate of the net present value of its future cash flows. But since CAP does not change, the valuation does not go up by very much. This leads to a key lesson for high-tech management teams:

The impact of better execution on stock price, assuming no change to the Competitive Advantage Period, is inherently modest.

You cannot execute your way to a Microsoft, Cisco, or Intel stock price. As long as your Competitive Advantage Period is on par with the rest of the sector, there is only so much area under the curve you can add through raising your rate of return.

This helps explain the extraordinary variation in valuations, for example, among various companies in the high-tech sector. A quick metric for this variation is a comparison among ratios of the market capitalization of a company divided by its previous four quarters of revenue, or the *price/sales ratio*. For hypergrowth markets in particular, this is a far better indicator of relative valuation than the more familiar price/earnings, or P/E, ratio. The reason is that competitive advantage in a hypergrowth market (or a potentially hypergrowth market in the case of momentum investing) is a function of winning market share, and revenues correlate to market share far more closely than earnings do.

Here are the ratios of four relatively pure "execution plays" in the PC industry from the "Stock Ticker" section of the July/August 1997 issue of *Upside*:

COMPANY	MARKET CAP	REVENUES	RATIO
Dell	$18.6B	$7.8B	2.4
Compaq	$27.7B	$18.7B	1.5
Gateway 2000	$5.3B	$5.3B	1.0
Tandy	$3.1B	$6.1B	0.5

As of this writing, Dell, with its focus on direct marketing over the phone and now over the Web, is outexecuting the rest of the industry as indicated by its operating margins and various measures of operational excellence. Tandy, by contrast, is underperforming the industry and is in the process of exiting its abortive attempt to be a superstore distributor. Compaq is still the market leader among the pure plays, but it has not demonstrated it can move away from its dealer-centric model to be competitive. (Since this table was compiled, it has acquired Tandem, which implies a whole other set of distribution ideas at the high end of the market, but which should not change the need to watch its margins for the low end.) Gateway provides an excellent contrast to Dell, as it too is a strong low-cost provider, but with less of a corporate presence.

Now, the point to note in all this is that the ratio gap between Dell, the best in class, and Tandy, the worst, is 2.4 to 0.5. That's a variation of 1.9 between best and worst in class in the PC industry, an industry that differentiates itself primarily on execution. Let's contrast it to a comparable list of computer networking companies, this one from the August 1997 issue of *Red Herring*:

COMPANY	MARKET CAP	REVENUES	RATIO
Ascend	$7.2B	$0.6B	10.8
Cascade	$3.7B	$0.4B	9.8
Cisco	$46.0B	$5.4B	8.5
3COM	$8.9B	$3.0B	2.9
Bay Networks	$4.8B	$2.1B	2.2

Here the *relative* variation is about the same—5 to 1 from top to bottom—but the absolute values of the price/sales ratios (market cap divided by revenues) are much, much larger. This is *not* primarily a function of execution. Arguably the best company at pure execution on this list is 3COM. Compare its ratio to that of Cisco's, and you get a feeling for the market capitalization effect of a gorilla's competitive advantage. Bay, as a direct competitor with Cisco, is another good comparison for this effect. But what about Ascend and Cascade (who merged shortly after this listing)? Why are they higher than Cisco?

Several principles are operating here in parallel.

1: Each company is the market leader in the space it dominates: Ascend in remote data access into the telephone network, providing equipment to get all the traffic onto the backbone; Cascade in ATM and frame relay switches, which speed the hauling of all that data along the backbone.

2: Each of these categories has enormous potential for growth, so they have lots of headroom to exploit their gorilla advantages.

3: The law of small numbers is operating here—it is easier to increase small numbers by a given percentage amount than large ones. Both companies are an order of magnitude smaller than Cisco, and even adding their market capitalization together, they do not equal a quarter of Cisco's market cap.

The gap in price/sales ratios between Dell, the leader in the PC list, and Cisco, the leader in the networking hardware list, is more than 3 to 1. The difference lies primarily in barriers to entry. Cisco has a much stronger hold on the networking hardware market than Dell has on the PC market, which results in a longer Competitive Advantage Period resulting in a higher valuation. Dell cannot match this kind of competitive advantage; all its superior execution can be copied. The market gives Dell a premium for its efforts within category, but does not give it the huge boost in capitalization that a gorilla with proprietary competitive advantage gets.

With that thought in mind, let us now turn to see specifically how CAP chart analysis incorporates competitive advantage into the valuation process.

EXTENDING COMPETITIVE ADVANTAGE

In the simplest case, a competitive advantage can be extended within an existing market without resulting in any tornado effects. Here is what such a change looks like:

Figure 4.11 The Impact of Lengthening the Competitive Advantage Period

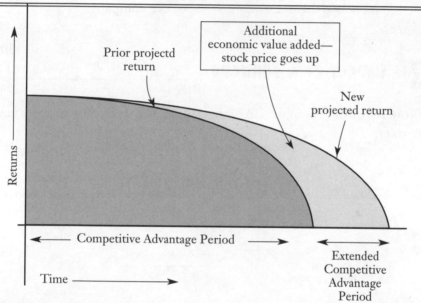

This diagram describes what happened to IBM's stock price in 1996 and 1997. At the beginning of the period, IBM's price/sales ratio was hovering around 0.8. By the middle of 1997 it was at 1.1. This represents over a $20 billion change in market capitalization. The biggest thing to change over that period was not IBM's ability to execute, but instead the competitive dynamics within its major market, enterprise computers. Specifically, the length of the competitive advantage period changed for the mainframe computer, a market category in which IBM has undisputed dominance. The market realized that the new paradigm (client/server architecture), in its new manifestation (network computing), far from supplanting the mainframe as it was expected to do, was actually going to *extend* the mainframe's useful life.

The result was an upside surprise, not in earnings, but in perceived competitive advantage (which, of course, is expected to turn into improved earnings going forward). When this happens in a market dominated by an aging gorilla, it simply pumps more life into the old fellow's body. It does not, however, represent a shift in advantage the way a tornado does, and therefore the ratio does not leap up the way it will in the next case we look at. But it does give the stock price a good shot in the arm, because extending the competitive advantage period increases the net present value of the company.

THE IMPACT OF A TORNADO

Now it is time to apply CAP analysis to the dynamics of a tornado market.

Figure 4.12 The Impact of the Tornado

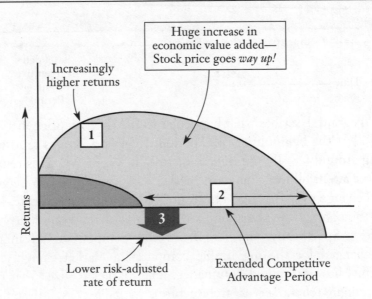

Recall that inside the tornado, demand for a given category of product escalates dramatically, outstripping the marketplace's ability to supply it. The marketplace, in turn, ramps up its supply capabilities as fast as it can, but no matter how fast that is, it still cannot catch up to demand. Growth curves, therefore, are inherently limited by the inability of companies to deploy any more investment. In this state, the return on invested capital is the highest imaginable. So the vertical axis starting point is very high (see the area marked "1").

At the same time, with the onset of the tornado, the new category of product, taken as a whole, is taking over the marketplace from some older approach. Think of this competition initially as category vs. category, not company vs. company. Just based on the dynamics of the Technology Adoption Life Cycle, we can project a whole new industry will come into being, served by a whole new value chain with a decade or more of business to do just replacing the old infrastructure and rolling out the new. Thus one can envision a CAP chart for the new category where its competitive advantage escalates dramatically, from an earlier niche-based advantage to one now based on a hypergrowth mass market. This has the effect of driving the horizontal axis reflecting Competitive Advantage Period way out to the right (see the area marked "2").

Finally, once a mass market enters the hypergrowth phase, the risk that invested capital would somehow be lost decreases dramatically. This lowers the baseline of the figure (see the area marked "3"), further increasing the area representing economic value added.

Overall, the dramatic increase in area under the curve represents the powerful allure of investing in tornado markets. Seemingly overnight the valuation of a category of companies leaps ahead by factors that simply have no precedent in ordinary business.

Every company in the category participates in this initial expansion in valuation. That is why we advocate that investors who have located a tornado opportunity buy the basket of companies participating in the new dynamics without regard to which one they feel is most likely to become the gorilla. At this stage there is little downside in owning the lesser companies in this basket, whereas there is huge opportunity lost in mistakenly excluding the one company that does become the gorilla.

FROM CATEGORY VALUATION TO COMPANY VALUATION

The previous CAP chart illustrates the impact of a tornado on an entire sector of companies, each of which participates in some way in the new category. We call this the *category capitalization*. The market then apportions this to the competitive set of companies that are each seeking share from the others for their part of the tornado opportunity.

At the outset the market tends to "distribute" the category valuation among these companies based on their respective market shares:

Figure 4.13 The Impact of Market Share

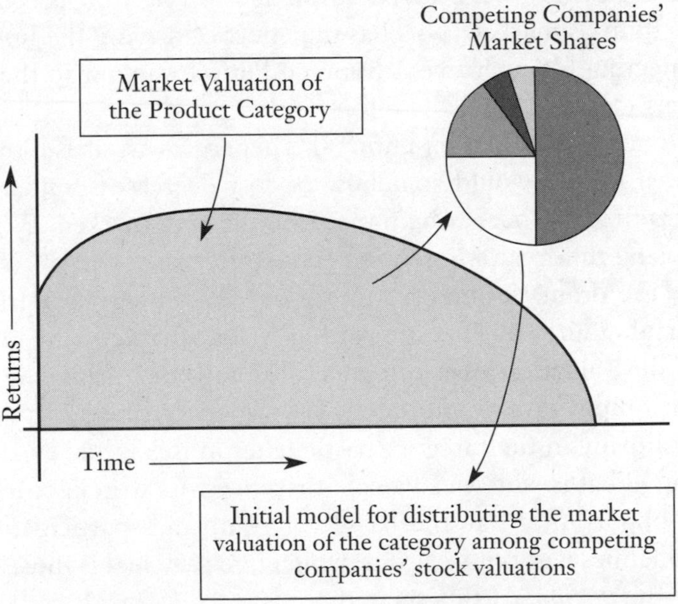

Competing Companies'
Market Shares

Market Valuation of
the Product Category

Returns

Time

Initial model for distributing the market
valuation of the category among competing
companies' stock valuations

The idea here is simple. The category is going to displace an existing infrastructure to the benefit of all its members. It is possible that new entrants could come in, but the speed of a tornado mitigates against them having much of an impact. Instead, the "first movers" have all the advantage. That advantage has begun to sort itself out into a market-share hierarchy, made up of a strong candidate for gorilla and some number of chimps and/or monkeys. Going forward, the valuation of each company will change according to how well it fares compared to its competitors.

The ideal way to follow this market battle as a whole would be to track the sum of the market capitalization changes of all the companies participating in the category. Unfortunately, many companies participate in more than one market category, and thus changes in their valuation are only partially based on their success or failure in this category. Pure plays, by contrast, give a much clearer picture of what is going on. In a world of pure plays, share of total market capitalization of the category is the perfect representation of the progress of the gorilla game.

Here is how the gorilla's CAP chart stacks up against the overall category's:

Figure 4.14 Gorilla CAP vs. Category CAP

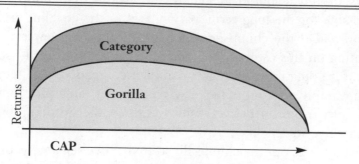

Note that the gorilla's Competitive Advantage Period is exactly the same length as the category's. The market assumes, given all its advantages, that the last company left standing in this category will always be the gorilla. So its CAP goes all the way to the end of the category's CAP. This is a distinctive feature of the gorilla and only the gorilla. It is the only company that is assumed to be immune to the risk of a shake-out.

Note also how much of the total EVA the gorilla is hogging. The market assumes that the gorilla, again given all its advantages, will be able to earn higher returns than any of its competitors. Thus it gets not only the longest EVA curve, but the fattest one as well.

Compare that with the chimps:

Figure 4.15 Gorilla CAP vs. Chimp CAP

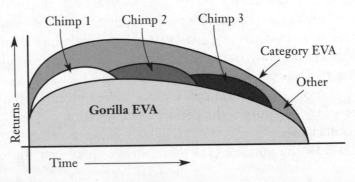

Chimps have to make room for themselves in the squashed area above the gorilla. This makes for somewhat flat EVA curves. Their CAPs are much shorter as well. The reason is that chimp strategy is not stable for the long term, particularly in the enabling technology sector, and if the chimp does not act to get into new categories—counting on this category to sustain its valuation instead—sooner or later it is going to disappoint. With its incompatible architecture, the chimp simply runs out of niche market areas it can exploit, and forced back into the mass market, falls victim to the gorilla's dominating competitive advantage.

If you broke out the chimps illustrated above separately, their CAP charts would tell the story of "The Three Little Chimps":

Figure 4.16 The Three Little Chimps

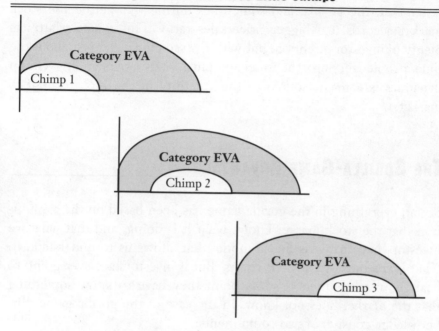

The first little chimp got into the market with the gorilla, fought to be the gorilla, and lost. As that loss became clear, the market withdrew its support, and its EVA collapsed. The second little chimp got into the market late, but with a second-generation innovation that challenged the gorilla effectively. At the same time, because of the collapse of the first chimp, it could absorb some of the EVA territory that the first little chimp had previously occupied. But eventually the gorilla responded to the second chimp's innovation, and manipulated the standards to block the second little chimp's progress, and it too fell victim. All along there had been a third little chimp, never number one and never number two, but always number three. With the demise of the other two little chimps, it finally rose to prominence. Unfortunately, that put it squarely in the sights of the gorilla, who set about knocking it down to size.

This is a fable, of course, although the reader will discover a marked resemblance between it and the history of the relational database market that we discuss in depth in Chapter 6. The key point here is that CAP charts for chimps are shorter and flatter than those of gorillas.

However, there is always a period when the chimp is actually growing faster than the gorilla, and sometimes during this period the stock market accords it a bigger price/sales ratio. This typically attracts plenty of investor attention, but with the sad effect that just about the time people get into the stock, it tanks. Misunderstanding chimp dynamics is a major source of the volatility in the high-tech stock market.

THE GORILLA-GAME ADVANTAGE

So far, everything in the gorilla game has been based on the assumption that the stock market knows what it is doing, and that what we investors have to do is find a model that allows us to understand it. That is the purpose of CAP charts. But if investors are ever going to beat the market, then at some point they have to know something that the market does not know. In the case of the gorilla game, this knowledge consists of two components:

1: The stock market will underestimate the returns that a gorilla can earn in a tornado market because they are so deviant from the value of market growth in other sectors.

2: The market will underestimate the length of the Competitive Advantage Period because it too is so deviant from CAPs in other sectors.

Of course, eventually the market will catch itself making these mistakes, and correct matters. But it will do so in fits and starts, something akin to peristaltic action, as the following chart illustrates:

Figure 4.17 The Progress of a Gorilla Stock: Successive Revaluations

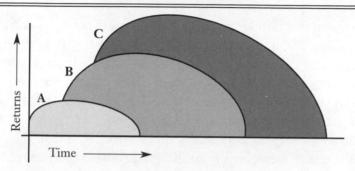

As the chart shows, investors begin by acknowledging a hyper-growth return stock as represented by Area A. This tracks accurately to the early stages of the tornado, but doesn't go far enough. Investors are simply not ready to believe that the tornado can continue or that the gorilla is going to be as powerful as it eventually becomes. But it does! The gorilla company keeps reporting significant upside surprises to expectations. So a new CAP chart (Area B) is forecast. Once again, investor expectations still do not appreciate the full impact of the tornado. After all, Area B is three times as large as the original CAP chart (Area A). A company with a market capitalization of $500 million has quickly become a company with a market capitalization of $1.5 billion. Surely that is enough! But it's not! The company again reports a significant upside to expectations, even against the revised set of expectations, and eventually the market cap explodes again, generating yet another CAP chart (Area C).

Gorilla-game investors know this succession of revaluations must happen, because the high-tech market development models upon which the philosophy is based insist that it must happen. Therefore, they buy into the category at the beginning of the tornado, regardless of the current valuation, confident that it will increase dramatically going forward. At the beginning all is well, but there comes a time when the gorilla-game investor's faith is tested—at the end of the tornado!

END-OF-TORNADO CORRECTIONS

We have seen that during the tornado, the market corrects itself upward to compensate for insufficient expectations. Eventually, however, these expectations do catch up with reality. This normally happens just as the tornado starts to decelerate. Now the market actually goes too far the other way, projecting a tornado out indefinitely just at the moment when in fact it is beginning to fade. As a result, the next set of reports from the sector surprise and disappoint the market, and all the companies in the sector, including the gorilla, go through a "correction."

Here's what surprising Wall Street looks like in the language of CAP charts:

Figure 4.18 The Impact of Surprising Wall Street

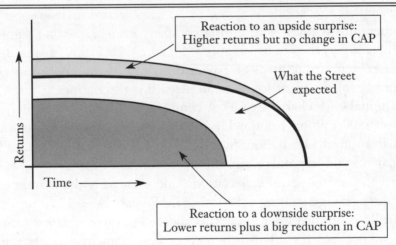

This chart helps explain a pair of questions that are deeply puzzling to management teams and investors alike:

1: Why is the stock market so punitive when high-tech companies announce even a modest shortfall in revenues or earnings?

2: Why is the market not correspondingly generous when these same companies announce a substantial positive surprise?

To read the chart, start with the heavy black curve that bounds the white space. This represents the market's current expectations for returns and CAP. Now let's suppose the company surprises with upside returns. The market puts those into its recalculation of the net present value of the firm, but it does not change its CAP. This creates the shaded area above the white space, the additional economic value added expected from future returns. But why no new CAP? Because the news came as a surprise, and the market has no information that the competitive dynamics in the category have changed. So while the upside surprise does increase the company's market capitalization, the additional amount is relatively modest.

By contrast, if the company surprises with downside returns, the market not only subtracts them on the vertical axis, reducing the formula for return, but it also clips the horizontal axis as well. In other words, this time it *does* change CAP. Why this time? Because the company did not warn it! The reaction here may not be conscious, but it is wise, for in the absence of any warning, there is a good chance the company has encountered an unexpected change in its competitive position and reacted by simply denying it.

This is not as uncommon as it might seem. No management team voluntarily admits to any condition that will lower its stock price. All teams keep struggling to keep the price up. This means that for several quarters they pull out all their stops to hit their numbers, often doing so by pulling in business from future quarters to make the current quarter fit what "the Street" expects. So when the team finally does fail to hit their numbers, it often means that their competitive position has severely eroded, and thus their CAP should be adjusted downward dramatically.

When the market lowers its expectations of returns and foreshortens the CAP at the same time, it is punishment indeed. Look how much area under the curve is lost! It is typical for a high-tech company at such a juncture—even a gorilla—to lose a third or more of its market capitalization in a single day! This, in turn, almost always attracts shareholder lawsuits, because surely such a collapse could only be the result of fraud. In fact, it is normally not fraud at all, but simply the fearsome dynamics of tornado markets at work.

When gorilla companies report revenues and earnings that disappoint, and their stock prices get dramatically lowered as a result, the key thing to keep in mind is that gorillas—and usually the gorillas alone—have a truly sustainable CAP that will reassert itself strongly on Main Street. This means they really do warrant holding, even though at the time it won't seem that way. When we get to our rules for investing, rather than trying to anticipate this moment of disappointment, we are going to recommend that the gorilla-game investor "hold" through it and indeed use this event to buy even more shares. At the same time, we think the professional investor, looking at the same market dynamics, will be able to construct hedges that can curtail some of this downside without giving up much of the upside.

But the main way to protect the gorilla-game portfolio from the end-of-tornado crash is to sell off the chimps long before it comes. These companies do not, as a rule, come back after the crash with anything like the gorilla's vigor. As chimps come out of the tornado, they find themselves fighting a strongly empowered gorilla who is becoming increasingly networked into the rest of the industry. As long as they make no mistakes, chimps can continue their game, but as soon as they stumble, their partners desert them, and while their current customers stick by them, they find it nearly impossible to attract any new ones. This does not bode well for anyone but the gorilla.

THE DEATH OF A GORILLA

With its competitors on the run, and the market playing right into its hands, a gorilla can't lose, right? Well, almost right. There is one condition that the gorilla must face on its own: mortality.

As pointed out in Chapters 2 and 3, the primary threat to a gorilla's market dominance is the undermining of the discontinuous innovation it rode to power by a newer, up-and-coming discontinuous innovation. If the marketplace goes with the new paradigm, the stock market forecasts a gradual conversion from the old to the new. This in turn implies some future time when the conversion is sufficiently complete that the competitive advantage of the old gorilla has been neutralized.

It takes a pair of CAP charts to show the full extent of how the market corrects the aging gorilla's market capitalization, and it is not a pretty sight.

Figure 4.19 The Death of a Gorilla, Part 1: Competitive Advantage Consumed

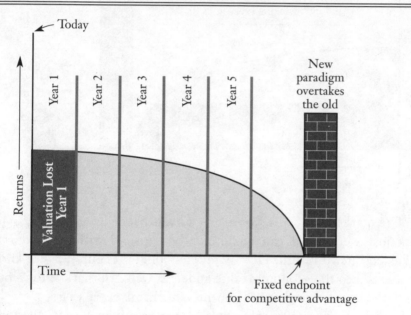

This is the first of the two charts. It positions the upcoming conversion to the new paradigm as an immovable object blocking future returns from the existing category at some point in the future. This means that CAP cannot grow any further to the right. But time marches on, so every year the area under the curve is diminished. The shaded rectangle on the left represents the loss in valuation just in the first year of this process. Since the area under the curve equals valuation, this means the stock price of the company is irrevocably hammered. Worse, since the market can anticipate this entire future in the present, it eliminates even the possibility of upside from its calculation of the net present value of the company, which knocks the stock price down even more.

But wait, it gets worse. Here is the second of the two charts.

Figure 4.20 The Death of a Gorilla, Part 2: Raising the Risk-adjusted Return

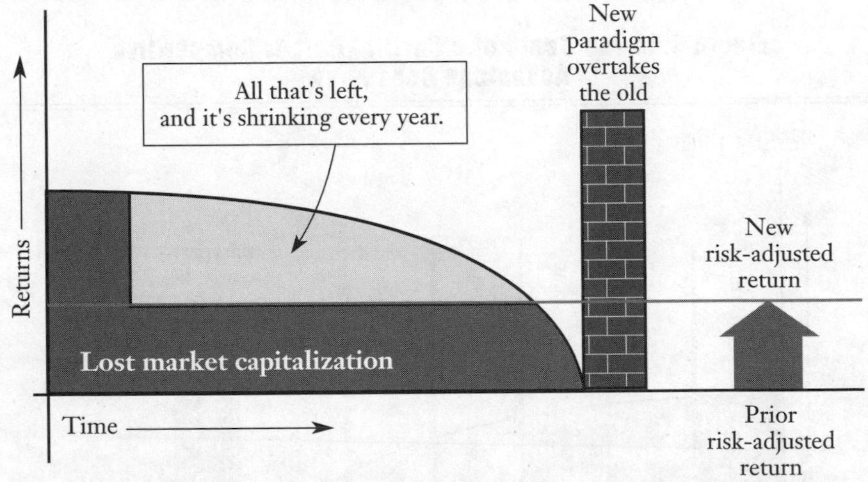

The market says, look, you aren't a healthy gorilla any more, so the risk just went up. I can no longer be satisfied with my old risk-adjusted rate of return. Here is my new one. Of course, as we know, that eats into the economic value added as well. All that's left is a piti-ful little wedge, and that will continue to shrink every year.

Such is the fate of an aging gorilla that has all its eggs in one tech-nology basket. In 1996 and 1997 the most painful examples have been Novell and Apple, both of which have made extraordinary contribu-tions to the computer industry, neither of which is given much chance of a viable future. The conversion to Windows NT as the LAN protocol standard going forward supplants Novell Netware, and the conversion to Windows as a desktop operating system stan-dard supplants Apple's Mac OS.

The first people to register this impact are always the industry partners, for they are deeply immersed in the competitive dynamics of the industry, and see early which way the wind is blowing. Last to see it, or rather acknowledge it, are the customers, for they are so tied down by their switching costs that they go into denial. Somewhere in between, the financial community catches on, and that is when the stock goes south. The drop-off in stock price, in turn, accelerates the defection of the partners, further reducing the value of the company's product offers, in a negative parody of network effects.

It is extremely difficult to pull out of one of these death spirals, as the shareholders and management of Wang, NBI, Lanier, Prime, Data General, Four Phase, Control Data, Unisys, Honeywell, Dun & Bradstreet, Knowledgeware, Cullinet, MicroPro, Ashton-Tate, and Borland will all be willing to testify. The technology wave moves on, and despite the fact that each of these companies had either gorilla or substantial chimp positions at one time, they are now either no longer in existence or relegated to a minor role in markets where they once ruled.

The consequences, then, of a blocked CAP are disastrous. Realizing this gives us a new perspective on what is traditionally criticized as the irrational volatility of stock prices in the high-tech sector. Far from being irrational, this volatility reflects genuine changes in competitive advantage and risk-adjusted rates of return that are very good first-order approximations for a very rational response mechanism. In other words, the waves may be high and violent, but they are still obeying the laws of physics.

THE IMPLICATIONS FOR THE GORILLA-GAME INVESTOR

Let us close this section by summarizing the key principles of investment that we have illustrated.

1: For any company listed, the stock market consistently seeks equilibrium around a market capitalization that accurately reflects the net present value of the company's projected future returns over and above its risk-adjusted rate of return. This economic value added is in effect a measure of the "good deal" an investor gets.

2: In the short term, however, the stock market is not good at pricing the stocks of companies in tornadoes, or the stocks of gorillas on Main Street. In both cases the correct valuation appears drastically overvalued. So instead, investors price these companies "closer to the mean." Since this mean consists of a mixture of a few companies in hypergrowth markets and a whole lot that are not, it seriously misrepresents the dynamics of hypergrowth.

3: The consequences of this misrepresentation are wonderful indeed for gorilla-game investors. It means, essentially, that we can buy low and sell high.

That is, because the market does not anticipate the full power of real tornadoes, it does not fully price these phenomena into the valuations of the participating companies, at least not until very late in the game. And because it does not anticipate the persistence of the gorilla's competitive advantage going forward onto Main Street, it persists in underpricing the gorilla relative to the chimps and monkeys, again until very late in the game—usually only after one or more chimps have died off. This double dose of persistent underpricing provides the foundation of the gorilla game. Capturing the huge appreciation that gorilla stocks enjoy as a result of it is the reward for playing the gorilla game well.

And on that thought we bring this section of the book to a close. You now have the complete theoretical basis for the gorilla game. It is time to move on, that is, from discussing *why* the game works and to focus instead on *how*.

Part 2

THE RULES OF THE GAME

5

Mapping the Terrain
THE SELECTION PROCESS BEGINS

In this second section of the book we are going to take you on a gorilla hunt. This will be an environmentally correct procedure—we don't want to kill the gorilla, we just want to buy a share of the company. But the important thing here is that we are interested in *a single species of investment*. There are many animals in the forest—lions, elephants, zebras, and the like. During our safari we will have occasion to point out these other forms of wildlife, but only in passing. We are going after gorillas, and gorillas only.

We stress this point at the outset for several reasons. First, the overwhelming bulk of the companies with whom the three of us do business are not gorillas. We want to reiterate that we have no desire to slight their value or to suggest in any way that they are unworthy of capital investment. Many of them are great investments. But they are not *gorilla investments*, and therefore they are going to be excluded from the *gorilla game*.

Second, the most explosive marketplace right now in high tech is the Internet, and we are going to make some gorilla-game recommendations on investing in that space in the last chapter of this book. However, many, if not most, of the leading companies in that marketplace *will not be included!* Again, this is not to challenge their leadership positions, or to suggest we understand the Internet better than the analysts who specialize in it, or to suggest that these leading companies are not worthy of investment. It is not even to suggest that these companies will not generate the highest returns in the sector—they may. It is most definitely to say, however, that regardless of how they perform, they are not operating as gorillas, and therefore they are not part of the gorilla game.

The reason this is so significant, the reason we are so adamant about this point, is that we make claims in this book about the safety of investing in high tech following the gorilla-game rules. These claims are not transferable to other animals. The gorilla may be a vegetarian, but the lion is not. For private investors in particular, who are operating with modest capital and a low tolerance for downside risk, we want you to stay close to the guide. More adventurous hunters will no doubt wander off a bit, but to the degree they do, management cannot responsible for their health and safety.

SECTORING THE TERRAIN

Whenever you hunt for anything, you need a map and a way of sectoring the search space so that you focus on the most likely places to find what you are looking for. Investing in high-tech stocks is no different. While the industry as a whole is complex and ever changing, there is a relatively stable consensus about boundary conditions in general. In this chapter we are going to offer an overview of the marketplace, and then focus on the places we think are most likely to be gorilla habitats.

At the highest level, we divide the high-tech world into four mega-sectors:

- Computer systems
- Vertical market systems
- Semiconductors
- Services

The focus of this book is almost entirely within the computer systems sector. All three case studies subsequent to this chapter come from this sector, as do the overwhelming bulk of our examples. That is because this is where all three of us do business every day. It is our natural hunting area, if you will. Before we dive into it, however, let us take a brief look at the other three major sectors on this map so that you can understand what gorilla-game opportunities they offer.

VERTICAL MARKET SYSTEMS

Vertical market systems refer to technology-enabled offerings that are devoted to a single market. Some of the most visible of these include:

- Medical equipment for health care, where companies such as Hewlett-Packard and General Electric have major operations.

- Exploration and production systems for oil and gas, led by Halliburton, Schlumberger, and others.

- Computer hardware and avionics software for aerospace and defense, the focus of well-known companies such as Lockheed-Martin and Rockwell.

- Switches and cellular base stations for telephony, where Lucent and Northern Telecom represent North America's strongest entrants.

- Fabrication equipment for the semiconductor industry, where Applied Materials and Lam Research are leaders.

Vertical markets like these generate huge spending for technology-enabled offers, and all of the companies named have multi-billion-dollar positions in them. But the markets operate apart from the market for computer systems in general, behaving instead like "bowling alley forever" markets. That is, they tend to crown their own local gorillas, demand highly specialized responses from them, and build long-term relationships that pose high barriers to entry for new competitors. Companies in this sector tend to have stable market capitalization and low volatility because they have long-term visibility into their customer demand and are relatively protected from sideswipes from some new technology. That's the good news.

The bad news from a gorilla game point of view is that it is much harder for a new gorilla to break into this club, new technologies being much more likely to get coopted by the existing hierarchy of vendors. Thus the primary gorilla candidates are the existing players. That in itself might not be too bad, except that there is an upper limit to their expansion, set by the limits of the vertical market—there are no mass markets for any of these devices, nor is there ever likely to be. As a result, vertical market vendors can take money from each other, or cannibalize their own contracts, but they have a much harder time creating new money.

It is still possible to have local tornadoes, of course. As a rule, however, they are harder to see, particularly for an outside investor, and in any event they will not scale beyond the limits of the local market. Hence, our recommendation to gorilla-game investors is, do not play the gorilla game here unless you happen to be employed in one of these markets or are willing to do the extra homework necessary to navigate your way.

SEMICONDUCTORS

The semiconductor industry provides the basis for the recurring tornadoes in all the rest of the high-tech sector. Its continuing ability to shrink the size and increase the density of electronic circuits has the effect of doubling the price/performance of chip-based processing power every eighteen months. This, in turn, allows companies to drive down the price point of their existing offers and undertake new ones, which only a few years previously were priced out of reach for all but the most deep-pocketed customers. In 1997, for example, continuous-speech voice recognition software, which has been feasible for more than a decade, has finally become a desktop offering, priced under $100, all because PC processors and memory now match what only mainframes could offer a few years ago. And the same goes for all the traffic that the Internet is bearing—impossible under the old cost of circuitry, but not under the new.

The semiconductor industry subdivides into some readily understandable categories—*microprocessors* and *memories*, in particular, are both familiar to any PC user—and some arcane ones, such as DSP (digital signal processing) chips, analog and mixed-signal devices, graphics accelerators, ASICs (application-specific integrated circuits), and the like. Overall, it is a highly specialized field and not readily handled in a book intended for wider audiences. It is also not our normal stomping grounds. Therefore, we have also put this sector outside the limits of our target terrain.

We want to be clear, however, that this is a gorilla habitat nonetheless. That is, the semiconductor industry does operate by the rules of the gorilla game, and all the principles we espouse are as applicable here as they are in the computer systems sector. There are numerous proprietary architectures, and there are high switching costs once a value chain commits to one or another, so this marketplace has and will continue to generate a strong complement of gorillas in addition to a lot of kings and princes. In 1997, for example, a company called Rambus looks to be a strong gorilla candidate in the emerging market for next-generation memories. It is just that to play the game in the semiconductor sector demands a highly specialized investor with highly specialized information. Once again, if you have occasion to be such an investor, we wish you good hunting.

SERVICES

The good news about services is that everybody understands these businesses. And what wonderful businesses they are, too! Whereas all the product-oriented companies in high tech must live or die with whether their architecture gets accepted or not, service companies don't have any such worries. Whatever architecture wins, that's the one we'll work on. Oh, you have one of the other ones? Well, we'll work on that one too, though our fees may be a bit higher. Compaq, HP, and IBM are all in a cutthroat competition against one another for winning NT server sales? No problem, we'll carry all three product lines, and may the best one win. Don't want to buy a product at all? How about outsourcing the function to us, and we'll handle all this stuff for you. How about just doing business over the Internet—we can set you up overnight. Cross over to our site, and all your sins will be washed away.

Yes, there is much to like in a services-based business, and only one caveat for the purposes of this book: *There are no gorillas in this sector.*

Gorillas, as we have stressed repeatedly, are the beneficiaries of proprietary architectures with high switching costs. Architectures live in products and in products only. To be fair, there are analogs to architecture in various types of service companies, and we shall look into these as we survey the terrain. Moreover, there are network effects and switching costs of a sort, and these have the same positive customer-retention impact in services as they do in the gorilla game. But at the end of the day, there is nothing in this sector that remotely compares with gorilla power. We are out in the veldt. There simply are no gorillas here.

This is not bad news. Services companies are relatively safe investments, and the best generate excellent returns. They do not generate gorilla returns, however, and before we move on, it behooves us to see why.

The services sector of high tech breaks out into the following categories:

- Professional services
- Distribution services
- Transaction services
- Information services
- Entertainment programming

Here's how each stacks up against the gorilla-game investment profile.

PROFESSIONAL SERVICES

Professional services companies in high tech tend to come in two main flavors—systems integrators who focus on the technical complexity of installing new systems, and business consultancies who support the reengineering of business processes required to benefit from any new system. Both come into prominence wherever complexity creates barriers between customers and the systems they want to deploy. Complexity, however, as we shall illustrate in the next chapter, is the prime enemy of tornadoes. To cope with it requires all the things that tornadoes hate—attention to detail, custom solutions, vendor expertise, and the like. These are scarce resources, and firms lucky or skillful enough to assemble them find they have trouble scaling to meet hypergrowth demands. Typically, therefore, tornadoes occur as professional services firms exit, not enter, a market.

From a power perspective, professional services firms differentiate themselves based on their methodologies, or what they are wont to call their *intellectual property*. This is something akin to a proprietary architecture, but it does not create serious switching costs, as the high turnover rate in consulting relationships makes clear. Moreover, while their customer-intimate relationships are able to create some level of network effects, professional services firms are able to leverage these more in the early market than during the tornado.

At the end of the day, professional services in high tech, like their cousins in advertising, accounting, and other sectors, must reestablish their leadership credentials with every customer every day or risk losing their accounts. By contrast, gorillas can abuse their customers for extended periods of time and still keep them by virtue of architectural lock-in. Abuse is not the recommended strategy, to be sure, but the fact that it is tolerable tells a great deal about the difference in power between the two types of firms.

DISTRIBUTION SERVICES

In contrast to professional services, distribution services do come into prominence during a tornado. These are service firms that help resell products to give them greater market exposure than a single company's sales force could achieve. In a tornado, the new value chain needs all the help it can get to process the influx of new customers, and thus turns to distribution services early.

The problem with distribution services as an investment is that what they offer is inherently a commodity. That is, they differentiate themselves almost entirely on *execution*. This means they have very low switching costs, such that one firm can replace another as soon as its offer is even a little bit better. There is just too little to prevent their vendor-customers from changing over to a competitor's service. As a result, while these firms can—indeed, must—scale to very high volumes, they can never get their profit margins up to anything like gorilla levels. To be sure, the bigger they are, the longer the CAP chart you could project for them—because in commodity markets, scale counts. But you can never get a fat CAP chart for them, never get returns that are significantly in excess of the minimum risk-adjusted return rate, and therefore never generate the good deal in economic value added that a gorilla represents. For these reasons, distribution services companies are not part of the gorilla game.

TRANSACTION SERVICES

Transaction services, as opposed to professional services, are bought not as one-time projects paid for on a fee basis, but instead are consumed recurrently and are typically paid for by subscription or a pay-as-you-go charge. Telephone calls, FedEx packages, airline tickets, dry cleaning, and movies are all sold as transaction services. In high tech, the Internet is consumed as a transaction service, with Internet access being the initial payment transaction, and e-mail and Web browsing being the primary usage transactions to date. But even product companies, once they get to Main Street, will make an increasing portion of their revenues from transaction services in the form of product maintenance, technical support, outsourcing, and the like.

Transaction services offer a particularly attractive business model because once the system's infrastructure is built out, and once revenues exceed fixed costs, the variable costs are so low that virtually every incremental bit of revenue drops straight to the bottom line. Market-leading transaction services franchises such as the SABRE System and AT&T Long Distance, therefore, are some of the most profitable enterprises on the planet. So why, then, aren't UUNet, Yahoo, or America Online part of the gorilla game?

First of all, the two conditions for getting these enterprises profitable are extremely hard to meet, especially during a tornado market.

Building out systems infrastructure is hugely expensive, as the business plans for any of these companies make painfully clear. You have to charge a lot of transaction fees for a very long time to even approximate it. Historically, most successful transaction services franchises come into being on the back of publicly funded, not privately funded, infrastructure. The original Internet itself represents such a publicly funded entity. But now the commercialization and scaling up of the Internet is being funded privately, at potentially ruinous costs. It is not clear that this model can ever pay its investors back. So that is strike one.

Strike two is getting the revenues. Where will they come from? Subscription fees, we have already discovered, are not enough. Consumers and business customers alike are too price-sensitive. For a while we thought transaction-processing fees would be the source, but the volume of transactions that one could charge a fee for is still very low in the Internet space. Maybe someday. Charging for information is a third possibility, and maybe someday it too will come through, but for now there is so much free information on the Internet that paid-for info is being shunted aside. All this clears the way for the current knight on white horse—advertising. Internet sites, most business plans now assume, will act like TV channels— they will attract viewers, and these viewers' eyeballs can be sold to advertisers.

Let's assume that this model stabilizes. (Please note, however, that it hasn't yet, so investors should garner a higher risk-adjusted premium for going forward.) Now the problem is to get the costs under the revenues. Again, there are all kinds of ideas about how this might be done, but little track record to date to show that it has been done. Indeed, the press repeatedly calls attention to the fact that the best-known sites are as yet unprofitable. Moreover, there are whole industries, like the airline industry, that appear to be constitutionally unprofitable. There is no guarantee, in other words, that this model will ever work. So that is strike two.

Strike three, for us, is actually a slider, which may or may not have hit the outside corner. (This is where you really need an umpire.) It has to do with our core issue: proprietary architecture and high switching costs. In a transaction services business, the analog to proprietary architecture is *brand*, and the analog to switching costs is *community*. The TV shows *Seinfeld*, *Friends*, and *Frazier* are brands. So are Yahoo and America Online. The TV shows are also communities—they have definable demographics, and moreover, they create word-of-mouth communities as people talk to each other about the episodes. Yahoo and AOL thus have the potential to provide not only the topics of conversation but also the medium—be it a chat room or a threaded discussion group.

So let's assume that the winning sites achieve this kind of status. (Please note, however, that this too has yet to come to pass, so investors should garner a second upward adjustment in their risk premium.) Now the question is, what are the switching costs? On TV, they are not very great. That's why the ratings shift around so much. Why will they be higher on the Internet? Does anybody think they would even approximate the switching costs of replacing even a modestly successful product architecture?

The answer is no. Therefore the notion that these companies could be gorillas simply does not hold. The risks they entail are much greater, and the security of their leadership positions, once achieved, is more precarious. They must, therefore, be some other kind of animal—*python* might be a good choice. Once again, we are not saying that pythons are not worthy of investment (although in this case, the danger may be higher than usual). Nor is it to say that their stocks will not appreciate dramatically in the next few years. They may beat every other stock on the market, for all we know. But if they do, it will not be because of the dynamics of the gorilla game. Some other dynamic will have to explain it. The transaction services sector is not a gorilla habitat.

INFORMATION SERVICES AND ENTERTAINMENT PROGRAMMING

Information services and entertainment programming represent two forms of valued content that are distributed typically by a transaction service. While either one can go into hypergrowth relatively easily and profitably, neither of them is ever based on proprietary architectures; nor can they create high switching costs from a technology point of view. Instead, their Competitive Advantage Period is best estimated by the popularity of their brand.

In the information services sector, there are plenty of great brands today, including *The Wall Street Journal*, CNN, and Bloomberg. Databases such as Nexus and Dialog have traditionally charged a premium for access to their records. There is a kind of switching cost in the space, in part based on habit, in part on familiarity with the site's tools, in part on the feeling that this site has the "best" or "right" information. But these switching costs are not comparable to architectural switching costs, and therefore the power they generate is much less.

In the entertainment space, as we noted above, popular brands—we would include movie stars in this set—have enormous competitive advantage. But they too do not create the kind of switching costs that keep gorillas in power. In Hollywood, in particular, you are only as good as your last movie. Once again, nice place to visit, but no gorillas.

That concludes our tour of the services sector. As you will have noticed, it is a part of the forest that is teeming with life. There are lots of investments here, but since none of them is a gorilla, we are going to move on.

COMPUTER SYSTEMS

We have now come full circle back to the computer systems sector of high tech, which is the domain proper for the gorilla game, because it is the primary home of *proprietary architectures* with *high switching costs*. This is a pretty complex arena overall, and there are as many ways of sorting it out as there are publications that cover it. What we offer here is, we believe, a fairly middle-of-the-road approach designed primarily to help you to group companies by competitive set and value-chain participation.

Figure 5.1 The Computer Systems Sector

	GLOBAL & ENTERPRISE	CAMPUS, DEPARTMENT AND WORKGROUP	PERSONAL AND CONSUMER
SOFTWARE			
Applications			
End-User			
OLTP	SAP, Oracle, PeopleSoft, Baan	PeopleSoft HR, Vantive, Remedy, Clarify	Intuit QuickBooks
DSS	Cognos, Business Objects, SAS	Arbor, Seagate	Microsoft Excel
Productivity		Autodesk, Cadence, Adobe, Macromedia	Microsoft Office
Edutainment		Jostens Learning	Electronic Arts, Broderbund
Communications			
Mail & messaging	Lotus Notes, Netscape, IBM PROFS	PictureTel, MS Mail	America OnLine
Information	Netscape, Verity (New)	Reed Elsevier, Verity (Old)	Netscape, AOL, MS Explorer
Systems			
Operating Systems	HP UX, IBM MVS	MS Windows NT, Sun Solaris, IBM OS/2, SCO	MS Windows 95, Macintosh
Networking	Novell (New)	Novell (Old)	
Database	Oracle, Sybase, Informix	ODI, Versant, Objectivity, MS SQL Server	MS Access, Paradox
Middleware	Security Dynamics, Sterling, Yahoo (Old)	Wang (New)	Progressive Networks
Tools	Computer Assoc., Forte, Dynasty, Powersoft	Visual Basic, Java	Symantec
HARDWARE			
Networking	Ascend, Cascade, Cisco	Bay Networks, Cabletron, Cisco	3Com, USR, Global Village
Computers	IBM, Digital, NCR, HP,	Compaq, Sun, DG, SGI, HP, Dell, Apple	Apple, Packard Bell, Gateway, Micron
Peripherals	EMC, IBM, StorageTek	Xerox (New), InFocus	HP, Iomega, Radius, Fax (New)
Office Equipment (Obsolete)		Xerox (Old), Wang (Old)	Fax (Old)

As you can see by Fig. 5.1, the sector breaks down into multiple subsectors while at the same time breaking out by size of the customer domain. These lines of division represent the way the industry has aggregated over time into different clumps. A clump has a characteristic set of leading vendors, and we have tried to list a representative set for each. No doubt we have left someone out who should have been included (which we will hear about), but the point here really is just to give a feeling for the space, not an exhaustive list of the citizenry.

CATEGORIZE BY SCOPE: BIG, MEDIUM, AND SMALL

The first thing you should notice are three long columns, each laid out according to the scale of a different target customer: Global and enterprise; campus, departmental, and workgroup; and personal and consumer.

These market sectors developed historically from big to small. Initially, that is, the computer industry was an enterprise-only affair, as IBM and others created systems interoperable on a global basis. Then the minicomputer came along to address a more local set of constituencies whose needs were sufficiently unique and diverse that corporate computing simply could not keep up with them. At the high end, this might be a division; at the low end, a workgroup or department—and for the most part all these systems were confined, at least initially, to a single campus. And finally a third domain emerged with the rise of personal computing, initially confined to the office desktop, then expanding into the home, first in the guise of work-at-home systems and eventually as true family computers.

At the outset these three spheres developed relatively independently. More recently, with the rise of client/server computing, which deliberately links the enterprise to the desktop, and the rise of the Internet, which links the desktop to the globe, they have become increasingly interwoven. Nonetheless, these boundary lines are still operative in most of high tech, and will continue to be for some time to come.

The reasons for this are several:

- First, all technology needs to be prioritized relative to a set of typically conflicting goals—low cost, high performance, rapid time to market, consumer appeal, ease of use, ease of support, and the like. By subsectoring into enterprise, department, and desktop, the industry is able to take a first pass at resolving these conflicts in different ways for different constituencies.

- Second, complexity for the most part increases with scale, which leads to high-end professional services concentrating in the enterprise space, and low-end transaction-based distribution services focusing on departmental users. Moreover, at the low end there is a great deal of consumer-style purchasing, which can leverage classic branding and packaged-goods marketing investments, whereas at the high end there is more emphasis on relationship marketing.

- Finally, by staying on one side or the other of any of these divides, competitors can temporarily avoid each other and focus their energies on developing new markets rather than fighting each other over old ones.

That being said, however, a large part of the normal competitive dynamics in high tech has to do with "horizontal" movement on this chart. That is, expansionist firms successful in one domain naturally think to grow across the chart into an adjacent one. This in turn often creates gorilla collisions, which cause once-secure hierarchies to be thrown into turmoil, the market suddenly becoming unsure as to which of these two gorillas will be the dominant one going forward. As noted earlier, such collisions present real challenges to the gorilla-game investor, and we shall spend a fair amount of time in subsequent chapters pondering how to respond to them.

CATEGORIZE BY TYPE: A TAXONOMY OF SYSTEMS

So much for the columns in our chart. Now let's turn to the rows. These represent divisions by product category. They also represent lines of competition. The vendors in any one cell are all competing against one another, and in the future are likely to compete against the other companies on their row. They are much less likely to compete against companies on other rows, it being more typical to partner with them. Of course, when a vendor leaps rows, all bets are off, and it makes for very exciting times.

The rows themselves aggregate into sectors. These are useful to sort out the general lay of the land. The oldest sector dividing line in the computer industry is the one between *hardware* and *software*. It still holds, but just barely. The problem is that more and more of the value in a hardware system is actually created in software, so that traditional hardware companies now employ more software designers and programmers than they do mechanical or electrical engineers; and even the latter, when you look at the tools they now use, look more like software programmers. Nonetheless, from a market point of view, the distinction has held up via the concept of the *platform*, which is traditionally made of hardware, and the *application*, which is traditionally defined in software.

This leaves, however, a murky middle ground of software that helps link the outward-facing application domain with the inward-facing hardware domain. This space is filled by *system software*. The classic stack of a computer-based system, then, as we illustrated in a previous chapter, consists of enabling hardware on the bottom, enabling system software filling up the middle, and value-delivering *application software* on top. While there is some rivalry between these three sectors, for the most part they combine rather than compete to create value.

If we go down a level in each sector, the hardware subsector breaks down into *computers* at the core, surrounded by *peripheral systems*, which serve to get data into the system, to store and retrieve it, or to present it back out—all of which is connected to the world via *networking hardware*. At one time there was a competing category in the office, called *office equipment*, which did not contain any computers; but it has now become obsolete.

Application software, in turn, breaks down into *end-user applications* and *communications applications*. When people talk about the shift in the computer industry from computing to communicating, they are noting that the old growth came primarily from end-user applications but that a lot of the new growth comes from communications applications. That being duly noted, by far the biggest driver of computer systems investment has been the automation of everyday business transactions, what the industry calls *online transaction processing* (OLTP). These applications include the traditional business systems—financials, inventory, order entry, and the like. They build large databases of customer activity which, in turn, management wants to analyze. This creates the need for the second major category of software, *decision support systems* (DSS), which create reports and graphs that present and interpret the results of operations.

With the rise of the PC and then the technical workstation, a third major category of application software emerged, called *productivity software*, which is focused more on the individual than the business process. And as PCs entered the home, a fourth category emerged, which has managed to find its way back to more than one office desktop, called *entertainment software*.

Finally, with the rise of networks, another class of application came into being, focused on communications rather than computing. At the outset the killer app here was electronic mail, which later grew to take on group interactions under the guise of "groupware" like Lotus Notes. Together, they are *mail and messaging*, although there will be some confusion going forward, as "messaging" of a different sort is also becoming a category inside system software. All this networking, in turn, has led us to the Internet and to the free availability of huge amounts of information on the World Wide Web; and that in turn is creating a second class of communications application software focused on helping people access, publish, and subscribe to various sources of information. These *information applications* represent some of the fastest-growing categories in the current marketplace.

Beneath all this application software, and riding on top of enabling layers of hardware, drifts a rather amorphous and hard-to-define middle layer of *system software*. In its worst moments, the industry throws up its hand in despair at defining this layer, and just calls it all *glue*. But we have to do a little better than that.

At the bottom of the middle, if you will bear with us, is the *operating system*. It manages all the interactions between the hardware and the rest of the software. It contains within it a file management system, but for storing and retrieving complex data used by many different applications, the industry looks to *database* software. To write the applications that use the system there is a whole other class of software called *tools and languages*, typically very specialized but sometimes becoming highly visible, as is the case with Java.

This leaves two final areas, both of which have become problematic in recent years. The first of these is *networking software*, which manages the connections of one computer to another, something that used to be a subset of the operating systems responsibility, but is increasingly coming under the domain of the networking hardware vendors. This puts operating systems and networking hardware vendors on a collision course, setting up what could be the gorilla collision of all time between Microsoft and Cisco.

The other area is *middleware*. This really is glue, the category being a catchall for highly useful software that has yet to be legitimized into its own category. The rise of networked computing has created huge needs in the middleware space, so we will be seeing lots more of this stuff, but the marketplace has no easy way of processing it. The problem is that middleware, by its very nature, is intimately connected with all the other types of system software and thus encroaches on all the established fiefdoms in the marketplace. In order to gain power, the category must break free from the others. But since it takes a specialist to understand what exactly the middleware is doing, and since specialists are known to disagree, it is virtually impossible to get clarity on this stuff. Most middleware comes to prominence only after it has been acquired or absorbed by an established player in some other category of system software; so despite all the tornado winds blowing around the category, it is typically not a candidate for the gorilla game.

But virtually every other category outlined in this section is. In particular, the bulk of the gorilla sightings we expect in the latter part of the twentieth and outset of the twenty-first centuries will be in three areas:

1: Computers and networking hardware.

2: Application software, specifically communications applications, with a secondary focus on OLTP and DSS.

3: System software, specifically operating systems and networking software.

In our view, those are the current active market domains that are likely to sponsor discontinuous innovations with proprietary architectures and high switching costs. To the degree that any other domain behaves comparably, it too should become part of the gorilla game. The first question to ask, in either case, is, *Has anybody seen signs of a tornado around here?* To answer that question, let's now turn to the next chapter.

6

Stalking the Gorilla

IN SEARCH OF HYPERGROWTH MARKETS

The goal of all investing is to outperform the market. If that were not the goal, we could all put our money in indexed funds and go home. The purpose of the gorilla game is to provide a platform for consistently outperforming the market in the sector of high tech.

There are only two ways to outperform the market—outreact it on a frequent basis (execute on the same insights and information that others use but do so faster than everyone else) or outthink it (execute on different insights and information than others use). Outthinking is actually a form of outreacting, but on a much slower time scale. That is, the "outthinker" sees upcoming events before they hit the market's radar, and acts on them ahead of the market.

Since the market is designed to be the consummate read-and-react mechanism, it is difficult for even skilled, well-situated professional investors to outreact it. For private investors, operating at a greater distance from the market and with fewer aids, it is that much harder, and in our view not a winning game. So instead of trying to help you outreact the market, our goal is to help you outthink it.

Outthinking the market is not as hard as it might sound, for the market does not think—it does not have ideas. Investors do have ideas, of course, and over time, as an idea becomes prevalent among large numbers of investors, it becomes priced into the market's valuations. But that takes time.

In the case of high tech, the market currently has a very weak idea of the tornado, one that is still distorted by ideas that are pertinent to other types of markets but not to high tech. As a result, the market has an inadequate mechanism for pricing the net present value of future tornado events into stock valuations. Investors with a clearer idea of the tornado should be able to outthink, and thus outreact, the market provided they are armed with:

1: *Decision models* that show what patterns to look for in an emerging technology-based marketplace and how to respond to them.

2: *Research practices* that show how to extract these patterns from the current publicly available information on a day-to-day basis, such that they can routinely track down tornadoes before the rest of the market gets there.

This chapter and the next will focus on the *decision models* side of this equation. These are, if you will, the rules of the gorilla game. It is time, in other words, to start the gorilla game in practice, and that means we have to go in search of tornadoes.

THE TORNADO WATCH

Those of you who grew up in areas prone to tornadoes learned at an early age that there is a big difference between a *tornado watch* and a *tornado warning*. A *tornado watch* is an alert to the public that conditions exist for a tornado, but no tornadoes have yet been spotted. A *tornado warning*, however, is an alert to the public that a tornado has been spotted and anyone in its proximity should seek cover. To get the maximum returns from the gorilla game, you have to engage in the tornado watch. If you wait for a tornado warning, you can still play the game, but the first jump in stock price appreciation will already have passed you by.

Not all tornado watches, of course, result in tornado occurrences. The conditions have to be just so for a tornado to form—air temperature, ground conditions, time of year, and the like. The same is true for technology tornadoes—making them somewhat rare as well.

Unfortunately, the press that reports on high tech creates just the opposite impression. Most new product categories get overhyped to the point that much of the market begins to believe that the tornado will touch down soon. The problem is, most emerging markets never make it to the tornado. We need to stop thinking Hollywood and start thinking Darwin.

Most new product categories quickly die off in the chasm. They are mutations, after all, and nature does not deal kindly with new-comers. Other hardier species hang on in the chasm, only to find that some other product category has leaped over them. They too get left behind. Still other product categories make it to the bowling alley but never leave, their value being perpetually confined to a handful of niche markets. Setting all these aside, it is the rare category indeed that is able not only to elbow its way into the mainstream market but actually to reengineer the marketplace to accept a new mass market offer.

A tornado watch is a search for this type of product category, one that exhibits signs of being likely to undergo hypergrowth at some unspecifiable future time. You are not going to try to predict *when* the category will go inside the tornado, only *if* it will in fact do so at some point. The key, then, is to know what to look for.

It is here that the real work of the gorilla game begins. There is simply no substitute for industry knowledge when it comes to looking in the right places for emerging tornado opportunities. The good news, however, is that it is just work, and the bulk of it can be done by subscribing to the basic trade magazines, along with habitually scanning the newswires that cover high tech. The point is, insider knowledge is not a prerequisite. Indeed, we believe it often can be a deterrent to good investment decisions, as the industry frequently gets caught up in a swirl of hype that even a modestly sober outsider could see through at a glance.

The bulk of the tornado watch consists of scanning the publicly available information focused on high tech. It is not an easy task, and it is therefore the first and primary way by which gorilla gamers sepa-rate themselves from the "average investor." (Actually, we have never met any investors who perceive themselves to be "average." However, most of our colleagues believe that most other investors are at best average, so we continue to use the term.) Scanning alone, however, is not enough. You also have to know what to scan for.

IT'S ALL ABOUT VALUE CHAINS

To detect the emergence of a tornado, you have to take into account its internal dynamics. Here is the key principle to keep in mind:

Tornadoes occur when—and only when—a new *value chain* comes into existence.

A value chain is a linked set of products and services that delivers something of value to an end customer. It can be visualized as follows:

Figure 6.1 The High-Tech Value Chain

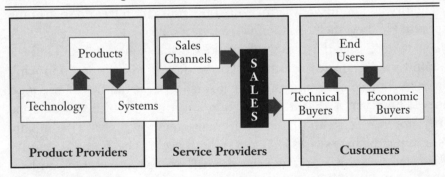

Value chains break into three chunks—a beginning, a middle, and an end, as Aristotle would say—as follows:

- The beginning of a value chain, shown on the left-hand side of the chart, is where the product offerings get assembled. It is typically made up of technology providers, component manufacturers, subsystems assemblers, all leading up to a product offer. This is the domain of product architectures, and where the gorillas live. Everyone else in the chain, however, must cooperate for these architectures to get adopted.

▪ The end of the chain, on the right-hand side of the chart, is the customer side. In business-to-business markets, there are typically three constituencies within the customer organization that must cooperate effectively for the value to get all the way through to making a bottom-line impact—the technical buyers, the end users, and the economic buyers. In consumer markets these roles tend to merge into one, except for markets where parents (economic buyers) are buying for children (end users, and in many households, also the technical buyers). Altogether, customers are the folk who pay for the value chain end-to-end, if and only if they receive appropriate value.

▪ Finally, the middle of the value chain tends to be occupied by service providers who help integrate multiple products into systems, then sell and support the products, and finally, often within the customer organization, help install the new systems and train the end users. These are typically the ones that make or break the creation of any new value chain. They cannot become gorillas themselves, as we have been careful to argue, but they are critical to the gorilla game.

To read the diagram from left to right, in the case of a discontinuous innovation, technology of a new and unique capability is being incorporated into products, which propose new and highly differentiated benefits to customers. For these benefits to be realized, the new products must be integrated into the world's existing systems, and the resultant *whole product* must be sellable through a sales channel. That channel, in turn, must make a sale to the customer, who then must have the technical capabilities to internalize the new system. At this point, if the end users adopt the new system, and it makes them more productive, then, *and only then*, do the economic buyers see a return on their purchase investment. Creating a new value chain, in other words, is not a slam dunk.

Now value-chain analysis is a business practice that was originally developed to improve focus on existing mature markets. In that context the idea is to see who is adding the real value and where, and what steps are being done more out of habit than necessity, so that companies can cut out non-value-adding steps and increase the value-adding content of their overall offer. It is an important process to follow, but it is for mature markets—not what a gorilla gamer cares about.

In emerging markets, however, there is a different use for value-chain analysis. Here the problem typically is that value is not getting all the way through to the customer. The role of value-chain analysis is to discover why not. Typically it is because some link in the value chain is weak. As a result, the entire value proposition is weakened, and only a little value, if any, is leaking through to the economic buyer who pays for the entire chain. In such cases, the market simply does not develop. By contrast, when value chains really do work, and value really does get all the way through to the economic buyers, then everyone is motivated to ramp up their investment in the category, and the market grows. Indeed, it is fair to say that a market is nothing more or less than an institutionalized value chain, and the better the circulation of value, the more dynamic the market.

When a technology-based market has yet to emerge, when it has not yet made it across the chasm and into a mass market tornado, that means there is something wrong with the value chain that needs to be fixed. *Always*. Gorilla-game investors can use this principle to track the status of emerging markets in terms of the current and future status of their value chains. By definition, the chains they are tracking are not working optimally at present, for if they were, they would already be inside the tornado. By definition they must work if the market is ever to go into hypergrowth.

The key questions to ask, then, are:

1: Can this value chain develop into a tornado mass market?

2: If so, what conditions are currently holding it back?

3: Are these constraining conditions likely to be removed?

4: If so, when is the *last remaining constraint* likely to be removed, and by whom?

When the last remaining constraint goes, assuming there is a genuine mass market value proposition that has never before been tapped, then the tornado begins.

THE EXAMPLE OF THE PC

Let's apply this line of thinking to the original PC tornado. Recall that back in the early 1980s there was a burgeoning PC industry, led by Apple with its Apple II, and including Commodore, Atari, Amiga, and others. All of them were utilizing microprocessor technologies that allowed them to offer a low-cost, desktop-sized computer. But there was not much software for these computers—you were supposed to write your own, using a language called BASIC some guy named Gates was working on—nor were there many outlets for them, although the Byte Shop was beginning to grow its franchise. Businesses were not taking these devices seriously in the executive suite, but engineers and other early-adopting end users were bringing them into projects, especially with the advent of a new software program for the Apple II, called Visicalc, which introduced the idea of a spreadsheet.

This is a classic tornado watch situation. Let's apply the key questions:

1: *Can this value chain develop into a tornado mass market?*
The personal computer's promise was one on every desktop. So, yes, if the value chain ever really got clicking, it would indeed be a mass market.

2: *If so, what conditions are currently holding it back?*
Several things were holding it back:

A. Technical buyers in business were waiting to see what IBM would do. At the time, no major Information Technology (IT) organization felt comfortable unless IBM supported an initiative.

B. Consumers lacked made-to-order products that could provide value "out of the box" to anyone other than a technology enthusiast. Specifically, there had not yet emerged a killer app, although both word processing and spreadsheets looked promising.

C. Stores were waiting to see the market develop, although Macy's, Sears, and others were showcasing some of these products in displays.

3: *Are these constraining conditions likely to be removed?*
At the time it looked quite likely that all would be removed. The question on everyone's mind was, when?

4: *If so, when is the last remaining constraint likely to be removed, and by whom?*
It was pretty clear that the last remaining constraint was IBM itself. Its support was needed by both the business customer and the sales channel to warrant the adoption risk of taking on a dramatically discontinuous innovation.

Everyone in the market went into hypergrowth upon IBM's entry. Intel's microprocessor business simply took off, allowing it to exit an unprofitable memory chip business a few years later. Microsoft's empire was born, giving it control over every desktop in the IBM and PC-clone domain. Sales of application software from Lotus (1-2-3), MicroPro (WordStar), and Ashton-Tate (dBase) all went through the roof. Huge chains of systems and service providers sprang up overnight, led by Computerland and Businessland. These chains sold not only IBM PCs, but also products from Apple, Commodore, and others. Even though the gorilla was preordained, these companies won too. Tornadoes, like rising tides, float all boats.

THE EXAMPLE OF THE WORLD WIDE WEB

That's one example of a tornado watch fulfilled. Let's apply the same line of thinking now to the World Wide Web, arguably still in the midst of its first tornado around browsers and Web servers, with a whole host of others forecast. But watch out! There's a trick embedded in this one, as Bill Gates found out.

Recall that back in the early 1990s there was a burgeoning on-line services industry, led by America Online, Prodigy, and CompuServe—with a big bad wolf called Microsoft huffing and puffing at the door, promising something to be called Microsoft Network. All of these services were utilizing modem technologies and public networks that allowed them to offer low-cost access to electronic mail and information services. But there was no easy interoperability among them, and the amount of information on any one, while intriguing, was not quite compelling. High-tech businesses were taking these services seriously as a means for software distribution and customer support for their technically sophisticated customers and partners, as Compuserve's success demonstrated; but consumers were holding back, as witnessed by Prodigy's continuing disappointing results. The public networks were simply a transport mechanism, and only Unix professionals knew about the Internet and how to navigate its protocols. The World Wide Web existed only among academic and governmental institutions; on-line communities like The Well were better known.

Let's try out our questions again:

1: *Can this value chain develop into a tornado mass market?*
Yes. The experience of America Online in particular was very encouraging. They had removed the user interface problem for "the rest of us," and were showing success in creating on-line communities. E-mail and chat rooms, in particular, were looking like possible killer apps.

2: *If so, what conditions are currently holding it back?*
Several things were holding it back:

A. There was a systems problem in the lack of a unifying standard to unite competing on-line services. Each had its own installed base that was pretty much confined to that system. Technological gurus routinely listed three or four services for e-mail on their business cards. Corporate customers had their own in-house e-mail based on proprietary products from Microsoft, Lotus, IBM, and others.

B. There was no good sales channel. The product category was fragmented, and the entry price low, which meant that resellers would have to stock lots of units with a low yield per unit—not a good business for them.

C. There was no standard way for buying or selling on-line content. Users were nervous about incurring charges that might escalate out of control, and database providers had no model for knowing what their data was worth.

3: *Are these constraining conditions likely to be removed?*
At the time it looked quite likely that all would be removed. But here is the kicker. *Nobody thought that the Internet or the World Wide Web was the key!* Everybody thought this problem was going to be solved by Microsoft.

4: *If so, when is the last remaining constraint likely to be removed, and by whom?*
In 1994 it was pretty clear that the last remaining constraints would be removed in 1995, when Microsoft would release Windows 95, which would have a button on its interface that automatically connected the user back to Microsoft Network. This link would pre-empt all other proprietary on-line services. The threat of monopoly control was so obvious that it generated a petition to the Justice Department on behalf of the rest of the industry.

Then, out of nowhere, the World Wide Web showed up! All of a sudden there emerged an alternative set of answers to these same four questions, and astoundingly, these answers were dramatically better than the first set. They were:

1: *Can this value chain develop into a tornado mass market?*
All of the previous reasons to anticipate a mass market still held, but in addition, there was a whole new community of Internet users already in the market, including a slew of college graduates and undergraduates who had gained free Internet access via their universities'

".edu" accounts, and who had already figured out how compelling it was to stay in touch with high school pals by e-mail.

2: *If so, what conditions are currently holding it back?*

Here again we have the same things that held us back before, the same weak links in the value chain:

A. No unifying standard to unite systems.

B. No good sales channel.

C. No standard for buying and selling content.

But look below at how these constraints get removed in Internet terms.

3: *Are these constraining conditions likely to be removed?*

The World Wide Web eliminated all the key constraints in a single blow:

A. *The Web is the standard.*

The client software is the browser, and the server software is the Web server. HTTP is the transport protocol, and HTML is the document standard. End of story.

B. *The Web is its own sales channel.*

You do not need any storefronts. It's all software, and it all can be downloaded. But how can this possibly work economically? Because . . .

C. *All content is free, including Web browsers.*

Content providers did not like this answer, but that turned out not to matter. Going forward, the economic model of the Web appears certain to be that of a free broadcast medium supported by advertising.

4: *If so, when is the last remaining constraint likely to be removed, and by whom?*

The answer was *now*, and the company was *Netscape!* And that is why its stock hit the stratosphere upon IPO. Its browser and Web server software begat the Web revolution, and it was a gorilla almost at birth!

Now, we should note that since that IPO, Microsoft, to its enduring credit and the delight of its shareholders, has made a phenomenal competitive response. But what is interesting about that response is that it *has always acknowledged Netscape as the gorilla*. Microsoft cloned Netscape's browser all throughout 1996 to catch up, and its strategy for overthrowing Netscape's gorilla position is not to beat it at its own game, but to change the rules by embedding the browser into Windows, and thereby putting the game back on its original course. We already had a look at this in a previous chapter, under the topic "When Gorillas Collide," and we will revisit it in our final discussion of gorilla games in the Internet space. Suffice it to say, it is one of the preeminent business events of the decade, and its consequences are still rippling through the industry.

To sum up, the point of these two examples of the PC industry and the World Wide Web has been to illustrate how to use a handful of key questions to surface tornado opportunities and to track their development. The focus should always be first on obstacles, then on enablers. There are all kinds of optimistic signals in any emerging high-tech market, but unless they herald the elimination of a tornado obstacle, we just aren't interested in them.

THE OBSTACLE IS COMPLEXITY, THE RELIEF IS AN ENABLER

The driver behind value-chain creation is wealth creation. Wherever new money can be made, a free market will ferret out a way to make it. The more new wealth that can be brought into existence, the greater the number of people who can participate in that new wealth; and the faster it can all happen, the greater the force with which it will happen. This is the essence of the tornado.

When the opportunity for wealth creation is real, and tornadoes still fail to form, the enemy is almost always *complexity*. There are two main types of complexity that can prevent a tornado from forming, and in both cases there is a corresponding enabler that can break the back of that complexity.

ADOPTION COMPLEXITY AND THE KILLER APP

This obstacle lives at the customer end of the value chain. Typically, either the product is too hard to install or use, or the customer benefit is too foreign to the target user population. In either case, the "positive returns" feedback loop so necessary to a tornado keeps getting interrupted as customer after customer pauses to say, "I don't get it."

The result of adoption complexity is hesitation and doubt. There is no buildup of universal unmet demand such that the marketplace can take demand for granted. This in turn prevents the value chain from devoting itself solely to the problems of ramping up supply. After a while solution providers get distracted into pursuing other market opportunities. The market does grow, but the tornado never comes.

To drive the emergence of a tornado, there must be a powerful customer benefit at the end of the value chain—a killer application. This consists of a single, common offering for which there is a temporarily unlimited demand, allowing the value chain to focus all its efforts on ramping up supply. If the market has to oscillate between creating more demand and then creating more supply, it will ratchet up but will not form a tornado. Hypergrowth requires the condition of being able to take intense sustained customer demand for granted. In the case of the PC, for example, the first killer app was word processing, and the second was spreadsheets.

In the case of the World Wide Web the initial tornado application was browsing; the second, a "rediscovery" of e-mail, this time on the Internet; the third, marketing communication via a Web site; and the fourth, using all of these applications to create an *Intranet* for internal communications.

Killer apps tend to be familiar, not discontinuous, at the level of the end user's experience. This makes them easy to adopt. Word processing, for example, replaced a system of typewriters that had long ago conditioned users to think in terms of tabs, margins, pages, files, and folders. In the case of spreadsheets, they replaced columnar tabs that had long ago conditioned us to think in terms of rows, columns, and cell formulas. The more familiar the application paradigm, the faster the herd gets with the new program.

IMPLEMENTATION COMPLEXITY AND THE WHOLE PRODUCT

This problem hits the product and service providers' end of the value chain. The solution template, or whole product, is too complex to replicate easily, reliably, and consistently, so although the customer wants the benefits, and thus the market wants to go into hypergrowth, the solution providers cannot scale their offerings fast enough to get things off the ground. After a while the customer base gets tired of waiting around and wanders off to explore other opportunities.

This has been the case to date with geo-spatial information systems (GIS), which provide maps for various business and governmental purposes; Lotus Notes, providing information sharing among knowledge-based organizations; and with data warehouses that promise to offer management unlimited bird's-eye views into operations. All three promise great benefits, and users by and large would support greater deployment of any of them. But they are all so discontinuous with the current technological infrastructure, require so much customization to be effective, and demand so much data administration, that it is virtually impossible for any of them to generate a mass market.

The objective in a tornado is to field an offer that can withstand the pressures of hypergrowth. The end result must be that independent solution providers can produce effectively identical results without communicating directly with each other. This allows each individual effort to spontaneously contribute to the larger, self-organizing mass market. Hypergrowth requires a simple formula that can be iterated over and over again, without any centralized command and control.

The cellular phone industry is built up of just such a whole product. Cellular systems formed in different parts of the country by different companies are able to interoperate and merge just because the fundamental solution set is well characterized and standardized. Or take the CAD industry, which had been confined for decades to small niche markets that could afford $50,000 workstations and up. Autodesk in the late 1980s was able to field a tornado offer based on a PC and its own flagship product AutoCad, in large part by keeping the complexity down to a level where independent resellers could design and assemble a standard system for their customers.

Subsequently, by opening up its program to third-party add-ons, it was able to further scale its market without introducing additional costs or complexity.

In sum, the tornado rewards a whole product that gives up some high-end features in order to be more readily delivered to the marketplace at large.

CONTINUITY PLUS DISCONTINUITY CREATES THE TORNADO

What makes customers so willing to go along with the tornado is the *continuity* of the killer app with their current lives. It is not fundamentally disruptive to them, but instead gives them a great new benefit that they can readily integrate into their current lives. So in looking for tornado opportunities, look for *continuity at the customers' end of the value chain*.

What creates a new value chain, on the other hand, is the *discontinuity* of the technology, which requires reengineering some part of the marketplace to bring it to market. Here we must have fundamental disruption, or the existing vested interests will simply coopt the opportunity, and no new wealth-creating institutions emerge. So in looking for tornado opportunities, look for *discontinuity on the suppliers' end of the value chain*.

This is the critical combination—a discontinuous technology that allows a new value chain of vendors to displace the current establishment, thereby creating new sources of wealth to invest in, and a continuous benefit that allows a customer base to adopt en masse, thereby creating the tornado surge in demand.

RECAPPING THE LESSONS OF THIS CHAPTER

Two critical lessons have been presented that must be internalized. They are:

1: When evaluating tornado market opportunities, maintain focus on the state of the value chain, asking the following questions over and over again:

A. *Can this value chain develop into a tornado mass market?*

If the answer is no, leave the sector. There will be no gorillas coming around here anytime soon. If the answer is yes, continue.

B. *If so, what conditions are currently holding it back?*

This is where you earn your stripes as a gorilla gamer. Nobody ever really knows the answer to this question, so the goal is to assemble ideas about it, and then take your own view. That view will drive the next phase of your tornado watch, as represented by the final two questions.

C. *Are these constraining conditions likely to be removed?*

As an investor, you need to imagine what it might take to remove the obstacles you have identified as the key blocking forces holding back the tornado's formation. Once you have ideas, you can start evaluating the offers from particular companies to see if they might do the trick.

D. *If so, when is the last remaining constraint likely to be removed, and by whom?*

This is a key caveat about betting on any breakthrough in a traffic jam. It doesn't do any good if the jam just re-forms a mile or two down the highway. In other words, until the value chain is operating effectively end to end, no value gets through. That's why it is important to postulate the *last* remaining constraint.

2: As you are looking at constraints and their removal, remember the critical factor is the need to overcome complexity. As we said, complexity comes in two main forms, each overcome by a characteristic enabler:

A. Adoption complexity, overcome by the killer app.

B. Solution complexity, overcome by a streamlined whole product.

As progress is made in one of these two areas, the blocking function shifts over to the other. It is not until both are solved that the tornado can be released.

So much for the tornado watch. With these principles under your belt, we think you can go out and find tornado markets. We think you can, in other words, locate potential gorillas. Now the question is, *What would you do if you found one?*

7

Capturing the Gorilla

THE BUYING AND SELLING OF HIGH-TECH STOCKS

We are now halfway through the book, and there is no more contextual knowledge to provide. It is now time for procedural knowledge: How does one actually play the gorilla game?

At the highest level, the principles of gorilla game are as simple as they are powerful. As we stated in Chapter 1, they are:

- Find markets transitioning into hypergrowth.

- Buy the basket of stocks that represent all the companies that have a clear shot at being the gorilla.

- As the gorilla emerges, sell off the rest of the basket and consolidate your holdings in the gorilla.

- Plan to hold the gorilla for the long term.

- Sell the gorilla only when a new category, based on an alternative technology, threatens to eradicate its power.

That's it. That is the gorilla game. It's that simple.

Of course, like anything that simple, it begs a ton of questions, and each merits a fair amount of discussion. That's why you are reading a book and not an e-mail. To take on these questions in a logical sequence, this chapter will proceed as follows:

1: When should I buy?

2: What should I buy?

3: What should I hold and for how long?

4: What should I sell and when?

5: What should I do with all the information I get in the mean-time?

These are all questions that keep investors up at night (and often logged on to America Online or the Internet), but our goal is to put them to bed directly.

In the process of answering them we are going to generate the Ten Rules for Playing the Gorilla Game. These are summarized at the end of the chapter. Those of you who like to know where you are going before you get there can take a peek at them now.

We should say at the outset that we are of two minds about so-called rules for investing in general. On the one hand, we don't believe that any set of rules captures the full responsibility of investing, or the many judgments that are required to process any real-world opportunity. On the other hand, the discipline of writing out these rules and having them critiqued by our colleagues has forced to the surface a whole raft of challenging issues that would have been easy to duck otherwise. So we offer these rules as our model of how to make actionable the view of the stock market we have presented, and we are standing by them as they are written. Waffling adds no value. We hope they make sense as is. We hope they will make even more sense after you read this chapter.

WHEN SHOULD I BUY?

Okay. You have been scanning the technological universe, and you have found some categories that you think are potential future tornadoes. When should you actually buy into the category?

There are two times to make your first purchase of a stock in the gorilla game. For application software, you buy in the bowling alley. For enabling technologies, including all hardware and system software, you buy at the beginning of the tornado. Here's how the reasoning plays out.

Rule 1. If the category is application software, buy in the bowling alley.

The ideal time to buy into any future tornado is before the market has recognized its true potential. That way you get the maximum return from the upside surprise. At the same time, the ideal moment is also when there is virtually no downside risk from the market not crossing the chasm. This means the earliest time to buy is in the bowling alley, and that is a good time for getting into software applications, specifically OLTP applications focused on managing business processes. This category includes financials, human resources, manufacturing requirements planning, supply-chain management, factory floor control systems, sales force automation, customer support, customer service, and the like.

Software applications are good buys in the bowling alley because even those companies that will not become gorillas still produce good returns. Markets for business application software never completely consolidate, the way they do with enabling technologies, so chimps have more winning options. Once a customer purchases a particular vendor's application, it is very hard for another vendor—even a gorilla—to overcome the switching-cost barrier and take that customer away. Application markets still generate gorillas, to be sure, and these gorillas still have all their customary advantages when it comes to garnering new customers. But they cannot be quite so predatory at the expense of their competition. Moreover, software application markets do not tend to generate monkeys as readily as other markets—it is almost impossible to really clone an application, particularly one that has a set of application-specific databases associated with it—so the chimps tend not to get undercut on price. As a result, buying a whole bunch of future chimps, which is a normal occurrence when investing in applications in the bowling alley, has relatively little downside risk.

The attraction, then, of buying application software companies in the bowling alley is that you can get pretty decent returns on all your stocks, *and* you get a fistful of tickets to a gorilla game. For the conservative investor, this is really the best kind of bet. With your downside relatively well hedged, your only significant remaining concern is simply the opportunity cost of tying up all your capital in a category that may never tornado.

Following Rule 1, and assuming all the companies were public at the time, you would have made the following investments over the past fifteen years:

- Accounting software packages for IBM mainframes in the early 1980s, including MSA, McCormick & Dodge, and Cullinet, with the ultimate gorilla being the merged MSA/McCormick & Dodge that became Dun & Bradstreet. This you would have sold off in 1992, once it became clear that client/server financials (substitution threat) would displace mainframe applications.

- Materials requirements planning (MRP)—later to become manufacturing requirements planning (MRP II)—packages for proprietary minicomputers in the mid-1980s. These would have included ASK, the leader on the HP 3000, and SSA, the leader on the IBM AS/400. These you would have sold in 1991, when it became clear that Unix computers (another substitution threat) would undermine the market for the proprietary minicomputer platforms these applications run on.

- Client/server financials and MRP systems, including SAP, Oracle, PeopleSoft, and Baan, which you would have bought in 1993 and would still be holding. Beginning in 1995, however, you would have started shifting more and more of your investment to SAP as their gorilla position became clear, dominating the Fortune 500 class of customer. In the middle of this shift, however, you would have learned that many in the market question whether SAP will be able to scale down its offers to attack the middle market effectively. Since the middle market is projected as the one with highest future growth, you would have begun rebalancing your portfolio in 1996 and 1997 by reinvesting in the other three vendors named above. This mild form of hedging is representative of the sort of freedom you can get in an applications market, but that you cannot get in an enabling software or hardware marketplace.

■ Customer support packages for client/server systems in the mid-1990s, including Clarify, Vantive, and Scopus, which as of this writing are still in the bowling alley, and which you would be examining for tornado tendencies. At the same time, you would have bought Remedy, which is in a related category called *help desk* software, because it was responding to the same business needs for in-house customer support that the others were doing for commercial customer support. Then in late 1996, you would have begun looking seriously at adding Siebel and Aurum, which are both vendors of "sales force automation" packages, because you would have been hearing about the possibility of a superset of applications emerging, called customer interaction systems, that might take over the front office the way enterprise requirements planning packages have taken over the back office.

So, with a wave of our magic wand, we have taken you into and out of a whole raft of investments. What can we learn from this? First, there were lots of choices in each category—indeed, we could have added more. That reflects the fragmentary nature of application software markets. Second, we telegraphed our selling strategy for gorillas, which will be formally presented later in the chapter—sell only on substitution threat (the death of the gorilla). The final point is that the real skill in application software investing, something that will build over time and cannot readily be put into rules, is to gain a feel for whether the category will:

1: Stay bowling alley forever, a fate that has to date befallen project management, computer-aided design, and document management.

2: Go into a true mass market tornado, as financial packages, e-mail, and word processing all have done.

3: Get coopted into a supercategory, as word processing, spread-sheets, and presentation applications all got swept up into a category called office automation suites.

If the category does stay bowling alley forever, you will exit it when you see no more bowling pins to knock down. If it does go into a mass market, you will play by the Ten Rules. But if it gets coopted into a supercategory, you will be faced with an ambiguous situation—is this a substitution threat (well, maybe—it certainly was when Aldus Persuasion fell victim to Microsoft Office with its bundled PowerPoint) or a market expansion (as it has been for PeopleSoft, which started with a leadership position in human resources and has extended into a strong chimp position in the supercategory of enter-prise resource planning)? Questions like these really will keep you up at night, and all we really have to recommend is taking a glass of warm milk.

Turning now to enabling technology, we can add a complement to our first rule, as follows:

Rule 2. If the category is enabling hardware or software, buy at the start of the tornado.

Unlike the relatively civilized world of application software, where multiple winners can emerge within a single gorilla game, with enabling technologies, be they software or hardware, there is a much more violent consolidation creating much more of a winner-takes-all outcome. These technologies *do* lend themselves to cloning, which means monkeys will enter the fray, adding to the market mass of the "standard" system and threatening to erode chimp pricepoints from below. Moreover, here gorillas *can* steal the chimp's customers because, as long as the application software doesn't change, the end user doesn't really care who owns the underlying plumbing. The swing vote, therefore, goes to application partners writing the soft-ware, not the customers buying it, and these partners, despite their fear and loathing of gorilla power, end up succumbing to the allure of the cheaper, more reliable results that a single standard infrastructure provides.

For companies providing enabling-technology hardware and software, the stakes are high and the losses painful. Spend gazillions developing and introducing a new candidate standard, and you may experience the fate of:

- LAN Manager, a local area networking standard Microsoft promoted heavily in the 1990s. The world went with Novell Netware instead.

- Open Desktop, a Unix-based Intel workstation standard sponsored by SCO, Compaq, and Relational Technology Inc. The dogs just did not eat this dog food, so the market stayed with Sun and HP workstations, and with Wintel PCs.

- OpenDoc, a document exchange standard championed by Apple and IBM. The industry went with Microsoft's OLE instead.

- VG AnyLAN, a 100-megabit networking standard cosponsored by HP and IBM. The industry instead went with 3COM and Intel's Fast Ethernet alternative.

Companies who invested resources in any of these systems—and the investors who backed them—simply came up empty.

But the risk does not stop there. Even if the enabling technology does get adopted on a bowling alley basis, it is not a given that it will scale further to become a tornado. This has been the fate, to date, of asynchronous transfer mode (ATM) networking technology, which just a few years ago was touted as a huge tornado in progress, but thus far has only been adopted in niche markets. Such has been the fate as well of solid-state storage (intended to replace disk drives), PCMCIA cards, smart cards, optical disk drives, infrared data ports, and the fibre-channel networking protocol. Because of the huge research and development expenditures needed to bring these kinds of fundamental technologies to market, anything less than a tornado normally does not create acceptable returns—something like the current blockbuster mentality in the film and book industries. As a result, many of the technologies just listed, even though some have gained strong niche-market acceptance, are typically deemed failures.

That said, however, we now must counter with a single observation:

The amount of wealth generated by an enabling-technology tornado that creates a true gorilla dwarfs any other investment returns on the planet.

This is the Super Bowl, the Oscars, and the Grammies all rolled into one. To not play here at all is to hate yourself in the morning.

Balancing, then, the desire for gain with the risk of picking wrong, we think it is best with enabling technologies to *wait until a strong tornado signal has emerged* and then get in on the game. At that time it may already be possible to sense who the emerging gorilla will be and weight your investment accordingly. But we would not advocate picking the gorilla ahead of the market. The whole point of the gorilla game is to confine one's gambles to picking the right category for investment and not to extend them into picking the right company. Let the market do that for you, and then consolidate.

Following Rule 2, and assuming all of the following companies were public at the time, over the past fifteen years, you would have:

- Bought the minicomputer stocks in 1984—Digital, Prime, Data General—peeling back to Digital in 1987, exiting Digital in 1992 when it became clear Unix would substitute for the proprietary systems.

- Bought Microsoft and Apple as microcomputer operating system plays, backing out of Apple in 1992 with the mass acceptance of Windows 3.0.

- Bought the personal computer microprocessor companies in 1986—Intel, Motorola, and AMD—and by 1990 peeled back to just the gorilla, Intel, which you would still hold.

- Bought the relational database companies in 1987—Oracle, Relational Technology Inc., and Informix—and by 1989 shed all but the gorilla, Oracle, which you would still hold (although nervously, in light of Microsoft's Back Office initiatives). It is possible you would have bought Sybase after it went public in 1991; if so, you would have sold it in 1994, probably taking a loss due to the steep downturn it had that year upon reporting its first quarter.

- Bought the inter-networking hardware companies in 1991—specifically the router tornado being driven by Cisco and Wellfleet (the latter merged later with SynOptics to form Bay Networks)—and by 1995 consolidated them to Cisco, which you would still hold.

In 1997 your portfolio would be concentrated in Microsoft, Intel, Oracle, and Cisco, and you wouldn't even be bothering to read this book, your more pressing concerns being the wallpaper selection for your pied-á-terre in London, and whether you should buy a one-sixteenth share in the Lear Jet that Tiger Woods has a piece of.

It's Not about WHICH—It's Only about WHEN

The key to gorilla game investing, as the above examples illustrate, is not to focus on *which* stocks to pick, but rather on *when* to buy into a particular category. This substantially reduces the downside risk of investing, and positions one to capture the acceleration when it hits. In the short term, the rising tide of the coming tornado will float all boats. The challenge in an enabling-technology investment basket is to get out of the chimps before tornado dynamics crater their stock price. The key to that is early detection of the gorilla and making the corresponding adjustment to your portfolio.

The biggest downside risk is when an enabling technology simply does not tornado. You can lose a big chunk of your investment the day the market wakes up to this outcome. That is why we recommend against investing in any pre-tornado concept plays. Yes, if the market does tornado, people who bought in advance of this event will make a huge killing, and that could have been you, had you only . . . But that way lies madness. Instead we recommend you be a little late to the tornado party, making sure it is authentically under way, just to protect yourself.

So, how can you tell *when?*

■ For *software applications*, where the signal is established presence in the bowling alley, the specific criterion you are looking for is the following:

> The application has been "designed into" the business processes of at least one specific vertical market, such that for the companies inside that segment, *not buying* is a bigger risk than buying.

This signal would have told you to buy desktop publishing software in 1987, with Aldus (page layout software for self-published newsletters) as your lead company. It would have gotten you to buy into the client/server applications companies in 1993, with PeopleSoft (human resource applications) and Oracle and SAP (financials for high-tech companies) as your lead companies. It would have gotten you to buy the customer service applications in 1995 (high-tech and telephone company customer support) with Vantive, Scopus, and Clarify all having 50% or more of their revenues coming from those niches.

The importance of this signal for applications companies cannot be overstated. If any one of these companies can dominate even a single niche, that company has longevity for itself. The market indeed may gravitate to some other standard, but because of switching costs, the niche under dominance assuredly will not. The line-of-business executives who govern the buying decisions in the niche will instead look to their local leader to take them forward into new systems. This means that that company can maintain a privileged relationship with a defensible set of customers, and has first rights to serve up to that customer base any future technology. This is not the upside that is generated from the tornado, to be sure, but in stark contrast to *concept* investments, it virtually eliminates all short- to medium-term downside.

■ By contrast, with *enabling technologies*, there is no customer intimacy with line-of-business buyers, since only the IT experts understand the technology issues underneath the covers. IT organizations, having been burned many times before, are much more likely to wait for the tornado before committing their companies to a new standard. That is why gorilla-game investors should also wait until the IT-driven tornado has arrived before they buy into enabling-technology market opportunities.

A good signal to begin tornado buying is when trade magazines stop printing articles questioning the readiness of a new technology for prime time and start printing ones focused on who is the emerging market leader. *ComputerWorld*, *InformationWeek*, and *CIO* are particularly useful for the computer industry sector, because all three magazines target IT executives who must weigh the risk of premature commitment to a technology against the risk of being left behind.

In 1996 these magazines gave the nod to two new paradigms, thereby signaling the start of their tornadoes:

A. Putting up Web sites on the Internet.

B. Rolling out Windows NT as the standard workgroup operating system.

A companion signal occurs on Wall Street at the same time. The category of companies involved surprises analysts two quarters in a row by returning revenues and earnings in excess of what was forecast. This is a frequent symptom of hypergrowth, where companies simply cannot spend enough to catch up to the growth in their top-line revenues. These executives do not forecast this hypergrowth in full because it is unprecedented, and because Wall Street is continually admonishing them to be conservative.

Of course, these are only indicators, and "your mileage may vary," as the car industry is wont to say. In such situations you simply have to keep returning to first principles and mapping the pattern you are seeking to the data you are receiving. Here also is where the benefit comes from participating in a good chat room or threaded discussion, where you can bounce ideas off of other interested gorilla gamers before you make your call.

What Should I Buy?

A key point of this book is to create an investment process that gets above-market returns from investing in gorilla companies. So the obvious question is, how do you predict which one company will become the gorilla? To which the simple answer is, *don't try!*

Instead of placing your entire investment in one stock, hoping it will become the gorilla, you play the gorilla game by investing in *all* the companies with a reasonable chance at becoming the gorilla. That does not mean investing in all the companies competing in a particular product category. Rather, it means identifying the two to four companies that have a legitimate shot at becoming the gorilla, what we might call the gorilla candidates.

While the eventual gorilla is hard to predict at the outset of a tornado market, gorilla *candidates* are fairly easy to spot. When the press writes about the product category, they will almost always cite a small list of representative companies. Once the same list of companies starts showing up over and over—and very quickly it will—these become the gorilla candidates. Moreover, the sequence in which the companies are listed represents the current consensus on their power ranking, with the favored gorilla candidate always listed first. If the market attracts financial analysts into following it, when they cover the product category they too will make perfectly clear who they think the front-runners are. When high-tech companies in other product categories need to partner with one of the vendors in the emerging product category, they too signal their views by always calling on the gorilla candidates first. At industry trade shows it is the gorilla candidates who will have a "buzz" in their booth—everyone wants to learn about them.

This type of conversation surrounds both applications and enabling technologies, but in the case of the latter you have to watch out for "religious wars." Because power centralizes so dramatically with enabling technologies, the market expects to see only a single winner, which in turn spurs all competitors to declare victory early and often. And as companies' PR agencies get more and more clever about garnering prestigious endorsements, it turns out to be a real problem sorting through all the hype to find out what is real. The best indicators in these cases are the partners who must interface or port their products onto these new platforms. Do not be fooled, however, by partner press releases that announce strategic relationships—these all too often represent companies simply covering all their bases, and many of these commitments will be left unfulfilled. Instead look for companies announcing their *second* generation of products on the new infrastructure, ones that can tout actual customers and some demonstrable marketplace commitment. That suggests there really are some teeth behind that enabling-technology vendor's claim to having been designed in.

All in all, the market follows the model of a presidential primary—early on two or three candidates emerge to become the serious contenders, while others begin to fall back, and still others drop out of the race completely. Once this happens it's highly unlikely that anyone but a front-runner will get the party's—or in our case, the market's—nomination. Consequently, our what-to-buy rule is:

Rule 3: Buy a basket comprising *all* the gorilla candidates—usually at least two, sometimes three, and normally no more than four companies.

Why not just do the best research possible and use it to choose just one? There are two reasons:

1: It's next to impossible to pick who will be the gorilla.

2: It's not worth the effort or the risk anyway.

Buying the basket works because stocks inside the tornado offer significant upside but only limited downside. The upside from investing in the basket of gorilla candidates is significant, even though the eventual chimps and monkeys do not appreciate as much as the gorilla. At minimum, chimps usually do not depreciate in a tornado, at least not until after you have had clear and repeated signals to sell them off and reinvest the proceeds in the gorilla winner.

Throughout the next few chapters we'll use numerous examples to illustrate the concept of buying the basket of gorilla candidates, but for now consider the following two examples.

MICROPROCESSORS FOR MICROCOMPUTERS

In the late 1970s three companies were locked in a battle for supremacy in the microcomputer microprocessor market—Intel, Motorola, and Zilog. By 1983, however, the three companies racing to become the gorilla were Intel, Motorola, and Advanced Micro Devices. Intel had become the key supplier to IBM, AMD was granted a license to produce the Intel design, and Motorola became the supplier to Apple Computer.

The PC crossed the chasm somewhere in 1985, after IBM's successful launch of the IBM PC/AT in August of 1984. The first wave of pragmatist adopters turned out to be financial managers who used it to run spreadsheets, most notably Lotus 1-2-3. The tornado for the rest of us, driven by word processing, followed shortly thereafter.

As such, 1985 would have been the earliest time to start purchasing the CPU stocks (remember, they are enabling technologies, so we start in the tornado, not the bowling alley). Even if you had waited until the last day of 1986 to buy your stock—fully two years after the first PC applications began to tornado—you would have generated a substantial return on investment over the next ten years. Here's what happened to the stocks of all microcomputer CPU gorilla candidates:

WHO	STOCK PRICE* DEC. 31, 1986	STOCK PRICE DEC. 31, 1996	10-YEAR RETURN	EVENTUAL STATUS
Intel	$3.50	130.9375	3641%	Gorilla
Motorola	$8.91	61.25	587%	Chimp
AMD	$13.75	25.75	87%	Monkey

* Split Adjusted

Granted, none of these stocks was a pure play in CPUs—each of these companies had substantial businesses in other product lines. However, it was clear to many by late 1986 that the PC business would revolutionize not only the industry but also the world, and that the microprocessor was the key hardware element of that revolution. Betting on the PC tornado to catapult these companies forward was not far-fetched. In fact, IBM had already signaled as much with its 1986 purchase of 12% of Intel for $250 million.

LOCAL AREA NETWORK OPERATING SYSTEMS

PC local area network operating systems began to tornado around 1987, when departments in medium-sized companies wanted to run networked versions of word processing software (primarily WordPerfect) and/or networked versions of spreadsheets (mostly Lotus 1-2-3), as well as communicate with each other via e-mail and print their files out on a shared printer. As the good word-of-mouth spread, a number of companies got into the game. There were three gorilla candidates in the LAN operating system product category: Novell, 3COM, and Banyan Systems (3COM later dropped out of the market, licensing its 3PLUS product to Microsoft, who marketed it as LAN Manager).

The product category grew tremendously after 1987, and in early 1988 the market crowned a gorilla, Novell, whose stock took off like a rocket. Its revenues grew from $183 million in 1987 to $933 million in 1992. Here's a look at the stock performance of the three gorilla candidates:

Who (Product)	Stock price* Dec. 31, 1987	Stock price* Dec. 31, 1992	5-year return	Eventual status
Novell (Netware)	$ 3.00	28.50	850%	Gorilla
3COM (3PLUS)	$ 5.00	7.41	48.2%	Chimp[1]
Banyan (Vines)**	$ 12.50	21.00	68%	Chimp[2]

* Split Adjusted
** Went public on August 7, 1992—This is a 5–month return

Combining both of these examples, any investor who had simply stuck a bunch of cash in all six of these stocks, then forgotten about them for several years, would have done very well. Buying and holding the basket in a tornado category is not a high-risk use of capital. Nonetheless, that is not what we advocate. Selling is just as much a part of the gorilla game as buying and holding, as the following sections will make clear.

What Should I Hold and for How Long?

You have bought the basket, and the category has gone into the tornado, and you are feeling very good about this, talking to your friends, getting kudos from your spouse. You know what you have to do at a time like this, don't you? Worry, what else?

Buyer's remorse is a well-documented phenomenon in consumer markets, but it pales in comparison to *seller's remorse* in stock investments: I sold too early—I sold too late—I should have sold—I shouldn't have sold. There is no way around these insecurities. There is, however, a right way to handle them.

That process should be based on asking yourself two key questions:

1: Was the decision-making process that I followed good or bad?

2: Was the outcome of the decision good or bad?

Now, when good processes produce good results, life makes sense, and all is well. When bad processes produce bad results, all may not be well, but life still makes sense, and the intelligent person learns from the experience. The hardest outcomes to handle, it turns out, are when bad processes produce good results and vice versa. Here most people make the mistake of preferring the good result with the bad process. This is painfully short-sighted and must lead to confusion and grief later.

Instead, the correct response is to prefer the good process even when it generates a bad result. This is because the goal of prudent risk-taking is *not* to never fail; the goal is instead to win a lot more times than you lose. Good process is the key to that outcome. If you abandon good process just because you didn't win this one time, you lose the winning edge. Similarly, if you abandon good process just because you got lucky with a bad process, you are also going to lose the winning edge.

Success in the gorilla game demands having a good process for holding vs. selling high-tech stocks. In most other sectors of the economy, where tornadoes are not common, *long-term holding* is the best strategy. That is because the better companies, the execution leaders or kings, will tend to outperform the category year in and year out. Massive shifts in power are rare, and churning your stocks in pursuit of incremental advantages has proved to be unrewarding.

In high tech, on the other hand, massive shifts of power are routine, so patient holding is not rewarded! Think instead of crossing a frozen river that is just breaking up—you have to leap from ice floe to ice floe to get across, always keeping your eye on the next configuration, never just walking straight ahead. You still hold in this model, but with nowhere near the faithfulness as in other sectors.

Specifically, here are the rules we recommend:

RULE FOR HOLDING GORILLAS

The most holdable stock in high tech is the gorilla. You want to have stock in this company, both inside the tornado and when the market matures onto Main Street. Even if this company never finds another tornado, and is never again able to generate spectacular growth with exceptional returns due to the tornado's phenomenal updraft in sales and profits, it will still enjoy a prolonged CAP in its existing category of dominance. It will significantly outperform the competing companies in its sector.

Although the stock market figures this out, meaning after a while your investment is not based on any privileged knowledge or understanding, the market still tends to *price to the mean*, slightly discounting the gorilla's advantage and slightly overpricing the chimps and monkeys. This leads to recurrent corrections, and every so often the market must reprice the gorilla upward, either because it is surprised by upside earnings or it sees now how the gorilla's competitive advantage is extending out further than it had originally thought.

(A note in passing: The stock market is an "it," and by conventional usage, things we call "it" cannot think. Nonetheless, we will continue to attribute intelligence to it. Our view is that the stock market operates like a hive of bees. It exhibits behavior that, in light of its ends, appears both rational and considered. Now, in fact, these responses are simply selected from a much larger population of random responses, and what we are really witnessing is a Darwinian mechanism that generates the illusion of rationality. That being said, of course, the same concepts could just as easily be applied to people. So we feel there is at least as good a case for attributing intelligence to the stock market as to the human race.)

An even better investment—the "hold" of all "holds"—is a gorilla that is able to maneuver itself into future tornadoes by extending its competitive advantages into adjacent technology sectors. Microsoft, Intel, Oracle, and Cisco have all demonstrated this ability to one degree or another, with Microsoft to date being the most astounding performer ever seen.

In this case, in addition to all the advantages of a single gorilla play, these stocks are building gorilla franchises one on top of the other. It is a land of multiple tornadoes, where you have both the stability of Main Street markets and the updraft on new hypergrowth markets bundled into the same stock. This is the stuff of financial legend.

But even here, blind holding is not a winning strategy. High-tech markets are ever-shifting terrains, and no company is exempt from being deposed, a lesson IBM taught many of us, much to our—and its—chagrin. Whenever a new technology successfully takes the stage, one or more traditional gorillas are bound to fall. And since new technologies are coming faster and faster, no hegemony is secure from substitution threat. There will come a time to sell Microsoft, Intel, Cisco, and Oracle—indeed, in the case of Oracle, unless it makes some more definitive response to Microsoft's incursions into relational databases than it has to date, the time may come relatively soon.

In the meantime, it is important to note that even the most successful gorillas will eventually underperform investor expectations and take a hit in their stock prices. As the stock market catches on to the gorilla advantage, investors continue to incorporate higher expectations into the stock price, until any error in execution causes a shortfall. This is to be expected.

These moments of shortfall, however, far from being times to sell gorilla stock, can be good times to buy more of it—if you believe the dynamics of the gorilla's advantage have not materially changed, and that, at the new price, the market has reverted to underpricing the value of the gorilla's CAP.

Rule 4. Hold gorilla stocks for the long term. Sell only on proven substitution threat.

RULE FOR HOLDING CHIMPS

After gorillas, the next most desirable holds are *application software chimps* if they have secured at least one dominant position in a niche market. As was explained, such a position of local dominance gives these companies a guarantee of longevity that hedges their stock against out-and-out collapse. They are, in effect, "local gorillas." At the same time, there is still upside in these chimps, for certain within their current categories, and possibly in light of further consolidations at some higher "super-category" level. Application chimps cease to be holds should it ever become clear they are truly boxed in to the niches they already serve and lack any reasonable play for expansion. From that point on they may still have years of good earnings, but their lack of maneuverability makes them sitting-duck targets for new technologies entering the market.

A very undesirable hold, by contrast, is an *enabling-technology chimp*. These companies made a bet to become the gorilla and lost that bet. They still are in a hypergrowth market, and they are currently showing all kinds of healthy signs, but the tornado model predicts that they are going to hit the wall and hit it hard. Holding these stocks in hopes of guessing the peak is not part of the gorilla game. Sell them early and put the money into the real gorilla.

Rule 5. Hold application software chimp stocks as long as they exhibit potential for further market expansion. Do not hold enabling-technology chimps.

RULE FOR HOLDING KINGS AND PRINCES

Kings and princes, you will recall, are market-leading companies in hypergrowth markets that do not have proprietary architectural control over their category and therefore cannot manipulate switching costs to their advantage. This means that the market is not biased to keep them in power the way it is biased to keep gorillas or niche-dominating chimps in power. The CAPs of kings and princes are based primarily on execution advantages, with kings having the edge due to larger economies of scale. The primary difference between them is size, not position; princes can hope to dethrone kings, whereas chimps can virtually never dethrone gorillas. As a result, kings are much less secure investments than gorillas, while princes are almost on the same footing with kings.

Kings and princes are attractive investments because execution-based advantages in a hypergrowth market can be formidable indeed, and often generate significantly long-lived CAPs. Upside surprises in revenues and earnings are just as accessible to kings as they are to gorillas. Moreover, in some gorilla games it is not clear until very late in the market's development whether the play for proprietary control will be won or lost. So it is not uncommon for a gorilla-game investor to find that a planned holding of gorillas and chimps has transformed itself into an actual holding of kings and princes. For all these reasons, kings and princes are part of the gorilla game. They just need to be handled carefully.

Our recommendation is to buy these companies as if they were any other gorilla candidate portfolio at the outset of the tornado, but to sell them much more aggressively. On an individual basis, we suggest you sell any of these companies if they stumble in the marketplace. On a category-wide basis, we suggest you sell off the entire collection as soon as the category's overall rate of revenue growth starts to decelerate. Following these rules, you will profit from the bloom of hypergrowth, probably give up some additional upside that you could have gotten by holding longer, and protect yourself against the inevitable loss in valuation once the lack of monopolistic barriers to entry permit price competition to erode profit margins.

Rule 6. Hold kings and princes lightly, selling individual stocks on a marketplace stumble and the category upon deceleration of hypergrowth.

RULE FOR HOLDING ALL OTHER STOCKS

In the pure gorilla game, there are no other holds. This means selling everything else—the why's and when's of which we will turn to in a moment. But there are numerous mitigating circumstances in the real world of investing that modify any pure game. The most common is that most companies are not pure plays, fielding instead a portfolio of products, some participating in tornado markets, others not. It is not usually obvious how much of the company's stock price is tied up in which parts of the market. So holding or selling increasingly becomes a matter of judgment.

At the outset, however, until you develop enough industry knowledge to activate your own judgment, we advocate playing strictly within the rules we outline here. These rules may not produce the very best decisions, but they are good at preventing truly awful ones. That's not bad place to start from.

WHAT SHOULD I SELL AND WHEN?

The basic rule of the gorilla game is buy gorilla candidates, wait for the gorilla to emerge, and sell everything else off. So the basic rule for selling is, as soon as you are certain a given company is not now, nor is ever likely to become, the gorilla, sell it off and put the proceeds into better gorilla candidates.

This strategy breaks down into three sub-strategies, which we call:

- Taking your losses.

- Consolidating your gains.

- Acting on gorilla collisions.

Here's how they play out.

Taking Your Losses

Relatively early on in any gorilla game, whether it starts in the bowling alley with application software, or in the tornado proper with enabling hardware and software, several companies will stumble for one reason or another. Don't just sell on a knee-jerk reaction. Instead, put these stocks on probation. Now, if at the same time they stumble there is also a gorilla candidate emerging, the likelihood that these companies could ever catch up is decreased dramatically, and you should sell them. But if you really are still unsure who the gorilla is going to be, then the stumbler is still a viable candidate, and you want to keep it in the basket.

Once you are reasonably sure that given companies are out of the game, sell their stock fast. Depending on what the market is doing at the time, you may well have to take a loss on these companies. This may make you want to hold on to them just a little bit longer, so they can get well and you can get your money out. Don't even think about it. Sell.

To think otherwise is to miss the point of the gorilla game. This is a basket-of-stocks game, not a single-stock play, and by selling you are simply moving assets from an underperforming square on the board to a higher-performing one. You know from the beginning of the game that all but one of the companies in each basket are going to fail in the quest to be the gorilla. So don't cling to ones that are out of the game. Just keep harvesting the assets and redeploying them into the stronger candidates.

Rule 7. Once it becomes clear to you that a company will never become a gorilla, sell its stock.

Consolidating Your Gains

The good news about playing the gorilla game is that the further you get into it, the stronger the remaining companies in play will be, so that your exit from one company to reinvest in another does not usually create a loss. Here too, however, it is still important to act decisively to increase the value and the security of your portfolio.

Now, normally when people talk about *portfolio strategy*, they are thinking about using diversification to reduce the risk of holding. What is counterintuitive about the gorilla game is that it uses *consolidation* to achieve this end. Here are the key concepts:

- The gorilla game does use *diversification* in the *portfolio* sense to reduce risk, by advocating that you invest in multiple tornado opportunities, each ideally reducing down to a single gorilla holding.

- The gorilla game also uses *diversification* to reduce the risk of *buying* high-tech equities, when it *is not clear* who is the gorilla. This is our buy-the-basket rule.

- But the gorilla game uses *consolidation* to reduce the risk of *holding* high-tech equities, once it *is clear* who is the gorilla.

For enabling technologies in particular, once it becomes clear which company is the gorilla, consolidating is critical. You should immediately pull out your stakes in all other candidates and put them into that stock. Recall that this type of game tends to concentrate power heavily in favor of the gorilla, so that when the chimps take a hit, they take a big hit. That is, at the same time that the market is still *underpricing* the gorilla, it is *overpricing* the chimp, sometimes radically so. That is because the risk-adjusted premium for a chimp should be much higher than for a gorilla. But the market has no way of making that distinction, so assigns both companies a "compromise" rate—one that is too high for the gorilla and too low for the chimp.

Being able to exit chimp stocks before they get knocked down is probably the biggest advantage the gorilla-game investor has over the market as a whole. Timing is critical here because the entire advantage is that you are anticipating an outcome that the market has not yet fully priced into any of the stocks.

In contrast to enabling technologies, for application software there is no reason for a hasty exit from a later-stage chimp, particularly if it has a gorilla-like status in some subsegment of the overall market. PeopleSoft may be a chimp in the overarching category of ERP, but it is a gorilla in human resources. This makes it an attractive hold, particularly in light of the emerging middle market for ERP, where SAP, the current gorilla, has struggled.

That being noted, the fundamental rule of the consolidation phase of the gorilla game is as follows:

Rule 8. Money taken out of non-gorilla stocks should immediately be reinvested in the remaining gorilla candidates.

ACTING ON GORILLA COLLISIONS

Not every day brings sunshine for a gorilla-game investor. Sometimes you buy a basket going into the tornado, and before your candidate gorillas can mature, something else happens. Internet investors who focused on Netscape were in this position at the end of 1996. At the beginning of the year, they had every reason to believe they had a healthy tornado in hand, led by a handsome young gorilla, until Microsoft came out of nowhere to spoil the party. What now?

It is time for what medical units call triage—cold-blooded assessment of damages, and swift action localized to where it can still make a difference. The first thing to do is get out of everything but the would-be gorillas immediately. Regardless of how bad things look after the first hit, by the rules of the gorilla game, they are going to get worse, not better, and the only companies that have a decent shot at weathering the storm are the would-be gorillas.

The reason you do not exit the would-be gorillas is that, for once in the market, you are going into a competition that does not have a predictable outcome. These are the moments when great companies are defined. They had a plan, it was a good plan, they were winning, and then bam! They got knocked off their feet. Now what will they do?

Most companies, to be frank, don't do very well. Some do, however, and it is usually more risky to break with your gorilla candidates at this point than to hold on. The would-be gorilla's market valuation has already been adjusted by the stock market—you have taken the hit—and therefore your downside is, for the time being, limited. But your upside is simply not clear. It *might* be excellent—but neither you nor the companies' management teams can tell for sure. It would be wrong, then, to precipitously leave this party. We advocate instead holding on, at least until the dust settles.

Rule 9. In a gorilla collision, hold your gorilla candidates until there has been a definitive outcome.

WHAT SHOULD I DO WITH ALL THE INFORMATION I GET IN THE MEANTIME?

One of the most attractive virtues of the gorilla game is that it puts a filter between you and the streams of investment information that wash over you on a daily basis. As you scan this flow, the goal should be to exclude, not include, new data—otherwise you are going to drown. Here are the filtering principles:

- *If it is not about a tornado, you don't want to know.*

This is particularly useful for excluding futurists at the front end of the technology adoption life cycle, and a whole raft of commentary on Main Street, including general assessments of the economy, discussions of interest rates, bull and bear markets, whether there is a good IPO climate or not, inflation, money supply, et cetera. You just don't care. None of them has the power to suppress or deflect a tornado, although they may change the speed of its progress.

- *If it is about a tornado, you want either bad news or facts.*

The purpose of this rule is to ensure you don't get caught up in the hype that inevitably surrounds both emerging tornadoes, and their evil twins, false tornado sightings.

Specifically, you want data that will help you answer the series of questions we posed in Chapter 4:

A. Is there a new value chain coming into existence? If so, you need to see evidence of this at every link of the chain.

B. Is there a niche market that can serve as an indicator for the coming tornado? If so, you want to know *everything* about it.

C. Is there a killer app? You want to know whether there is a killer app in sight or not, as it is always a key indicator.

D. What are the third-party partners doing? Following their lead usually takes you right into gorilla dynamics, and often right to the gorilla.

E. Is there proprietary architectural control in this market, and if so, who has it, and can they keep it? Here you want to probe *very* deeply, as this is a key underlying dynamic for the entire investment philosophy.

F. How high are the switching costs in this market, and what barriers to entry do they create? This is key to setting the length of CAPs both for gorillas and kings.

G. Finally, is there a new technology coming hard on the heels of this one that will foreshorten the length of its overall market life? This is the ultimate terminating force of a gorilla's CAP.

All in all, what you want to know about are changes in marketplace power that relate to tornado market dynamics, and that is all you want to know about. This leads to our final rule:

Rule 10. Most news has nothing to do with the gorilla game. Learn to ignore it.

This last rule is no doubt presumptuous, but throughout this book we have tried to cut through the layers of conventional wisdom in order to carve out a clear and reasonable program of investment. It is a Gordian knot type of problem, and if we wield our sword a bit cavalierly, we think it is better at the end of the day to slice the thing in two rather than be left in a tangle.

We are now at the end of Part 2 of this book. All the theory is in place, and all of the mechanics for gorilla game play have been described. The remainder of the book is made up of case studies and tips for how to put the theory into investment practice. By way of bringing this part to a close, here is a summary of the entire set of rules:

Ten Rules for Playing the Gorilla Game

Rule 1.   If the category is application software, begin buying in the bowling alley.

Rule 2.   If the category is enabling hardware or software, begin buying after the tornado has formed.

Rule 3.   Buy a basket comprising *all* the gorilla candidates— usually at least two, sometimes three, and normally no more than four companies.

Rule 4.   Hold gorilla stocks for the long term. Sell only on proven substitution threat.

Rule 5.   Hold application software chimp stocks as long as they exhibit potential for further market expansion. Do not hold enabling-technology chimps.

Rule 6.   Hold kings and princes lightly, selling individual stocks on a marketplace stumble and the category upon deceleration of hypergrowth.

Rule 7.   Once it becomes clear to you that a company will never become a gorilla, sell its stock.

Rule 8.   Money taken out of non-gorilla stocks should immediately be reinvested in the remaining gorilla candidates.

Rule 9.   In a gorilla collision, hold your gorilla candidates until there has been a definitive outcome.

Rule 10.   Most news has nothing to do with the gorilla game. Learn to ignore it.

Part 3

CASE STUDIES

8

Case Study 1: Oracle and the Relational Database Tornado

This section of the book presents three case studies of gorilla games somewhat in the spirit of Charles Dickens's *A Christmas Carol*. There Scrooge met the ghosts of Christmas past, Christmas present, and Christmas yet to come. In this chapter we will trace the rise of a gorilla game past, one whose outcome has been decided forever. In Chapter 9 we will turn to a gorilla game present, focusing on Cisco and the network hardware tornado, a game in which the gorilla has been crowned for now, but which still has some capability for surprise left in it. And in Chapter 10 we will present a gorilla game yet to come, looking at the customer service application software arena and three gorilla candidates it is spawning.

The goal of all three case studies is to answer a version of the question that the Watergate scandal made famous a quarter of a century ago: *What did the gorilla-game investors know, and when did they know it?* The idea is to walk through the Ten Rules for Playing the Gorilla Game and show how they play out in each of these three situations. As we do so, the reader will notice a progression from *hindsight* to *insight* to *foresight*. We confess, right now we are much better at hindsight than the other two, so that's why we're starting with the historical example.

Let us go back to May of 1988, and view the investment opportunity in relational databases as it might have looked to us at that time.

BACKGROUND FOR THE FIRST TORNADO

The category of relational databases emerged in the early 1980s. It was an outgrowth of the ever increasing need to deal with more and more data across more and more programs, and eventually across more and more computers. The first data management technology had been sequential files on magnetic tape. It was good for long runs of master files being updated with a batch of transactions. It was too cumbersome, however, when you wanted to access or update just a few records in the middle of the tape. Therefore it was supplemented with indexed files on hard disks, which solved the access problems nicely, but led to a huge proliferation of files, many of which had much of the same data inside them.

Having multiple copies of the same data leads to one copy getting updated while another is not, which in turn leads to unreliable data values. This led to the invention of a third technology, the database, in which the goal was to have one, and only one, copy of any data element. All programs were directed to a database manager to "check out and return" the data they needed. This ensured that all programs were working with the correct data, but created a bottleneck, especially in the response time it took for on-line transaction processing (OLTP). Vendors like IBM solved this problem with hierarchical databases that sped up the input transactions dramatically. But as with everything, there were trade-offs. To gain OLTP speed, hierarchical databases sacrificed both ease of use and flexibility in query and reporting.

When businesses woke up to the fact that computers were not just fast clerks, but were in fact the core of their management information systems, the demand for query and reporting flexibility skyrocketed. This created a demand for yet another class of products, variously called report-writers, decision support systems, or fourth-generation languages. The big hang-up with these products was that they all required a "shadow copy" of the OLTP database to work against, which meant that every night the on-line data had to be unloaded and transferred to the other system.

At this point relational databases entered the scene. Their claim was that they could support both OLTP and DSS from a single product. Initially, performance was so slow on the OLTP side that only laboratory and other low-volume-transaction applications were viable, but over time performance improved to the point where commercial OLTP was an option. On the decision support side, the products competed against a host of other fourth-generation languages, but gained a huge boost when Oracle standardized on IBM's SQL language. Almost overnight, this created a de facto standard for the category.

Now, IBM had the mainframe business locked up, and that was where it focused its SQL efforts via a product called DB2. It also had a strong minicomputer in the AS/400, but it did not use an SQL-oriented system, so IBM had no interest in SQL databases on minicomputers or, as it later turned out, on PCs. This left the field wide open for the relational database companies. Oracle, in particular, made its cause *portability*, porting its system to every viable platform in the market. Since every minicomputer needed a whole product, and since they all were focused on hardware rather than software, they welcomed Oracle's efforts and gave them full support (indeed, most even paid the company to port).

When Informix entered this market, it was already behind Oracle in size and market presence, but it saw an opportunity that Oracle did not, namely, the exploitation of the Unix market. At the time, this was not much of a market, its top offer being back office systems for dentists and doctors, based on microcomputer servers from companies like Altos, running a version of Unix from the Santa Cruz Operation, and being sold and serviced through small value-added resellers. Later on, however, it would turn out that Informix's focus on this technology was prescient.

A more direct competitor to Oracle was Relational Technology Inc. (later to be renamed Ingres, after its flagship product). It went straight after the same market of minicomputer databases for corporate

America, and in that booming market it grew at 50% per year through most of the 1980s. Unfortunately for RTI, however, Oracle was growing at 100% per year over the same period. Moreover, corporate America took a liking to Oracle's standardizing on SQL and imposed the same requirement on RTI. This flew in the face of the original Ingres architecture and caused them to lose precious ground just reengineering to meet the new standard.

But that would not have been visible in 1988. What the gorilla-game investor would have known at that point was:

- There was a tornado under way in the relational database category. Oracle had been growing at 100% for the decade, and by the end of 1988 was on a $500 million run-rate, with strong earnings.

- RTI was clearly second to Oracle, but had strong sales growth and good profitability.

- There was a Unix submarket, which Informix led, that was modestly interesting.

- IBM supported the SQL-relational model via DB2, and that was becoming the standard.

- Relational was the substitution technology of choice for hierarchical and other types of databases of the 1980s.

- There was a possible substitution threat for relational databases on the very far horizon called *object-oriented databases*, but they had not even gotten to the chasm.

Consulting *Computerworld*, which at the time was the leading trade press organ for enterprise systems hardware and software, one would have found Oracle to be the most visible of the three companies, with fifteen headlines in 1987 and twenty-five in 1988, compared to RTI (three and two, respectively) and Informix (five and four, respectively). This is a key indicator of market status.

Significantly greater press coverage is one of the key attributes of gorilla status, for the following reasons:

1: Gorillas get more alliance coverage because they get invited into more third-party relationships.

2: They get more coverage in round-up articles because they are included not only in the ones about their own markets, but also in broader round-ups discussing the overall state of the industry.

3: They get more customer stories because they have more customers.

4: They get more marginal coverage because they typically have more money to spend on public relations in general.

Another key indicator of status occurs both in trade and business press whenever an article lists the major companies in a given category. These companies are almost always listed in order of power, typically based on market share. At the very outset of *Computerworld's* coverage of the category, RTI was once listed ahead of Oracle in a December 1986 article on distributed databases. Thereafter, Oracle always preceded RTI, which in turn always preceded Informix, up until RTI's acquisition by ASK in 1990. This was simply pecking order at work. Since the gorilla game is based directly on the principle of pecking order, the press is a real ally in our efforts.

THE FIRST PURCHASE

Under these conditions, the gorilla-game investor would have bought either the basket, being unsure as yet of Oracle's dominance, or just Oracle, since all the signs were there. Let's assume that you bought the basket, being a mere mortal and frequently subject to confusion. Let's say you purchased shares on the June closing price of each stock. Because you felt Oracle was borderline gorilla, let's say you split their purchases, with 50% in Oracle and 25% in each of the other two. Here's your initial position:

Table 8.1

Action	Date	Adj. Price	Split Adj.	Price	Shares	Amount	Holding	Total
BOT ORCL	6/30/88	1³¹⁄₆₄	13.500x	$20.04	250	$5,000	250	$5,000
BOT IFMX	6/30/88	2²⁹⁄₃₂	8.000x	$23.25	108	$2,500		
BOT RTI	6/30/88					$2,500		

As we go along, we are going to keep a running total of your gorilla holdings based on how the market turned out eventually, So right now you have $5,000 in Oracle, the eventual gorilla.

Having thus diversified your position for risk reduction at the outset, you should now be looking to consolidate it as soon as possible around the gorilla, again for risk reduction. Each quarter going forward Oracle will announce record revenues and earnings, all the way up to 1990. Each of the other two will stumble along the way, in both cases taking a double bump downward. Both stumbles simply confirmed what was already pretty firm knowledge, that Oracle was the gorilla in this space.

At this point a gorilla-game investor invokes Rules 7 and 8, as follows:

Rule 7. Once it becomes clear to you that a company will never become a gorilla, sell its stock.

Rule 8. Money taken out of non-gorilla stocks should immediately be reinvested in the remaining gorilla candidates.

Following these rules, gorilla gamers would have exited Informix almost immediately, in July of 1988, when it lost roughly half its market cap for buying a company called Innovative and then missing its targets badly. Peg your exit price at the July closing, curse yourself roundly for not being more faithful to gorilla-game principles, and put the money into Oracle. Now your position looks like this:

Table 8.2

Action	Date	Adj. Price	Split Adj.	Price	Shares	Amount	Holding	Total
SLD IFMX	7/29/88	1 19⁄32	8.000x	$12.75	108	$1.371		
BOT ORCL	7/29/88	1 13⁄32	13.500x	$18.98	72	$1.371	322	$6,108

Time passes, and both Oracle and RTI continue to grow, but the latter grows at a much more modest rate. At this point you should be combing the trade press looking for reasons to get out of RTI, and if you had not reacted before, you would once you read the headline in the July 24, 1989 *Computerworld*: "RTI Shuffles into No. 2 spot." Gorilla-game status does not get any plainer than that, and looking at the size differential between RTI and Oracle, and the ongoing lament about RTI's inability to market itself effectively, you would have sold on the July closing price, if not before. You put the proceeds into Oracle, and your position now looks like this:

Table 8.3

Action	Date	Adj. Price	Split Adj.	Price	Shares	Amount	Holding	Total
SLD RTI	7/31/89	9⅛	1,000x	$ 9.13	138	$ 1,259		
BOT ORCL	7/31/89	2 9⁄32	6.75x	$ 15.40	82	$ 1,259	725	$ 11,165

At this point you are holding Oracle for the long term. It reports another quarter of hypergrowth in September of 1989, while RTI reports a loss, and loses 23% of its stock price in a day. You are feeling good about your gorilla-game strategy and are inclined to speak of it at cocktail parties. You feel even better when the following quarter, Oracle reports another quarter of hypergrowth. This gorilla-game stuff is a piece of cake. Your position at the December close of 1989 is:

Table 8.4

Action	Date	Adj. Price	Split Adj.	Price	Shares	Amount	Holding	Total
ORCL	12/29/89	3¹⁵⁄₃₂	6.750x	$23.41			725	$16,980

Rough Times Ahead

Sailing into 1990, you run smack into Oracle's first-quarter *loss!* Its stock drops 31%! Where are those gorilla-game authors, anyway—we'll sue 'em! After a day or two, you calm yourself and assess the situation as follows:

1: There is still no substitution threat on the horizon. Object-oriented databases are still pre-chasm. Hierarchical databases are in retreat. Relational is the dominant paradigm and looks to be so for a long, long time.

2: There is no competitor who can genuinely threaten Oracle's position. The other guys all stumbled first.

3: Oracle's problems, therefore, are management problems internal to itself and not market problems external to the company.

The principles of the gorilla game suggest that internal problems will work themselves out, and that far from selling on a gorilla stumble, you should buy. Bravely you step up to that bar and double your stake in Oracle (at roughly half the previous quarter's price).

Anxiously you await Oracle's fourth-quarter report (its fiscal year ends in May). You are delighted to learn that, although the days of 100% growth are long gone, the company can post a 58% increase in earnings on top of a 55% increase in revenue. The stock starts back up, and at the June 1990 close, your position looks like this:

Table 8.5

ACTION	DATE	ADJ. PRICE	SPLIT ADJ.	PRICE	SHARES	AMOUNT	HOLDING	TOTAL
BOT ORCL	4/16/90	$2^{13}\!/_{32}$	6.750x	$ 16.24	725	$ 11,779	1,450	$23,557
ORCL	6/29/90	$3^{27}\!/_{64}$	6.750x	$ 23.10			1,450	$33,501

Maybe these gorilla-game ideas aren't so bad after all, you decide. Then all hell breaks loose.

This time it's not just Oracle, it's everything. In the summer months of 1990 every major company in high tech takes a big hit. Hewlett-Packard loses almost half its market capitalization, so does Digital Equipment Corporation, so does Oracle—and those are the *good results!* Informix loses over two-thirds of its market cap, and Ingres (formerly RTI) is so maimed it has to be acquired by ASK Corporation.

Again you scream for the gorilla-game authors' heads, and this time you go so far as to buy a book on value investing! But after a few days, you once again cool down and once again assess the situation. None of your earlier analysis has been shaken. All that has happened is that a fourth factor—the state of the overall economy—has entered the fray. So you ask yourself, are computers somehow going out of fashion? Is there some reason to believe their time has passed?

When you conclude the answer is no, you realize again that, despite your churning intestines, you are faced with a *buying opportunity*, not a selling one. You wait a quarter to see how the sector is doing, and as you see HP and DEC and the others trending back up, you step up to the mark and, without telling your spouse (who is no doubt talking behind your back about your "investment theories"), and with nary a whisper of it on the cocktail circuit, you double up again on Oracle at the close of the year (the only good news is that it keeps getting cheaper to do so). Now your position looks like this:

Table 8.6

Action	Date	Adj. Price	Split Adj.	Price	Shares	Amount	Holding	Total
BOT ORCL	12/31/90	1¹¹⁄₆₄	6.750x	$7.91	1,450	$11,473	2,901	$22,946

Over the course of the next year, Oracle increasingly puts its house in order. It has used the crisis to install a new management team, recruit new board members, bring on a world-class CFO, restate its earnings (not once, but twice—not all that hypergrowth, it appears, was on the up and up). Ingres is no longer available as a pure-play investment in the category, and the trade press suggests that ASK is giving it low priority. Nothing makes you want to get back into Informix either, although it is also putting its house in order. At the end of 1991 your position looks like this:

Table 8.7

Action	Date	Adj. Price	Split Adj.	Price	Shares	Amount	Holding	Total
ORCL	12/31/91	2⁹⁄₆₄	6.750x	$14.45			2,901	$41,914

This is not bad for a post-tornado stock, where the gorilla maintains its market share, and you are ready to watch it gently increase its leverage going forward. What you were not expecting was for all heaven to break loose.

ENTER CLIENT/SERVER COMPUTING

Part of the collapse of the computer systems market in 1990 was due to the inability of distributed computing to provide a genuinely stable alternative to mainframe computing. By this time, the original deployment of minicomputer-based systems had peaked, and a new architecture connecting groups of PCs—the local area network—was in its ascendancy. To grow further, minicomputers had to go up the food chain, not down, and that was the targeted direction for distributed computing. But there were simply too many proprietary platforms that had to be connected by too many proprietary gateways for its approach to work. For some time, however, the Gartner Group and other industry analysts had proposed an alternative architecture, called client/server, which would standardize these interfaces and make them more replicable and scalable. In 1992 the last few remaining obstacles to client/server deployment were removed, as follows:

1: With Release 3.1, Windows finally replaced DOS as the desktop operating system of choice and provided a much-needed standard graphical interface client.

2: By 1992 Unix had gradually supplanted proprietary minicomputer operating systems, so that there was a relatively standard server environment available from virtually all major vendors.

3: Unix also brought with it TCP/IP, a networking protocol that provided a standard communications interface (this would later have major ramifications for the hypergrowth of the Internet).

4: Client/server application packages began to appear in 1992, led by Oracle Financials, PeopleSoft Human Resources, and Lawson Financials, later to be supplemented with SAP (the eventual gorilla in the ERP category), Baan, and a host of others.

With the obstacles successfully removed, the client/server tornado took off.

The question gorilla-game investors have to ask themselves at a point like this is, in which companies do I invest to take advantage of a systems-level tornado? Clearly Microsoft was going to be the client-side beneficiary. And with all the networking, there would be companies in this category as well (see Chapter 9 for this part of the story), and there would be applications companies (PeopleSoft and Oracle were the two publicly traded opportunities), and server hardware (Hewlett-Packard ended up being the gorilla in this competition, which was clear by the end of 1992), and relational database software (Oracle again). To be specific to the concerns of this chapter, *there was no alternative to a relational database in client/server architecture, and client/server was inside the tornado.*

With relational databases locked in, once again we can look to buy the basket or go with the old gorilla. As before, there were two attractive alternatives to Oracle, both of which had successfully marketed differentiated solutions that would be hard for Oracle to match. One of these was our old friend Informix who, under the leadership of Phil White, had pulled itself together after the merger with Innovative, streamlined its operations, and set about exploiting its Unix position in the market. By the last quarter of 1990, it was garnering this sort of comment from *Computerworld*: "Still, Informix's annual growth rate of 20% to 30% is modest compared with . . . industry leader Oracle Systems Corp's . . . rates of 50% or more. *Yet, Informix bests Oracle within the Unix marketplace*." (italics added). It would have been the company's superior Unix position that would cause a gorilla-game investor to put it in the basket. This would have been bolstered when in February of 1992 Informix surprised Wall Street with upside earnings and revenues—a performance that would continue for some time to come.

The other attractive alternative was a newcomer, Sybase, which had withdrawn its public offering in 1990 because of the terrible downturn in the sector, and gone public in 1991 instead. Sybase had taken advantage of RTI's fall from grace and Informix's struggles to leapfrog them both into second place in the relational database market. Moreover, it had done so specifically with the message of *client/server database*. Its growth rates were higher than either of its competitors, and it was the darling of Wall Street, which just happened to be the head bowling pin in its "crossing the chasm" strategy. As the world moved to client/server architecture, it looked like Sybase could come out the winner, and for the next three years it would outperform the category.

Neither of these competitors, however, had anything like Oracle's size, so you would have had no qualms about keeping the Oracle position in your portfolio strong. By mid-1992 Oracle too was surprising the Street with "robust" sales and "surging" earnings, to use the adjectives that *The Wall Street Journal* loves to employ. Let us suppose, then, that you added the other two, and because you were still licking your 1990 wounds a bit, did nothing to change your

Oracle holdings. And let's say you did so on the July close of 1992, when the rebound was clearly well under way. That would make your position look as follows:

Table 8.8

Action	Date	Adj. Price	Split Adj.	Price	Shares	Amount	Holding	Total
BOT IFMX	7/31/92	4 23/32	4.000x	$18.88	132	$2,500		
BOT SYBS	7/31/92	15 3/16	2.000x	$30.38	82	$2,500		

Once again, you have diversified at the outset to reduce your risk of entry. From this point on in the gorilla game, you are looking to consolidate to reduce your risk of holding. But in 1993 you would have had no news to sell on. All three companies' stocks rose handily. In May Informix was featured in a *Wall Street Journal* article lauding its market and management savvy, titled "Informix Rides High-Tech Wave with Unix System." The story fully validated the client/server tornado assumptions. At the same time, a subtitle might have given you pause: "Some Attribute Its Staying Power to Cost Controls, Growth in Europe." The phrase that should have rung a bell was *staying power*, the implication being that it was swimming against the tide. This is indeed what all chimps do, and with Oracle's growth continuing strongly—by year-end it was on a $2 billion run-rate—there were increasing signs that it was the gorilla of the new game as well.

Similarly, in 1993 Sybase got rave reviews. The trade press in particular lauded its growth with articles like this one in *Computerworld*: "Sybase sets its own direction; Early adopter of client/server sets sights on enterprise computing." It closed out 1993 with a record performance of 64% earnings gain based on a 68% revenue gain, putting the company on a $500 million run-rate—impressive to say the least, but still one-fourth of Oracle's.

By 1994, however, the trade press began to give a number of signals that it was time to sell Sybase. Here is a series of headlines from *Computerworld*:

- March 21, 1994: "PeopleSoft port to Sybase hits snags."

- March 28, 1994: "Sybase products remain disjointed."

- April 11, 1994: "Sybase misses database deadline."

- April 18, 1994: "Sybase/Microsoft split triggers user concerns."

You would not have known at the time what really lay behind any one of these headlines, although a later one on July 11 would have given you a second clue: "Sybase disputes report slamming System 10." Following up on this article, you would have discovered that application package vendors like PeopleSoft and SAP were having trouble porting to Sybase. Here's why.

Sybase's Release 10 lacked a technical feature called *row-level locking*, which meant it could not support the transaction response time requirements of very large installations. At the time, however, in the client/server tornado, three application vendors—SAP, Oracle, and PeopleSoft—were in an all-out war (eventually won by SAP) in which scalability and response time were key weapons. Not surprisingly, none of these vendors felt they could afford to support Sybase. Instead they all supported Oracle (and to a lesser extent, Informix), giving Oracle the database win almost every time they sold one of their applications. Sybase's sales performance began to suffer as it lost not only the sales these packages would have brought in, but the larger in-house standards battle as well.

Now, why was row-level locking so key in this battle? *Because it was a feature of Oracle's database architecture!* That is, all of these vendors were doing their primary development on Oracle, the gorilla, and they saw in row-level locking a way to enhance their performance, so they designed it into their applications. Once it was designed in, they simply had to have it. The truth is, had they started with Sybase, they might well have found an alternative path to the same goal. So it is not really the case that Sybase's design was a mistake. It was, however, fatally incompatible with Oracle's de facto standard. This is the kind of power that gorillas wield. And that is why it is imperative to exit chimps, to consolidate rather than diversify, in order to reduce risk.

But let us suppose you had trouble pulling the trigger on this news. You would kick yourself on the morning of July 21 when you would learn that the previous day the market took 15% of the value out of Sybase on a huge sell-off—*despite the company reporting a 72% earnings increase on a 65% revenue gain*. Ah well, live and learn. You sell now (even though, as it turns out, the stock will rebound some).

Assuming you sold your Sybase stock on July 21, 1994, and converted the proceeds to Oracle, your position now looks like this:

Table 8.9

Action	Date	Adj. Price	Split Adj.	Price	Shares	Amount	Holding	Total
SLD SYBS	7/21/94	41¼	1.000x	$41.25	165	$6.790		
BOT ORCL	7/21/94	10³¹⁄₃₂	3.375x	$37.02	183	$6.790	5,985	$221,561

At this point, you might very well have also sold Informix. It was running third behind Sybase, and although it was continuing to report very good results, it was no real threat to Oracle's future. In that case, all your money would be "safely" consolidated in Oracle, and your position would look like this:

Table 8.10

Action	Date	Adj. Price	Split Adj.	Price	Shares	Amount	Holding	Total
SLD IFMX	7/21/94	9⅜	2.000x	$18.75	265	$4,967		
BOT ORCL	7/21/94	10³¹⁄₃₂	3.375x	$37.02	134	$4,967	6,119	$226,528

If you did not get out of Informix in 1994, perhaps this headline from *Computerworld* on March 20, 1995, would have given you sufficient stimulus: "Informix fights also-ran image." Now, there is no shame in fighting such an image, but it should make clear to any reader of this book that the company is in no danger of becoming a gorilla, and therefore should not be part of a gorilla-game portfolio. Therefore, you would have exited Informix at the latest by the end of March 1995.

SCORING THE EFFORT

Here are your final results, as of the middle of 1997:

Table 8.11

ACTION	DATE	ADJ. PRICE	SPLIT ADJ.	PRICE	SHARES	AMOUNT	HOLDING	TOTAL
ORCL	8/29/97	38 1/8	1.000x	$38.13			20,652	$787,361

Here is a graphical view of the relational database gorilla game history. Note: In order to make clear the comparative value of a gorilla vs. a chimp or monkey, we have created a new form of chart, which we will use throughout the remainder of this book. In this type of chart, the initial value of an investment in each stock is set arbitrarily at $1000. This puts all stocks on an equal footing (something that stock price charts do not). The chart then displays what happens to the value of that holding over time. This makes for easy comparison among their performances.

Figure 8.1 Gorilla Game : 6/88 to 8/97

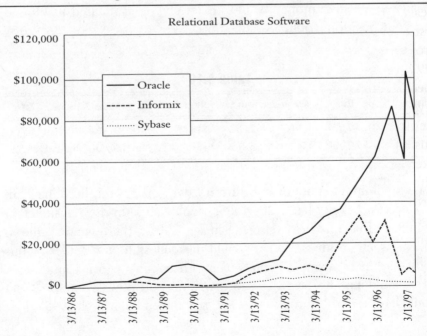

The chart shows two moments of gorilla victory for Oracle. The first of these came in the 1998–1990 period, when it broke away from Informix and RTI (RTI is not illustrated). The second began with the high-tech recovery in 1992 and has never looked back. The distance between Oracle and its competitors today is staggering—unless you understand the dynamics of the gorilla game.

So how did you fare playing this game? You bought all three stocks in July of 1992. You sold off Sybase in July of 1994 on the downtick. You sold off Informix either at the same time or in March of 1995. Each time, you put the money back into Oracle.

What are the results? Well, you missed the rebound of Sybase in the latter half of 1994; but more important, you missed the collapse of the stock on its first-quarter 1995 loss. Even though it subsequently rebounded somewhat from that catastrophe, it was no longer able to sustain its database positioning, and by 1996 was repositioning itself for the Internet and away from packaged client/server application support. By mid-1997 it was in limbo as the market waited to see what progress it could make on this repositioning.

As for Informix, in hindsight you definitely got out too soon, your ideal exit being at the beginning of 1996. But you missed its 1996 first-quarter drop, and more important, its 1997 first-quarter catastrophe, when like Sybase, it fell out of the game. As of the middle of 1997, Informix was painfully depositioned for any form of progress. Specifically, having become overly enamored of its next new technology, object-relational databases, it had sought to feature it in a bid to overtake Oracle, even though the product category had not even crossed the chasm. This turned out to be a very bad decision. It was taken however, somewhat out of desperation, as Informix needed to differentiate itself from Oracle's increasingly powerful de facto standard. The result was that customers hesitated to buy the new databases, but also held back from buying the old ones, deciding instead to buy Oracle took its retribution swiftly. There are no easy alternatives for a chimp in a gorilla's grasp.

In retrospect, Wall Street and the boards of Sybase and Informix did not appreciate the illusory nature of success inherent in the role of chimp in an enabling technology category. Because such categories support intense hypergrowth, they offer strong early rewards for credible initiatives. But because they ultimately consolidate around a single gorilla owner, there is only so much "chimp share" to be gained, after which each chimp hits the wall. Thus RTI had the chimp money in the 1980s, Sybase in the early 1990s, and Informix in the middle 1990s. At any given time, the market supported one gorilla, one strong chimp, and one weak chimp.

The key point for the gorilla-game investor, in any event, is a simple one. As soon as it is clear which company is the gorilla, consolidate your holdings and hang on.

UPCOMING GORILLA COLLISION— SELL OR HOLD?

So much for history. Going forward, it appears that the relational database market will actually move into a new phase, where the primary alternative to Oracle will no longer be other Unix-oriented databases but rather IBM DB/2 in the mainframe world and Microsoft SQL Server running as part of Back Office on the Windows NT operating system. The latter is part of an "adjacent tornado" in which NT is displacing Novell Netware as the primary LAN operating system. This positions Microsoft for a powerful assault on the low end of the client/server market.

At present both the Microsoft operating system and the database lack many components of enterprise computing. Indeed, despite Microsoft's ability to offer a more integrated solution, Oracle has successfully coopted the NT platform to date, in large part because corporations still want a portable database for enterprise computing, and SQL Server only runs on NT. They have no such objections, however, when it comes to LAN-based solutions, and there Microsoft is rapidly becoming the sole play.

Going forward, there is no obvious barrier to entry that Oracle can put up against Microsoft's future incursions. That is, between the local workgroup and the top of the enterprise there is no one line of defense. For a long time, to be sure, there should be little immediate threat, as Microsoft's gains will be at the low end of the food chain, and there is still a huge amount of high-end business to be done. But sooner or later, Oracle's competitive position threatens to become unsustainable, much the way that Cray's supercomputer position fell under Silicon Graphics' attack from below, and currently Silicon Graphics' position is being undercut by Intel.

So should the gorilla-game investor sell now? We don't think so. Too much can happen in the intervening period. Enterprise computing is inherently complex, and embracing complexity flies in the face of Microsoft's proven gorilla strategy. Moreover, the Internet is a monstrous wild card, as are the network computer and the Java language. Oracle's management team is ferociously competitive. Microsoft is stretching itself thinner and thinner. Oracle is attracting new allies as more and more of the industry coalesces in an anti-gorilla position under the banner "Anybody but Microsoft."

In short, the relational databaase market is coming up on a gorilla collision. In our view, this won't really be felt until the turn of the century at the earliest. That gives the contestants time to define and explore multiple alternatives. This makes for times that challenge the gorilla-game investor's patience because there is no single right answer to this problem. In this case, however, we would err on the side of nervous holding. Gorillas like Oracle have lots of power, and they are hard to knock out of the box, even by another gorilla.

There's another variable in this equation: If you sold Oracle, do you have a good place to put the proceeds? It would not be a good idea to throw your money into some other tornado about which you have little knowledge, regardless of how strongly recommended it comes. Gorilla-game investing requires too much domain knowledge. On the other hand, if you have another game in progress, and that gorilla's position is preferable, then a good alternative is to execute a hedge selling strategy, transferring some portion of your holdings in the threatened gorilla to safer ground.

LESSONS LEARNED _____

The key lessons of the relational database case history are as follows:

1: There were actually two tornadoes, the first based on proprietary minicomputers, the second based on client/server computing. Having earned the gorilla position in the first tornado, Oracle had first dibs to take it in the second one—another illustration of a good reason to hold gorillas.

2: Between the two tornadoes there was a lull—1990 to 1991—when even a gorilla's stock was not proof against a downturn. But as long as the gorilla's core advantages continue to obtain, downturns are *buying opportunities*.

3: Markets like a chimp—indeed, the chimp is often the market's darling—but only for a while. The market will not let the gorilla be overthrown, so the chimp is either hammered down by the gorilla or bypassed by some newer, hotter chimp.

4: Exiting chimps may leave some money on the table from subsequent upside performance, but it will save more money in the long term by avoiding the inevitable catastrophe on the downside.

5: When gorillas collide, things get dicey, but there is no quick easy fix. This is where creativity and thoughtfulness get rewarded.

With these in mind, let us now turn to the second case study, a gorilla game in progress.

9

Case Study 2: Cisco and the Network Hardware Tornado

In the previous chapter we noted that Oracle, an enabling software company, was the beneficiary of two computer-systems tornadoes, the first a move from mainframes to minicomputers, and the second a migration from server-centric to client/server applications. Today the company may stand on the verge of a third tornado if it can find ways to leverage its database technologies for the Internet.

A comparable history is at work with Cisco, a vendor of enabling hardware for data networking. During the 1990s the company has participated in four separate tornadoes, each of which has driven its growth and its market capitalization to new heights. All these hyper-growth markets have been fueled by the dramatic increase in demand for networked computing, both within corporations and beyond them. In order of appearance, the specific market sectors that Cisco has participated in are:

- Routers
- Intelligent hubs
- LAN switches
- Remote access devices

We are going to review the market development in each of these sectors to indicate what the gorilla-game investor would have seen at the time and what actions that would have driven. We will then sum up the results of the combined interaction of all markets by reviewing each of the rules of the gorilla game and how they would have been applied.

Readers will note that the structure of this chapter and the types of evidence it puts forward will be somewhat different from the previous one. That is because Chapter 8 looked at the marketplace through the eyes of Geoff Moore, and this one looks through the eyes of Paul Johnson. Paul, you will recall, is an analyst at BancAmerica Robertson Stephens. As might be expected, his view of the world tracks much more tightly to financial performance as reported on a quarterly basis. Following his path through the tornado will teach you some wonderful new tricks, as his fellow authors are delighted to testify.

SOME BACKGROUND ON CISCO

The 1980s was the decade of the PC, and towards its latter half it saw a huge rise in local area networks. For the most part, however, LANs were simply workgroups looped together by wire to share expensive peripherals, like a laser printer, and to share files. All that changed, however, with the advent of electronic mail.

Electronic mail, and all the extensions to it that have followed, including the World Wide Web, have driven meteoric escalations in demand for interconnecting computers. These connections have proliferated at every level of organization—from workgroup to workgroup, department to department, enterprise to enterprise, home to office, hotel to office, consumer to vendor, country to country, citizen to citizen. They have made the 1990s the decade of inter-networking, be it expanding outward from the LAN to the WAN (wide area network), or exploding inward, converting what used to be a simple hierarchy of LANs into a segmented and switched fabric that rivals the telephone system in its complexity.

None of this could have been accomplished without the emergence of an entirely new category of computer system called *networking hardware*. Not surprisingly, the category as a whole has created enormous wealth for investors during this decade, and no one has profited more than those who bought stock in Cisco Systems. From the time it went public in April 1990 until June 1997, Cisco's stock has appreciated by more than a hundredfold.

Cisco is a classic Silicon Valley success story. Founded by five techies from Stanford University, almost literally in a garage, the company went on to dominate the $15 billion market for data networking equipment in less than a decade. In June 1992 Cisco's revenues were essentially equivalent to those of rival Bay Networks, each with quarterly revenues of roughly $110 million. (The Bay Networks figure actually represents the sum of SynOptics and Wellfleet, who were later to merge to form Bay.) By mid-1997, five years later, Cisco's revenues had grown to be approximately three and a half times the size of Bay's. Please note that Bay's performance has hardly been a stumble: Its revenues had been growing by more than 30% per year during this period and its stock went up more than sixteen-fold from its IPO. But in the same five years, Cisco went from accounting for approximately 15% of the industry's profits to nearly 50%. As we have said repeatedly, differences of this magnitude cannot be explained by better management, strategy, or execution. Instead, they reflect the fundamental dynamics of the tornado, and there remains little doubt that Cisco has emerged as the gorilla of networking hardware.

The company was formed in 1984 by five engineers: The two most visible were Sandra Lerner and Len Bosack, who lived together and both worked at Stanford University. Lerner was in the business school and Bosack was in the computer science department. Although they worked on the same university campus, they could not send each other e-mail because of the disparate computer networks that each department had implemented. The business school ran on an HP 3000, while the engineering school ran on an HP 9000. Despite the fact that both computers came from the same company, the machines could not interoperate within a network. This was not an unusual state of affairs during the 1980s, for in most computer companies, each product team built its own vertically integrated end-to-end solution without reference to what other divisions were doing.

Irked and offended by this state of affairs, engineers in the engineering school built a computer system that would allow the two respective computer networks to interoperate. The engineers called this device a network router because it could "route" network traffic from one network to another. That is, it translated traffic from the business school's network to that of the computer science department, and vice versa. As a result, Lerner and Bosack could send e-mail back and forth to each other. Love will find a way.

At the same time, larger forces were at work—well, not larger than love, but larger than networking at Stanford. Engineers were attempting to scale up the Internet, and they faced a problem analagous to that which had troubled the company's founders. The problem was at once more simple and more complex. On the simplification side, every computer on the Internet spoke Unix and TCP/IP, the networking protocol. There was nothing like the HP 3000/9000 incompatibility problem. But there were interoperability issues nonetheless, because no two vendors' implementation of Unix is identical. And while the glitches themselves may have been minor by comparison, the fact that there were so many different computers in so many different interactions made the problem hugely complex. Transporting e-mail between this huge variety of disparate computer systems became a maintenance nightmare, and the time and effort it was taking to tweak these systems to communicate with each other was becoming a serious obstacle to the Internet's growth. The Cisco sales force took their story on the road, and it soon became obvious that Cisco Systems had solved this very problem.

Thus the router market was born. But at that stage, it was still in the early market. That is, most customers were technology enthusiasts from the public sector, not pragmatists from the private side. These users did not care about Cisco's financial performance, the company's size or its origin. They just needed a device to help scale up the Net. As customers, they did not need a sophisticated or competitive marketing program either. Indeed, in many cases it was they who sought out and found Cisco, not the other way around.

Even when Cisco began to take on corporate customers, their market was still pre-chasm. It was the visionaries, not the pragmatists, who were in command. One of Cisco's first corporate customers, for example, was Boeing. Their first application was simply an HP 3000 to 9000 link. But then they hooked that up to the Internet. And then they scaled that up to one of the first corporate intranets. At the end of the day, the company had undertaken nothing less than to create a seamless corporate-wide network in support of a massive reengineering of the business processes involved in designing and manufacturing its airplanes. In the process it too had discovered just how many disparate computer systems had found their way into its corridors. And in its search for a solution, it too had found Cisco, not the other way around.

MOMENTUM BEGINS

As work at Boeing and other early customers resulted in demonstrable success in tackling a truly thorny problem, corporate demand started to pick up elsewhere. Word-of-mouth endorsement of Cisco's industrial-strength approach began to spread among the pragmatists who ran the bulk of industry's networks. In addition, it was becoming clear that Cisco could service and support demanding corporate clients, a key skill needed to expand the market to pragmatist users. Business began to take off.

Cisco went public on April 20, 1990. Its original market capitalization was roughly $300 million, well under 1% of its market cap a scant seven years later. Table 9.1 shows quarterly revenue for the emerging router market for the five quarters before the company went public. As the table shows, Cisco accounted for roughly 85% of the market for network routers. Wellfleet Communications, still a private company at the time and one of the predecessor companies to Bay Networks, accounted for the other 15% of the market. Despite several attempts by other vendors to wrest this router market away from Cisco, its market share has remained in the mid-80% through 1997.

Table 9.1 Quarterly Router Market

	1989 MARCH	JUNE	SEPT.	DEC.	1990 MARCH
Routing Total	7.7	10.3	15.6	18.3	20.7
Qtr/Qtr growth		33.6%	52.1%	17.1%	13.4%
Yr/Yr growth					169.6%
Cisco Systems	7.7	10.3	14.1	16.1	17.9
relative share	100.0%	100.0%	90.3%	88.0%	86.3%
Qtr/Qtr growth		33.6%	37.4%	14.0%	11.2%
Yr/Yr growth					132.6%
Wellfleet (Precursor to Bay Networks)			1.5	2.2	2.8
relative share			9.7%	12.0%	13.7%
Qtr/Qtr growth				45.4%	29.5%

Source: Company reports

Market-share dominance of this type at the very outset of a market could signal either a gorilla game or a royalty (king/prince/serf) game. The persistence of such an imbalance over time, however, virtually always means the market leader has proprietary architectural control with high switching costs. Such was certainly the case with Cisco. When routers route to other routers, they typically use a proprietary protocol, such that Wellfleets can talk to Wellfleets, and Ciscos to Ciscos, but Cisco cannot talk to Wellfleet, or vice versa. In addition, each vendor used different network management, making a multivendor environment exceedingly difficult to manage. Once a company or sector starts down the path with one of these vendors, it becomes increasingly unlikely that it will even consider the other one. Since tornadoes always distribute their market shares asymmetrically, once Cisco had the lead, which they did in part due to their first-mover advantage, the game was over really even before it picked up full steam.

Here is what would have happened to a $1,000 investment in Cisco made on February 16, 1990:

Figure 9.1 Cisco

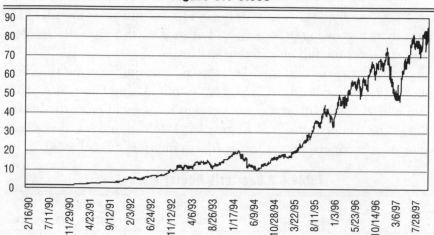

The $1,000 grew by a factor of ten in less than three years. It grew by a factor of twenty within four years, but then sank back down dramatically in 1994, giving back half its value. But then, as the gorilla, Cisco resurged, passing the 20x barrier again in 1995 and, as of July 1997, demonstrating in the space of seven and a half years a growth factor hovering around *eighty!* This is gorilla performance indeed.

But when would you, as a "real-world investor" have known to get on this bandwagon?

WHEN DID THE TORNADO START?

Over his years of following high tech on Wall Street, Paul Johnson has developed a simple rule of thumb for establishing the start of a tornado. It is this:

When year-to-year growth approaches or exceeds 100%, and when quarter-to-quarter growth also is rapidly accelerating, a tornado has begun.

The first part of this formula, the 100% part, ensures that the market meets the hypergrowth criterion. The second part, the idea that not only is it growing prodigiously, but its growth is actually accelerating, captures the full potential of the tornado.

For the network router market, this rule was met during the summer of 1990, shortly after Cisco went public. Using Cisco as a proxy for the market (Wellfleet was not yet public), we will mark the beginning of the router tornado as August 15, 1990—one week after Cisco reported its financial results for its fourth quarter of fiscal 1990.

Table 9.2 Quarterly Router Market

| | 1989 | | | | 1990 | | | |
	MARCH	JUNE	SEPT.	DEC.	MARCH	JUNE	SEPT.	DEC.
Routing Total	7.7	10.3	15.6	18.3	20.7	25.4	37.9	51.4
Qtr/Qtr growth		33.6%	52.1%	17.1%	13.4%	22.9%	49.0%	35.6%
Yr/Yr growth					169.6%	148.1%	143.1%	181.5%
Cisco Systems	7.7	10.3	14.1	16.1	17.9	21.8	32.8	43.9
relative share	100.0%	100.0%	90.3%	88.0%	86.3%	85.6%	86.5%	85.5%
Qtr/Qtr growth		33.6%	37.4%	14.0%	11.2%	22.0%	50.4%	34.2%
Yr/Yr growth					132.6%	112.5%	132.6%	173.7%
Wellfleet (Precursor to Bay Networks)			1.5	2.2	2.8	3.7	5.1	7.4
relative share			9.7%	12.0%	13.7%	14.4%	13.5%	14.5%
Qtr/Qtr growth			45.4%		29.5%	28.7%	40.5%	44.8%
Yr/Yr growth							240.6%	239.2%

Source: Company reports

Arguably, a gorilla gamer could have bought a few months sooner, at the Cisco IPO. It is hard to suggest, however, that anyone following our rules would have needed more evidence to buy Cisco. But this is typical of the gorilla game. A six-month window is a far different call to action than a six-hour or six-day window. Gorilla games move to the rhythm of quarterly reports, not stock tickers.

At this point, were there never to be any other inter-networking market but that for routers, we could predict an extremely attractive future for Cisco. But other things were brewing in the market, and whenever that is the case, there is always the opportunity for even greater expansion—or on the downside, a chance to lose all in a gorilla collision. In this case, the second category was *intelligent hubs*. Its market actually started developing prior to the router market, so it too was under a full head of steam by the time the router tornado broke.

INTELLIGENT HUBS—AN ADJACENT MARKET

While Cisco's routers were helping customers enable their disparate networks to communicate with each other, these same customers were struggling with another barrier of scaling up their networks—what might be called the "Christmas tree light problem." In the early days of minicomputer networks, which proliferated in the mid-1980s, terminals and computers were physically networked in the same fashion that Christmas tree lights are strung together, one to another in a chain, using a device called a bridge tap. This structure was easy to implement, but created a management nightmare when any device crashed or simply got unplugged. Because of the in-line structure, it was nearly impossible to determine which device had caused the network to fail.

A more structured way was needed to physically wire all devices to the network. Developments at Xerox PARC and elsewhere led to a new wiring topology based on a hub-and-spokes architecture. In this setup, where each device on the network is attached as a spoke, disruptive devices can be detected and isolated immediately. The architecture was termed *structured wiring*, and the device that connected all the spokes was called an *intelligent hub*—*hub* from the hub-and-spokes architecture, *intelligent* from the ability to manage the network's physical wiring.

Intelligent hubs allowed network administrators to control the network in ways that they could not achieve with older technologies. This lowered the cost of operating the network dramatically; and for the first time allowed network managers to roll out workgroups, and with the advent of network bridges, corporate-wide networks on a truly aggressive basis.

The market for intelligent hubs was pioneered by SynOptics Communications (which later merged with Wellfleet to form Bay Networks). Cabletron Systems entered the market right on SynOptics' heels, followed by a number of other vendors, including Chipcom and 3COM. SynOptics went public on August 19, 1988; Cabletron went public on May 30, 1989; and other hub vendors such as Chipcom went public thereafter. 3COM later acquired Chipcom in May 1996 for $775 million.

MARKET DEVELOPMENT

Unlike the market for network routers, the market for intelligent hubs did not go through an extended early-market phase. Although an innovation, to be sure, hubs were relatively continuous with existing infrastructure. That is, they could be inserted into existing network topologies without laying a lot of new wiring or modifying the network interface cards in the devices on the LAN. You simply plunked down the new hub and then plugged everybody in the neighborhood into it. And when you filled up one hub, you plunked down another. You could even plug hubs into hubs, but to really scale things up nicely, you connected them by *network bridges*. Even this architecture, however, ran up against scaling limits. Hubs do not scale beyond roughly one hundred people per segment, and bridges cannot handle high load. For really large networks, the only thing to serve was a router. In addition, routers were the only devices that could establish network-to-network connections over the WAN. So the two markets, hubs and routers, grew up together, as it were. Table 9.3 shows how all this played out in the market development for intelligent hubs.

Table 9.3 Quarterly Intelligent Hub Market

	1989				1990			
	MARCH	JUNE	SEPT.	DEC.	MARCH	JUNE	SEPT.	DEC.
Intelligent Hub Total	19.1	24.0	29.6	37.4	46.7	62.0	74.0	87.1
Qtr/Qtr growth		25.2%	23.5%	26.5%	24.7%	32.8%	19.4%	17.6%
Yr/Yr growth					143.8%	158.5%	150.0%	132.5%
Cabletron Systems	4.5	7.8	8.7	11.9	16.6	18.4	22.9	27.5
relative share	23.5%	32.5%	29.4%	31.8%	35.6%	29.7%	30.9%	31.6%
Qtr/Qtr growth		73.3%	11.5%	36.8%	39.5%	10.8%	24.5%	20.1%
Yr/Yr growth					268.9%	135.9%	163.2%	131.1%
SynOptics (Precursor to Bay Networks)	14.6	16.2	20.9	25.5	30.1	41.3	48.4	56.3
relative share	76.5%	67.5%	70.6%	68.2%	64.4%	66.5%	65.3%	64.6%
Qtr/Qtr growth		10.5%	29.2%	22.2%	17.8%	37.1%	17.2%	16.3%
Yr/Yr growth					105.4%	154.9%	131.2%	120.2%
Chipcom (Later Acquired by 3COM)						2.3	2.8	3.3
relative share						3.8%	3.8%	3.8%
Qtr/Qtr growth							18.9%	18.3%

Source: Company reports

INTELLIGENT HUBS GO INTO THE TORNADO

Using our same rule for dating, the intelligent hub market went into its tornado in the second quarter of 1990. We will mark the official start date as July 15, 1990—the same week that SynOptics reported the financial performance for the second quarter of its fiscal 1990 results.

Figure 9.2 Intelligent Hubs

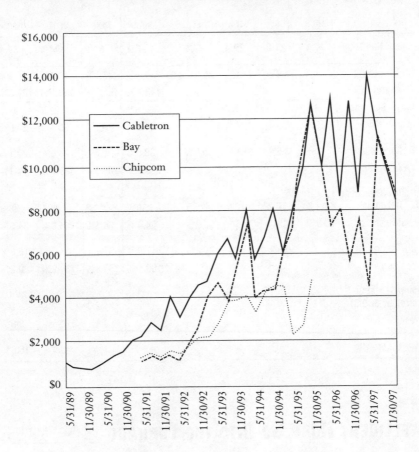

Going forward from 1990, the market for intelligent hubs took a very different path than the router market had. While SynOptics (the other precursor company to form Bay Networks) and Cabletron went on to dominate this product category, each company had similar market shares. When such a thing occurs, it signals a royalty (king/prince/serf) game, not a gorilla game. Indeed, when you analyze the architecture of intelligent hubs, you discover that the critical interface is set by an industry standard—the Ethernet protocol—and not by the hub device or its maker. Thus, while on the inside hubs are all different, on the outside they all look the same to the network, so that a SynOptics hub does talk to a Cabletron, and a Chipcom, and a 3COM.

This interoperability actually helps speed market development; hence, the much quicker arrival of the intelligent hub tornado compared to the router. But from the gorilla-game investor's point of view, the lack of proprietary architectural control means that no one company can dominate the market the way a gorilla can. While all these stocks appreciated, two of them breaking the 10x barrier at least for a time, none of them has gorilla power, and therefore they do not end up qualifying as long-term holds for the gorilla game.

CISCO PLACES A SIDE BET

While Cisco did not play in the intelligent hub market directly, the growth of the intelligent hub market contributed indirectly to its success. As hubs increased the density of network traffic, it became necessary to use routers in large networks simply as traffic cops to try to manage the ever increasing load placed on the backbone of the network. By segmenting large networks into smaller workgroups, and using routers to communicate between workgroup segments and the backbone, corporations could continue to scale their networks. Therefore, the growth of the intelligent hub market, and the number of workgroup networks by implication, further fueled Cisco's routing tornado.

In addition, Cisco developed a comarketing program with the three largest vendors of intelligent hubs: SynOptics, Cabletron, and Chipcom. Because corporations usually decided on an intelligent hub vendor before choosing a router vendor, these relations were extremely important to Cisco's continued success. Through this program, as corporations were making their selection of a router vendor, Cisco ensured that all of these vendors referenced their relationship with Cisco. Indeed, at one point Cisco and SynOptics looked at a sustained partnership, but as the industry forces trended toward consolidation, it became clear to both companies that theirs was to be a competitive relationship instead. In fact, that realization was one of the driving forces behind SynOptics' merger with Wellfleet, combining the number one intelligent hub company with the number two router company to create Bay Networks.

When the two did merge, Bay Networks was actually larger than Cisco, and there was talk of a new gorilla in the industry. Very quickly, however, the market whittled Bay back down to size as Cisco swept past it. This was hugely frustrating for the management at Bay, leading ultimately to wholesale changes in its executive ranks, because investors assumed that management teams must have erred badly. It was just a case, however, of a prince (SynOptics) plus a chimp (Wellfleet) being no match for a gorilla. This was made particularly true in light of two additional markets that were coming on-line at the same time. In both cases, the gorilla Cisco acquired presence in these markets and then leveraged its gorilla strength to create new areas of market dominance.

THE THIRD NETWORKING TORNADO BEGINS—THE MOVE TO LAN SWITCHES

By 1993 the networking industry was large and growing rapidly, comprising the markets for intelligent hubs, network routers, and LAN switches. Revenues that year would total approximately $3 billion, an increase of 85% from the prior year's total. Where did this new category of LAN switches come from? From the insatiable need to improve bandwidth.

Basically, networks were becoming victims of their own success. Network usage began to accelerate to the point that the current infrastructure simply could not handle the strain. The most obvious problem was *bandwidth*, the ability of the network to move traffic without delays. It is precisely analogous to the problem of overcrowded freeways. Intelligent hubs, in their original configuration, improved manageability but did not increase bandwidth. Network routers could increase bandwidth by segmenting network traffic into separate sections or workgroups; but routers were expensive, not particularly fast, and difficult to manage in large numbers. In the simplest sense, networks needed a new device—something that offered the simplicity of the intelligent hub architecture with some of the intelligence of the network router.

In late 1992 and early 1993 a new crop of networking hardware vendors got established to address the need for increased network bandwidth, and the product category they brought into existence was called *LAN switches—LAN* for local area network and *switches* for the ability to switch traffic from point to point. The word *switch* comes from the telephone industry, where every call is a point-to-point connection. By contrast, in Ethernet networks, every communication is on a party line, sharing the bandwidth with all the other calls on the line. By implementing a switched architecture, network managers would be able to relieve some of the congestion, giving high-volume traffic its own routes and leaving the byways free for the more typical user.

It turned out that the easiest place to put these LAN switches was right behind the intelligent hubs. From this vantage they could segment and route however demand dictated. But it soon became clear not only that there was a fair amount of duplication in this arrangement, but that replacing the intelligent hub altogether would increase the bandwidth even more dramatically. Thus if you were going to implement switches, you would probably do so at the expense of hubs. Nonetheless, at the beginning the two markets coexisted nicely because making any change to network architecture risked disruptions that few companies wanted to entertain. Over time, however, as network administrators became more comfortable with the transition of LAN switches replacing intelligent hubs, the market for LAN switches began to accelerate.

The market for LAN switches was pioneered predominantly by new, smaller networking vendors such as Kalpana, Synernetics, ALANTEC, Crescendo, Network Peripherals, and Grand Junction, all of which were privately held at the outset. Although LAN switches would eventually displace intelligent hubs in many, if not most, corporate networks, the initial market development was similar to other technology markets. The initial buyers were corporations with acute and specific bandwidth needs. LAN switches offer enormous increases in bandwidth, but required their own understanding, and sometimes a new network architecture. The early users were the ones with the most pain—they would be the most tolerant of the high costs of purchasing and supporting a whole new category of device. As the new vendors became more sophisticated in dealing with corporations, however, and as the devices themselves became more bug-free, demand began to accelerate to other corporations and more pragmatic users.

Table 9.4 shows the initial market growth for LAN switches.

Table 9.4 Quarterly LAN Switch Market (1993–94)

	1993				1994			
	MARCH	JUNE	SEPT.	DEC.	MARCH	JUNE	SEPT.	DEC.
LAN Switching Total	9.9	13.0	16.6	20.0	28.2	43.7	61.0	82.9
Qtr/Qtr growth		31.4%	27.3%	20.9%	40.5%	55.4%	39.3%	35.9%
Yr/Yr growth					184.2%	236.0%	267.8%	313.4%
Kalpana (acquired by Cisco)	3.0	3.5	4.0	5.0	8.0	9.0	9.0	15.0
relative share	30.3%	26.9%	24.1%	24.9%	28.4%	20.6%	14.8%	18.1%
Qtr/Qtr growth		16.7%	14.3%	25.0%	60.0%	12.5%	0.0%	66.7%
Yr/Yr growth					166.7%	157.1%	125.0%	200.0%
Crescendo (acquired by Cisco)					2.0	8.0	17.0	26.0
relative share					7.1%	18.3%	27.9%	31.4%
Qtr/Qtr growth						300.0%	112.5%	52.9%
Yr/Yr growth								
Synernetics (acquired by 3COM)	4.0	5.0	7.0	8.0	10.0	14.0	20.0	20.0
relative share	40.4%	38.4%	42.2%	39.9%	35.5%	32.0%	32.8%	24.1%
Qtr/Qtr growth		25.0%	40.0%	14.3%	25.0%	40.0%	42.9%	0.0%
Yr/Yr growth					150.0%	180.0%	185.7%	150.0%
ALANTEC (acquired by FORE Systems)	2.5	3.5	3.6	4.0	4.7	5.4	6.1	8.5
relative share	25.3%	27.0%	21.6%	20.2%	16.7%	12.4%	10.0%	10.3%
Qtr/Qtr growth		40.4%	1.6%	13.1%	16.3%	15.1%	12.2%	40.4%
Yr/Yr growth					87.6%	53.8%	69.9%	110.9%
Network Peripherals					0.6	2.2	3.4	6.0
relative share					2.3%	5.1%	5.5%	7.3%
Qtr/Qtr growth						244.2%	51.4%	78.5%

Source: Company reports

As Table 9.4 shows, the market for LAN switches had achieved a run-rate revenue stream of just over $100 million by early 1994, against a backdrop for the industry of roughly $3 billion. Although the revenues generated from LAN switching were still small, most industry observers believed that LAN switching would play a major role in the future of the networking industry.

By the rule of year-to-year growth, the tornado in LAN switches would have begun at the end of the first quarter of 1994. Since all the companies listed were privately held, however, there would have been no investment opportunity for the gorilla-game investor. We say "would have been" because all that was changed on September 23, 1993.

Cisco Enters the Game

On that day Cisco Systems, the gorilla in network routers, announced the acquisition of Crescendo Communications, a privately held networking vendor specializing in LAN switches. Although Crescendo was neither the largest nor the most important of the LAN switch vendors, this announcement sent a shock wave through the industry. At the time of the acquisition, Cisco dominated the market for network routers, and the company was now endorsing the market for switching. Although the LAN switch market had not yet entered its tornado, Cisco's endorsement was a critical catalyst to accelerating market acceptance of these products and technologies. Thus by the time the tornado started, Cisco was the only publicly traded equity that would allow the private investor to play in the LAN switch game.

Crescendo was Cisco's first acquisition. At the time, the price appeared to be high—for $100 million, Cisco was buying a private company with revenues of roughly $10 million per year. At ten times revenues, this looked like an expensive and risky deal for Cisco. But that was because we were looking at it through the traditional lens of mergers and acquisitions, which is typically based around consolidation in Main Street markets. Cisco was inventing a new form of gorilla attack, using its own highly valued stock as a currency to buy into adjacent product categories in, or about to enter, hypergrowth markets. This tactic had not been used significantly prior to Cisco—it was not part of the hypergrowth at Oracle, Microsoft, or Intel, for example. But Cisco showed the industry the way, both in outright acquisitions and in taking minority shareholder positions where technologies show promise but are not yet full-blown, and Microsoft and others have since followed. Leveraging the currency of a strong stock price has now become a fundamental weapon in the arsenal of all market-leader management teams, and no company gets to use it more powerfully than a gorilla.

Going forward from 1993, Cisco went on to acquire two additional privately held vendors of LAN switches to round out its product portfolio—Cisco paid $202 million in 1994 for Kalpana and paid $340 million in 1996 for Grand Junction. Cisco's revenues from LAN switching devices—those developed at the former Crescendo, Kalpana and Grand Junction, and those developed internally—generated revenues of approximately $2 billion in 1997. By then Cisco had captured the dominant share of this market, as Table 9.5 depicts.

Table 9.5 Quarterly LAN Switch Market (1996–97)

	1996				1997	
	MARCH	JUNE	SEPT.	DEC.	MARCH	JUNE
LAN Switching Total	598.9	779.3	904.8	1,025.5	1,130.7	1,259.4
Qtr/Qtr growth	25.6%	30.1%	16.1%	13.3%	10.3%	11.4%
Yr/Yr growth	329.5%	263.2%	194.8%	115.1%	88.8%	61.6%
Cisco Systems	240.0	323.0	385.0	450.0	500.0	586.0
relative share	40.1%	41.4%	42.6%	43.9%	44.2%	46.5%
Qtr/Qtr growth	37.1%	34.6%	19.2%	16.9%	11.1%	17.2%
Yr/Yr growth	313.8%	361.4%	250.0%	157.1%	108.3%	81.4%
3COM	120.0	149.0	177.0	197.0	205.0	242.0
relative share	20.0%	19.1%	19.6%	19.2%	18.1%	19.2%
Qtr/Qtr growth	9.1%	24.2%	18.8%	11.3%	4.1%	18.0%
Yr/Yr growth	185.7%	112.3%	86.3%	79.1%	70.8%	62.4%
Bay Networks	75.0	80.0	78.0	78.0	102.6	141.2
relative share	12.5%	10.3%	8.6%	7.6%	9.1%	11.2%
Qtr/Qtr growth	-16.7%	6.7%	-2.5%	0.0%	31.5%	37.6%
Yr/Yr growth	3650.0%	255.6%	136.4%	-13.3%	36.8%	76.5%
Cabletron Systems	61.8	101.5	131.0	145.8	165.0	160.0
relative share	10.3%	13.0%	14.5%	14.2%	14.6%	12.7%
Qtr/Qtr growth	134.3%	64.2%	29.1%	11.3%	13.2%	-3.0%
Yr/Yr growth		2060.3%	856.5%	452.2%	166.8%	57.6%
FORE Systems	65.5	71.7	85.3	96.9	86.1	80.1
relative share	10.9%	9.2%	9.4%	9.4%	7.6%	6.4%
Qtr/Qtr growth	19.7%	9.5%	19.0%	13.6%	-11.1%	-7.0%
Yr/Yr growth	122.3%	95.4%	96.3%	77.1%	31.5%	11.7%
Xylan	23.4	28.2	35.4	41.5	48.0	45.1
relative share	3.9%	3.6%	3.9%	4.0%	4.2%	3.6%
Qtr/Qtr growth	50.7%	20.5%	25.7%	17.0%	15.8%	-6.0%
Yr/Yr growth	1576%	526%	320%	167%	105%	60%
Network Peripherals	3.6	3.8	4.0	4.5	5.0	5.0
relative share	0.6%	0.5%	0.4%	0.4%	0.4%	0.4%
Qtr/Qtr growth	2.9%	5.6%	5.3%	12.5%	11.1%	0.0%
Yr/Yr growth	-45.3%	-36.0%	20.2%	28.6%	38.9%	31.6%

Source: Company reports

This chart demonstrates the ability of a gorilla to extend itself in adjacent categories through the power of acquisition. The concentration of power in Cisco looks like a gorilla's market share until we recall that it is, in fact, the sum of multiple market shares developed at the acquired companies. What helped these companies meld so well was that the architecture in LAN switching, as in intelligent hubs, is under proprietary control. Once again, any LAN switch can talk to any other LAN switch because the standard interface is Ethernet—all of the devices essentially offer Ethernet connectivity. As a result, Cisco has emerged as a powerful king, not a gorilla, in the LAN switching market, with 3COM coming in second as a strong prince.

A FOURTH TORNADO

By 1994 enterprise networks had grown to rival mainframes as the mission-critical backbone of the corporate information system. Network-based applications such as e-mail and client/server applications proliferated throughout most organizations. Networks had become one of the most important ways to share information throughout the corporation, from the CEO down to the line worker. At the same time, two other developments were brewing: mobility and the Internet.

The 1990s have seen, in addition to other hypergrowth markets, a meteoric rise in the laptop computer market, as more and more executives carry their work with them in these machines. One of the key drivers has been the need to stay in touch via e-mail while traveling. Indeed, the primary significant barrier remaining in this technology is the insistence of hotel management on blocking all available power and phone outlets with large, immobile pieces of furniture. Persistent executives, however, have moved enough of this stuff aside to create a mass market for remote access to networks.

Meanwhile, at the same time that enterprise networks were developing, the Internet was entering its own tornado. Not unlike its corporate brethren, the Internet also needs reliable remote access to make it available to individuals as well as corporations. While large corporations and frequent users sign up for dedicated lines to access the Internet, the rest of the world dials up to go on-line.

In either case, whether you are dialing in from the road to get on a corporate network, or dialing in from home, office, or the road to get into the Internet, you and your network provider are going to need *remote access devices*.

REMOTE ACCESS DEVICES

Essentially all remote access uses the traditional telephone network to communicate from one location to other. However, since the phone network was originally designed to handle voice calls only, computers need a specific device, called a *modem*, to communicate over the network. Modems are needed on each end of a connection to complete the computer telephone call.

Although modems had been around since the late 1960s, their use was limited initially because they were expensive and slow. Through the use of integrated circuits and aggressive marketing by many of the original modem manufacturers, however, starting in the early 1980s the price of modems fell rapidly, and their performance increased significantly. By the early 1990s a 14.4 kbps modem cost around $300 and allowed for a reasonable computer connection. Within the next few years, a 28.8 kbps modem at twice the speed was available at the same price. Price/performance was not at a point to cause a tornado in remote access, both inside corporations and on the Internet.

Modem technology is standards-controlled, not proprietary. All modems communicate with a standard language, or network protocol, and all operate at standard speed grades such as 14.4, 28.8, or 33.6. Modems supporting the same standards and speed ratings can interoperate even if they are from different vendors. Up through 1996, therefore, the market has been a royalty (king/prince/serf) game with no opportunity for proprietary architectural control. In 1997, however, rival modem manufacturers began introducing next-generation technologies that operate at close to 56 kbps, almost doubling the rate of performance once again. But this time, there are proprietary elements that would cause the market to shift from a royalty game to a gorilla game, a situation we will delve into further in Chapters 10 and 12, where we look at 1997 investment opportunities in the Internet sector.

As the number of computer users with access to fast modems and a telephone line began to accelerate in the early 1990s, supporting all of these users became a network management nightmare. Because each modem must speak to another modem, any corporation offering remote access essentially has to have a room full of computers connected to modems connected to telephone lines waiting to "answer the phone" from computer users dialing into the network. Enter any one of those rooms and you'll see: It really is a jungle in there.

This same problem existed on the Internet, except even more so. As use of e-mail began to grow, demand for dial-up access also began to accelerate among individual users. Any company wishing to offer dial-up access to its service had to have a room full of modems connected to a terminal server (basically a device to "terminate" a modem call to carry the remote computer's data directly into a network) to support its customers. After a while the number of modems became too large to manage, particularly when any of the devices failed to operate.

REMOTE ACCESS CONCENTRATORS

At this point, a few engineers at Ascend Communications and U.S. Robotics got the neat idea that if these individual modems could be integrated into a single device, the deployment of additional modems would become easier and the problem of managing all of the racks and racks of individual modems would become much easier. These original devices were called *modem concentrators*.

It became clear after a few users deployed these original devices that if more services and robust network management could be added to the device, it would further simplify network management and customer support. The leading vendors elected to add additional software to their device and position the new devices as a *remote access concentrator*, not just a modem concentrator. This last development proved to be an important catalyst in the early development of remote access for the Internet.

Table 9.6 shows the early market development for remote access concentrators.

Table 9.6 Quarterly Remote Access Concentrators

	1993				1994			
	MARCH	JUNE	SEPT.	DEC.	MARCH	JUNE	SEPT.	DEC.
Remote Access Total	20.3	18.3	19.1	23.4	22.3	30.6	50.5	64.1
Qtr/Qtr Growth		-9.8%	4.0%	22.5%	-4.4%	37.1%	64.9%	27.0%
Yr/Yr Growth					9.9%	67.1%	164.8%	174.4%
Ascend Communications	3.1	3.8	4.0	5.3	6.8	8.2	10.3	14.0
relative share	15.5%	20.5%	21.1%	22.6%	30.5%	26.9%	20.4%	21.8%
Qtr/Qtr Growth		19.5%	7.3%	31.2%	28.9%	20.8%	24.9%	36.1%
Yr/Yr Growth					116.9%	119.3%	155.3%	164.8%
Shiva Corporation	16.9	13.9	13.8	16.2	7.6	8.0	11.5	17.7
relative share	83.0%	75.9%	72.5%	69.4%	34.0%	26.1%	22.7%	27.6%
Qtr/Qtr Growth		-17.5%	-0.6%	17.2%	-53.1%	5.3%	43.1%	54.5%
Yr/Yr Growth					-54.9%	-42.5%	-17.2%	9.1%
US Robotics (acquired by 3COM)					6.0	12.0	17.0	23.0
relative share					26.9%	39.2%	33.7%	35.9%
Qtr/Qtr Growth						100.0%	41.7%	35.3%
Yr/Yr Growth								

Source: Company reports

Once again, using the simple rule of accelerating industry revenue growth, the market for remote access concentrators entered the tornado at the end of the second quarter of 1994. We will pick July 15, 1994 as the official start date—one week after Ascend reported the financial performance of its second quarter.

As the table shows, the early market was initially dominated by Shiva, who marketed primarily to corporations. Shiva's technology did incorporate proprietary elements, and had the market gone into the tornado at this stage, they might have become a gorilla in the corporate market. Meanwhile, Ascend Communications, who marketed primarily to Internet service providers (ISPs), could not impose architectural control on the customers. What it had instead was a dominant niche market presence in the Internet access sector, which made it a very strong prince overall. Before we could see how this battle would play out, U.S. Robotics entered the market with a nonproprietary, low-cost solution for corporations. This new product basically cut Shiva's market share in half because of the density, scalability, and price performance of its products. In addition, Shiva licensed part of its remote access software technology to Microsoft to be incorporated into Windows 95, making it harder for all of the vendors to differentiate their access products with client software. This competitive challenge had a devastating effect on Shiva's stock price, although the stock made an impressive comeback during 1996 as the company attempted to reposition itself as an alternate vendor to Ascend in the ISP market. Ascend, by contrast, was relatively immune to this development, because it was establishing itself as the dominate vendor into the market for Internet access. This market position did drive some economies of scale as well as moderate switching costs within its installed base. In the end, Ascend emerged as the key vendor to large ISPs, while U.S. Robotics emerged as the primary vendor to smaller ISPs because of its analog technology, and to the corporate market.

Going forward into 1995, Ascend and U.S. Robotics rose to prominence as strong princes, neither one able to knock the other one far enough back to establish a king status, both reasonably content to dominate in their home sectors of ISPs and corporations, respectively. Now the question arises, both for this chapter and for the industry as a whole, *where was Cisco in all this?*

Cisco has announced its intent to enter, and eventually dominate, the market for remote access concentrators. So far the company has been only moderately successful. Through a series of small acquisitions aimed at adding specific remote access and high-speed modem technology, Cisco has built its own remote access concentrators to compete with the entrenched vendors, Ascend and U.S. Robotics. Despite its efforts and stated desires to enter this market, however, Cisco has been unable to garner more than a 15% share of the market segment. U.S. Robotics merged with 3COM in mid-1997, and Ascend acquired Cascade Communications, a manufacturer of frame relay and ATM switches that are sold to ISPs and telephone carriers. Both of these corporate marriages will make it more difficult for Cisco to attack this market because the competitors now have more scale from which to compete with the established gorilla. Nevertheless, in light of Cisco's past successes in the industry, most observers expect the company to volley many more shots into the market segment before the game is over.

Here is the chart comparing $1,000 investments in the three key remote access concentrator vendors.

Figure 9.3 Remote Access

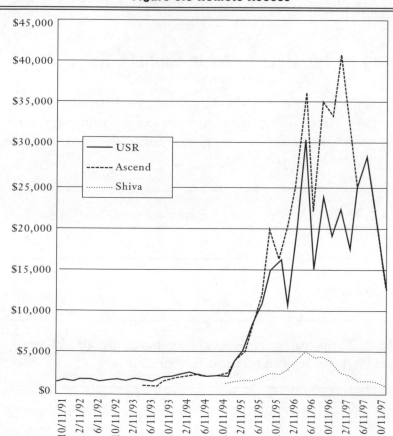

Note that Ascend and Shiva go public in 1994, the year that the tornado starts. Here we get dramatic returns from two of the three competitors, but notice that they are spiky, and do not sustain themselves. This is the effect of a royalty game as opposed to a gorilla game. When the market leaders do not have architectural control, other competitors can enter the market, drive down prices and thus returns, and shorten the Competitive Advantage Period, all of which reduces EVA and thus stock price.

This is why we advocate to "hold kings and princes lightly" and to sell off the category upon deceleration of hypergrowth. The big return potential is real but it is only temporarily sustainable. That is, the leaders have a time advantage during which they can extract near-monopolistic rents from the market, but they do not have a sustainable barrier to entry to perpetuate this competitive advantage indefinitely.

PLAYING BY THE RULES OF THE GORILLA GAME

In Chapter 7 we presented the Ten Rules for Playing the Gorilla Game. Let's review those rules now in conjunction with how a gorilla-game investor would have responded to the market for networking hardware devices.

Rule 1. If the category is application software, begin buying in the bowling alley.

Does not apply.

Rule 2. If the category is enabling hardware or software, begin buying after the tornado has formed.

Networking products are enabling technology, therefore the decision to buy should have occurred after the tornado had formed. As we determined above, the timing of each tornado was as follows:

Intelligent hubs	2nd quarter, 1990
Network routers	2nd quarter, 1990
LAN switching	1st quarter, 1994
Remote access	2nd quarter, 1994

Investors should have been attracted to, and invested in, all four markets. Although investors would have done very well in all four tornadoes over the ensuing years, the market for network routers was the only one to produce a true gorilla—Cisco Systems. The other three markets all produced industry structures along the royalty metaphor of king/prince/serf, as follows:

- The market for intelligent hubs produced two strong princes—SynOptics and Cabletron.

- The LAN switching market produced a king—Cisco (by way of three acquisitions and gorilla execution)—and a strong prince—3COM.

- The remote access market produced two strong princes—Ascend and U.S. Robotics—as well as a fatally weakened chimp—Shiva.

As we learned with the remote access market, at the beginning of the tornado it is not always clear whether a given market will develop around a gorilla game based on proprietary technology with high switching costs or whether it will default to a royalty game based primarily on execution dynamics. There is almost always a proprietary play possible, but as competitors in the marketplace become increasingly sensitive to its consequences, they work to block market development along those lines as best they can. It ends up, therefore, being far too subtle an issue for the private investor to penetrate at this point in the market's development. Later on it will become obvious after the fact; but that is then, and investment decisions are always now.

Therefore, we always assume that a gorilla-game investor will not be able to distinguish between kings and gorillas at the time of purchase and will indiscriminately buy candidates for either position.

Rule 3. Buy a basket comprising *all* the gorilla candidates—usually at least two, sometimes three, at most four companies.

Here's how our shopping basket would have been filled:

- In the market for network routers, the basket would have consisted of Cisco Systems and Wellfleet, although Wellfleet did not go public until July 30, 1991.

- In the market for intelligent hubs, the basket would have consisted of SynOptics, Cabletron, and Chipcom.

- In the market for LAN switches, the investment vehicles would have been Cisco and 3COM. As Cisco would have been in the portfolio already, the only decision would have related to 3COM. LAN switching, however, was a very small of a portion of the total 3COM revenue stream, and we do not believe this market would have qualified the company's stock for inclusion in the investment portfolio. As a result, other than possibly adding to the Cisco investment, the gorilla-game investor would not have participated in this market.

- In the market for remote access concentrators, the basket of stocks would have included Ascend Communications and U.S. Robotics, but not Shiva, since, by the time we entered the fray, they had already stumbled badly.

Rule 4. Hold gorilla stocks for the long term. Sell only on proven substitution threat.

As we have discussed, Cisco turned out to be the one true gorilla in the bunch. For its stock, the rule says simply to hold on to it through thick and thin. This rule was tested severely in 1994, when it appeared that the router tornado might end in a collision with the intelligent hub tornado, the latter somehow substituting for the former, initially in the application of segmenting LANs, with wider encroachments to follow. During this same period, however, the market saw the introduction of LAN switching devices, and the whole networking industry was temporarily thrown into chaos. Would these switches be the substitution threat to end both routers and hubs?

During this period, Cisco actually missed investors' financial expectations for a quarter and the stock was cut in half for a few months in mid-1994. It can happen in the best of families. Nonetheless, if you had asked yourself at any point in this process, is there a proven substitution threat that can take Cisco's power away, the answer would always have been, no, there are just fears of such a threat. They are not *proven*. This kind of fear is the constant companion of all investors, but it must not drive decisions, so the gorilla-game investor playing by these rules would have held on.

Rule 5. Hold application software chimp stocks as long as they exhibit potential for further market expansion.

Does not apply.

Rule 6. Hold kings and princes lightly, selling individual stocks on a stumble and selling the category upon deceleration of hypergrowth.

The companies that would have been part of our gorilla-game portfolio but that later would prove themselves to be princes in royalty games were SynOptics, Cabletron, and Chipcom in intelligent hubs and Ascend and U.S. Robotics in remote access devices. The rule for such stocks is to begin selling them once revenue growth for the entire market sector begins to slow. This way you get the benefit of the tornado but don't have to be dependent on the long-term stability of any one player in it.

For the intelligent hub market, the hypergrowth phase of the market began to slow in March 1994. For remote access devices, the market began to slow in September 1996.

Therefore the gorilla-game investor would have:

- Sold SynOptics in March 1994 (prince, market stopped accelerating).

- Sold Cabletron in March 1994 (prince, market stopped accelerating).

- Sold Chipcom in March 1994 (lesser prince, market stopped accelerating).

- Sold Ascend in September 1996 (prince, market stopped accelerating).

- Sold U.S. Robotics in September 1996 (prince, market stopped accelerating).

Rule 7. Once it becomes clear to you that a company will never become the gorilla, sell its stock.

The one company within the group that competed directly with a gorilla and lost, thereby becoming a chimp, was Wellfleet, later to be merged into Bay Networks. The market for network routers followed the gorilla game structure, and Cisco was crowned the gorilla in mid-1993. Investors at that time therefore would have:

- Sold Wellfleet in June 1993 (not a gorilla).

No doubt this seems harsh to many, and especially to anyone in the management structure of Wellfleet. So let us once again state, we are not saying that the company was no longer deserving of capital investment. We are not saying that it cannot generate excellent returns. All we are saying is that it has fallen out of an exceptionally restricted set of companies that form the basis of the gorilla game. In that context, the governing market model predicts that a chimp can *never* unseat a gorilla. Therefore, Wellfleet's gorilla opportunity goes to zero, and regardless of how good a company it is or how well it is doing, according to the rules of the gorilla game, it should be sold.

Rule 8. Money taken out of non-gorilla stocks should immediately be reinvested in the remaining gorilla candidates.

The money that was generated in selling off the entire intelligent hubs category in 1994 would have been reinvested in Cisco, for its ongoing position in the router market, and its emerging position in the LAN switch market, as well as in Ascend and U.S. Robotics, for their position in the emerging tornado category of remote access concentrators.

Here are the entire results of the networking hardware gorilla game put into a single table. We keep a running total of your holdings in Cisco to show how value develops around consolidating in the gorilla.

Table 9.7 Gorilla-Game Results

Action	Date	Price	Shares	Amount	Holding	Total
BOT SNPX	7/16/90	$28.27	177	$5,000		
BOT CS	7/16/90	$20.16	248	$5,000		
BOT CSCO	8/15/90	$23.75	211	$5,000	211	$5,000
BOT CHPM	5/31/91	$16.50	303	$5,000		
BOT WFLT	8/1/91	$22.78	219	$5,000		
SLD WFLT	7/15/93	$50.48	439	$22,160		
BOT CSCO	7/15/93	$52.25	424	$22,160	2,108	$110,160
BOT CSCO	4/15/94	$30.25	165	$5,000	4,382	$132,554
SLD SNPX	4/15/94	$20.38	354	$7,208		
SLD CHPM	4/15/94	$49.20	303	$14,908		
SLD CS	4/15/94	$103.28	248	$25,620		
BOT CSCO	4/15/94	$30.25	1,340	$40,528	5,722	$173,082
BOT ASND	7/15/94	$15.25	328	$5,000		
BOT USRX	7/15/94	$28.31	177	$5,000		
BOT SHVA	11/18/94	$31.50	159	$5,000		
SLD ASND	10/15/96	$64.75	2,623	$169,836		
SLD SHVA	10/15/96	$45.38	317	$14,405		
SLD USRX	10/15/96	$78.00	706	$55,099		
BOT CSCO	10/15/96	$65.88	3,633	$239,340	15,077	$993,176
CSCO TOTAL	8/29/97	$75.38			15,077	$1,136,404
Total Initial Portfolio						$45,000
Total Increase in Value of Portfolio						24x

After your initial basket purchase, your first act was to sell Wellfleet and buy Cisco. Note that your holding and Cisco has jumped dramatically over the interval. This is because the stock has split to 8x its original issue.

In April of 1994 you bought into Cisco again, plus you sold off other holdings and put those proceeds into Cisco as well. That put your stake at 5,722 shares worth just under $175,000.

In the same year of 1994, you started a new basket in remote access. That turned out not to be a gorilla game, but a royalty game, and so in 1996 you sold off the category in its entirety, having made a stupendous gain on your Ascend purchase, and put it into the long-term safe hold of the gorilla, Cisco.

As of the end of August 1997, your initial $25,000 in 1990—supplemented with an additional $20,000 in 1994—is now worth over $1.1 million, a gain of 24x, with a bright future still ahead of you.

Please note that 24x is far less than the theoretical maximum of "just investing in Cisco," but it accurately reflects the kind of hedging and false starts that real-world investing entails. And, of course, it is a far cry from what "normal investing" would generate.

Rule 9. In a gorilla collision, hold your gorilla candidates until there has been a definitive outcome.

This was the case that we discussed under Rule 4, where at the beginning of 1994 a potential collision between routers and intelligent hubs was further complicated by the introduction of LAN switching into the market. It had a disastrous local impact on all the stocks, but we held on until we could see a definitive outcome.

From time to time we have flirted with an alternative rule here, which would be to sell out the category until the smoke clears and then buy back in. At the end of the day, however, the signals for when to sell and then buy seemed so murky that we gave it up.

Rule 10. Most news has nothing to do with the gorilla game. Learn to ignore it.

In many respects, this is one of the most important of the rules, although it may be the hardest to live by. With hindsight it is clear that Cisco has become the gorilla of the networking industry. The stock has been exceptional, to date returning investors more than one hundred times the original investment in the IPO. Of these gains, a gorilla gamer would have participated in about half, buying in not at the time of the IPO but at the time of a confirmed tornado market. But if there were ever a use for the phrase "not half bad," surely this is it.

However, along the way there were numerous predictions of Cisco's impending death. With each new product category introduction, each new crop of competitors was quick to predict that the newly introduced product would have the effect of putting Cisco out of business. It is difficult to read announcements such as these recurrently and not feel that somehow one of them could be the fatal blow. It would have been particularly difficult to sit back and ignore all of these pronouncements if one had been fortunate enough to have invested in Cisco early in its life—shouldn't we get out now while the getting is good? As any company's valuation continues to increase at a very rapid rate, investment profits become tempting to cash, especially with all of the rhetoric floating around the industry.

Nevertheless, holding on to the gorilla for the entire life of the product category cycle is the critical strategy in the gorilla game. If you take your money out of the gorilla, you have to be able to say where you would put it that would be a better bet. By the principles of the gorilla game, there is no such place. That's what makes Rule 10 so critical.

WRAP-UP

Figure 9.4 Networking Industry

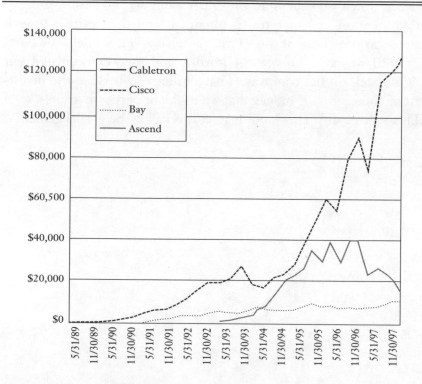

To bring this chapter to a close, an investor playing the gorilla game between 1990 and 1997 in the network hardware category, following the decision processes outlined in this chapter, and starting with $45,000, would now have $1,136,404. This is, of course, the classic punch line in all investment success stories. It is also *not* the point of this chapter. *Woulda*, *coulda*, and *shoulda* are not what the gorilla game is all about.

Instead, the key point all along has been to illustrate that playing the gorilla game does not take magic. Every decision we presented was rule-derived, not inspired, and was based largely on quarterly performance data. This data, to be sure, had to be interpreted with industry knowledge, but it was not insider knowledge. Rather, it consisted primarily of an analysis of whether the companies involved had proprietary architectural control with high switching costs or not. If such control was lacking, as was the case in intelligent hubs and remote access concentrators, the game diverted to a royalty game, in which we held on to the entire category of stocks as long as the momentum of hypergrowth obtained, and then exited. If such control was present, as it was in the router market, we held the portfolio until we saw who was the gorilla, and then consolidated our position back to that company. That gorilla also became the investment of choice for any money that we took out of royalty games.

That's all we did. This is not magic. It is called the gorilla game.

10

Case Study 3: Customer Service Software

A GAME IN PROGRESS

We now turn from the world of Paul Johnson, Wall Street analyst focused on networking hardware, to that of Tom Kippola, high-tech strategy consultant and private investor. In his latter role, he has begun to take an interest in an emerging tornado in client/server software for sales and customer service organizations. Unlike the previous two examples, this gorilla game is playing out in the *application software* domain where, the reader will recall, gorillas are a bit less fearsome, and chimps can stabilize their position for the long haul. It all leads to a very different kind of gorilla game, as you are about to see.

The key players in this particular sector of client/server applications come from two categories of software that developed independently but which by 1996 had begun to converge. The more mature of the two from a market development point of view is *client/server customer service applications*, among which three vendors, Vantive, Scopus, and Clarify, have developed strong positions. The other category, *client/server sales force automation*, has not progressed as far along in the Technology Adoption Life Cycle. Its leading vendors are two, Siebel Systems and Aurum, the latter of which was acquired by The Baan Company in 1997. Both categories play host to dozens of other companies besides the ones mentioned above, virtually all of which have made successful cases for either private or public investment; but Vantive, Scopus, Clarify, Siebel, and Aurum are the current market leaders and the reasonable gorilla candidates. Finally, there is a third category, which is often combined with the other two, called *help-desk* software, which hosts a very strong gorilla candidate named Remedy. The market dynamics in the help-desk arena, however, are very different, and until such time as Remedy offers something in one of these other two categories, we do not think it should be considered part of the set.

To set the stage for our discussion of these companies, we will first look at the larger context of client/server software applications in general. As we shall see, these developed first in the back office, and only more recently have moved out into the front office, the domain of customer service and sales. The two domains, however, are sufficiently parallel that we think the lessons learned in one can be applied to the other. With these lessons in hand we will then turn to the front office market and play out a gorilla game with the companies noted above.

One final characteristic that sets this gorilla game apart from the gorilla games in the previous two chapters is that it is *still a game in progress.* At the time of this writing, client/server software for neither customer service nor sales force automation is, in our view, inside the tornado. We are looking at them instead during the bowling alley phase, and it will be questionable whether sales force automation has even gotten that far. You will see that when you look at markets this early in the life cycle, it adds a lot of uncertainty to the process, so you may see us proceeding a bit more humbly than usual, as we practice walking in the gorilla-game investor's shoes without the benefit of hindsight.

BACKGROUND ON THE CLIENT/SERVER TORNADO

While customer support and sales force automation have not yet reached the tornado, they do participate in a larger class of software called *client/server enterprise applications*, which has. We have already had occasion to mention a number of the companies that have benefited from this hypergrowth market, including SAP, PeopleSoft, Oracle, and Baan. Now, because it sets the key framing context for the current gorilla game, we need to look at its overall structure more closely.

Client/server applications participate in what is arguably the fourth wave of computing since the computer industry's inception. The first wave was mainframe-based and focused on automating mission-critical business processes for large corporations and organizations, largely through the streamlining of records and calculations. Its primary beneficiary was the finance and accounting department, although over time these applications branched out into order entry, inventory, manufacturing, and distribution. The second wave came with the rise of the minicomputer. Computing was brought into the design and engineering functions and down onto the factory floor. At the same time, minicomputer-based word processing systems were beginning to have an impact in sales and consulting functions. Finally, smaller companies and divisions of larger companies were getting their own dedicated versions of what had heretofore been mainframe applications. Then a third wave came along, led by the PC, which completely reengineered the way individuals and work-groups interacted with information and each other. Applications here were highly standardized, requiring much less support and training, and thus easy to proliferate. Whereas today there are tens of thousands of mainframes, and hundreds of thousands of minicomputers, there are tens of millions of PCs.

At the end of the third wave, the world was heavily populated with computers of all shapes and sizes, none of which talked to each other very well. Industry analysts began to describe large-company computing infrastructures as "islands of automation." By 1990 it was clear to most companies that if all their different types of computers were supposed to interoperate with one another, a new computing model was needed as the enabler. Thus began the emergence of *client/server* computing as the fourth distinct wave of computing.

The model called for a new type of application software—client/server software—which would be composed of two or more pieces. While the *client* piece would run on a PC, the *server* piece could reside in any number of places—on a high-end PC, a midrange computer (proprietary minicomputer or Unix machine), or even a mainframe. Within a single system there can be multiple server types in this architecture, each dedicated to providing a specialized service, such as hosting the database, or running an application, or providing the user interface, or managing the network. Helping to keep all these clients and servers working together smoothly also called for new categories of system software and a whole new fabric of data communications technologies to provide the underlying connectivity.

The advantage of this wholesale change in architecture was twofold. First, at the high end, it disaggregated monolithic systems into workable sets of building blocks, allowing for systems to progress along several paths in parallel, each path proceeding at its own pace. This relieved a lot of pressure on overly centralized mainframe systems, which had for some time been a bottleneck to any rapid application deployment. At the same time, client/server architecture allowed systems to integrate a disordered proliferation of personal and workgroup systems into a manageable hierarchy, and give users access not only to local but also to corporate data. These changes had the effect of making information systems much more adaptive to change, so that as management teams were forced to reengineer their business processes, the IT side of the house could keep up. In industries undergoing rapid restructuring, such flexibility quickly grew from being desirable to being mandatory, and the client/server tornado was born.

CLIENT/SERVER APPLICATIONS FOR THE ENTERPRISE— A SUPERCATEGORY

When a new architecture replaces an old one, the initial surge of demand is just to get the old applications up and running in the new space. It is a wholesale swap-out, and in the case of client/server, it created a whole new supercategory called *enterprise client/server applications*. Financials, inventory, order entry, distribution, manufacturing—all the old systems had to be ported over to the new architecture. It was way too big a job to do with in-house staff or on a custom basis. Instead, it called into being a raft of application package vendors who flooded into the space to fill up the void.

As a collective group, these companies grew client/server application revenue from $187 million in 1991 to $5.9 billion in 1995. In the process a single company, SAP, emerged as the overall gorilla in the supercategory. Relatively unheard of prior to 1990 except in its home country of Germany, the company has risen to the position of fourth-largest independent software company in the world. And the domain it carved out for itself became known as *enterprise resource planning* (ERP), an extension of the manufacturing resource planning of an earlier era.

If we refer back to the Computer Systems Sector map in Chapter 5, ERP lives in the space called on-line transaction processing (OLTP) applications. This has been one of the real hot spots for the 1990s. It has attracted a lot of development, enough so that it needs to be subdivided further, as the following diagram indicates.

Figure 10.1

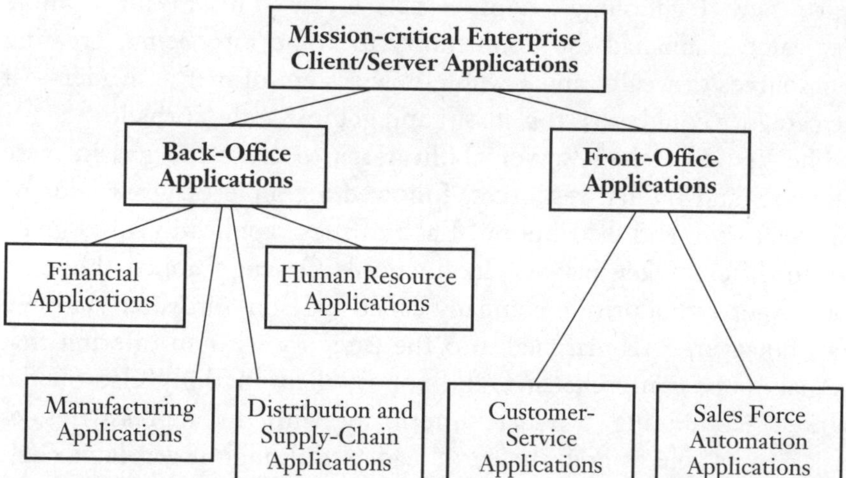

At the highest level of abstraction, the client/server applications supercategory can be split into *back office* and *front office* OLTP applications.

Back office applications automate processes in departments that do not regularly interact with customers. The key applications here include financials, manufacturing, distribution, supply-chain planning, and human resources. By contrast, front office applications automate processes in departments that *do* regularly interface with customers. The key applications here are customer service and sales force automation (SFA). Our focus for the gorilla game coverage in this chapter will be the front office, but since the back-office is further ahead in the life cycle, and since it has some lessons to teach us, let's stop briefly there before moving on.

Back Office Inside the Tornado

In 1990 back office applications were on Main Street when it came to traditional computing platforms of the mainframe, minicomputer, and PC. But when they all took up the cloak of client/server architecture, they turned themselves back into *discontinuous innovations* and had to prove themselves all over again. Client/server, therefore, initiated a new Technology Adoption Life Cycle. This meant a whole new value chain had the opportunity to come into being, creating new sources of wealth and a whole new system of market leaders—if the category could cross the chasm and get inside the tornado.

The first two client/server applications to cross the chasm were financials and human resources, followed a couple of years later by manufacturing and distribution. Each of these applications has given rise to different key players. In financials Oracle grabbed the early lead, along with a private company called Lawson Software. Within a year, however, SAP marched into the category with an offering that was far more comprehensive and robust than anything else on the market. Combining product superiority with an aggressive sales force, it was able to grab the early lead, and though it was later challenged by Oracle and PeopleSoft, it ultimately prevailed and was crowned the gorilla.

In human resources the tornado got under way at roughly the same time, but here the leader from the outset was PeopleSoft. It captured over 50% of the early HR market and has held that market share ever since. PeopleSoft's story is a classic example of using bowling alley strategy to cross the chasm. They got their value chain going early within the confines of a single department's concerns. This allowed them to achieve a local gorilla status in HR, which they have subsequently leveraged into gorilla candidacy both in financials and in manufacturing.

The manufacturing applications category was originally dominated by SAP, but more recently it has opened up in two ways that are creating additional possibilities. First of all, a series of value-adding applications has emerged and given rise to a raft of new vendors, including Manugistics and I2 in *supply-chain software* (with Datalogix being acquired by Oracle, and Red Pepper by PeopleSoft), Trilogy and Calico in *order configuration software*, and Sherpa and Aspect Development in *product data management software*. All of these categories add value on top of a basic ERP system. All of them also live currently in a curiously ambiguous state: Is their future to be a partner to the major ERP systems, or a competitor?

To date, that is, all these companies have a significant lead in functionality over the established ERP vendors; but going forward, if customers decide they want to have one-stop shopping, it is not clear what would prevent a major ERP vendor from just buying one or more of these companies and offering the capability itself. This in turn would put the new vendors in conflict with the very same sales channel that currently provides them comarketing support. For now, however, cooperation serves both parties, so there is a working alliance to develop the market together. But this begs the key question: How sustainable is the competitive advantage of these value-adding vendors? As we shall see in a moment, this same question gets raised in the front office space as well.

The other way that the ERP category has opened up is along the dimension of complexity. SAP is a very complex system to implement, and while the major corporations may not find that daunting, the rest of the planet does. This creates opportunities for alternative vendors as the market shifts from the largest customers to the middle tier.

Here is where Oracle, PeopleSoft, and Baan all seek to reassert their own market leadership. At the same time, going further downmarket, PC-based applications from vendors like Great Plains and others are now scaling up into the client/server space, leveraging the increasingly sophisticated Windows NT environment. And between these two endpoints are any number of intermediate strategies from companies like J.D. Edwards, Lawson, Platinum, SSA, and others, intended to carve out chunks of the middle-tier market using a vertical market focus. The net of all these approaches to date has simply been to provide customers with an attractive variety of choices, there being enough available market for most well-executed plans. But going forward, as this space becomes increasingly crowded, the issue of which of these companies can build sustainable competitive advantage will drive stock performance. Once again, there will be a direct parallel to this competition in the front office space.

FRONT OFFICE IN THE BOWLING ALLEY

Prior to client/server computing, the front office applications space had never made it to the tornado—in fact, it's arguable that it never crossed the chasm. While a number of large companies had installed customer service automation systems, or sales force automation systems, the offerings were typically custom-built from scratch. A few companies, such as Brock Systems, did offer prepackaged SFA applications, but the category never took off, in part because the laptop computer infrastructure was not really robust enough to support it, and in part because automating salespeople is a bit like herding cats.

From the early to the mid-1990s a number of factors changed the front office application landscape forever. The pressure came not from sales, however, but from service. The incredible success of the computer industry had created a huge headache. As the computer industry pumped out an ever-rising volume of products, the number of support calls to computer industry support centers rose astronomically. Moreover, since computer products all have to interact with one another, each time *anyone* introduced a new product, it created additional complexity for *everyone's* support desks. The demands on hardware and software vendor support centers rose geometrically. Companies first attacked this problem by hiring additional people to staff their support desks. Then they began to run out of qualified people, so they began hiring less-qualified people and training them. However, that didn't solve the problem either. It was not uncommon for an end user to call a support center and wait on hold for an hour before getting through to a support representative.

This *broken, mission-critical business process* is the primary market driver needed for crossing the chasm and starting a bowling alley market. Customer support departments sponsored the arrival of client/server customer support applications. If only one vendor had answered the call, that vendor would now be the gorilla in the space. But three vendors—Clarify, Scopus, and Vantive—all answered at roughly the same time. All three produced excellent software, all entered the market simultaneously, and thus no one company was able to gain an SAP-like dominance over the other two. In the micro-tornado of the first segment, which should have produced a micro-gorilla—that is, a definitive market leader for that segment—the result instead was three micro-chimps. Now, because the category has been so explosive, and because it clearly has opportunities to expand far beyond its initial niche, being a micro-chimp is not all that bad. But it is an unstable condition, and the market is watching closely to see what happens next.

Markets seek hierarchies if for no other reason than to speed purchase decisions. If there is no clear leader, then customer after customer feels compelled to go through lengthy evaluations and benchmarks. It drives everyone nuts, not only the vendors themselves but also their partners who are waiting on this decision in order to get their bids approved. So we expect the broad market to resolve itself into the more familiar gorilla/chimp 1/chimp 2 pattern over time. It is therefore, in our view, a gorilla game in progress. The questions now are, how would gorilla-game investors have learned about it, when would they have acted and on what information, and what would be the status of those actions as of September 1997?

THE CUSTOMER-SERVICE GORILLA GAME _____

By late 1995 the technology press had picked up on the rise of the customer service category, and by early 1996 the general business press was writing about it. The subtitle of an April 1996 *BusinessWeek* article read, "Customer support software is going gangbusters," and the article provided a brief overview of the category, including the growth rate, the players, and the trends. In June of 1996 *InformationWeek*, a popular computer-industry trade magazine, ran a special report on customer support systems. In the fall of 1996 *The Wall Street Journal* ran a profile of Dave Stamm, the CEO of Clarify, which called further attention to the category as a whole. Evidence was building that customer service systems had reached the bowling alley and were poised for dramatic growth.

Analysis of this evidence led to some interesting observations, as follows:

- Many of the articles that focused on the category, from both the technology and business press, listed a number of key buyers of the technology. A quick glance at those articles, along with a follow-up look at the Web sites of the three leading vendors, made it clear that well over half of all sales were to companies in high tech, either in the computing or telecommunications sectors. This suggested a bowling alley niche market was forming.

- Not only were numerous stories circulating in the press about the astronomical problem at high-tech support desks, but anyone who ever tried to call one of these support desks experienced the problem firsthand. Thus the compelling reason to buy—an essential factor needed to fuel adoption of a new technology—was being confirmed.

- The June 1996 article in *InformationWeek* cited a study by Computer Sciences Corp. of 346 information systems managers in North America. The study found that customer service automation led new systems development efforts, and that nearly 60% of the respondents were currently implementing such systems. By comparison, the responses further down the list included many of the traditional back office product categories, such as finance, inventory, distribution, and the like. This suggested that the pragmatist herd was moving.

- The same story stated that Cambridge Technology Partners (one of the fastest-growing professional computer service firms in the history of the computer industry), "is so bullish on demand for new customer service systems that it is concentrating 60% of its staff and marketing efforts in this area. Although the market is still somewhat immature, [the VP of Marketing at Cambridge] expects it to grow as much as tenfold in the next five years." Another member of the pragmatist herd weighs in.

By summer of 1996 a gorilla-game investor would have developed a hypothesis about the category that included the following:

1: The category had reached the bowling alley. The first bowling pin to cross the chasm was the computer industry, followed by the telecommunications industry. The financial services industry appeared to be the next likely industry to cross. All other industries still remained relatively unpenetrated, and therefore the category still had a huge number of potential adopters to create a tornado.

2: There were three gorilla candidates: Vantive, Scopus, and Clarify. None of the three had built a big enough lead to be considered a leading gorilla candidate. The eventual winner among these three would likely become the gorilla, and the other two would have strong chimp positions, *unless* one of the following two developments changed the dynamics of the category.

3: Another fast-growing front office category, sales force automation (SFA), was beginning to converge with the customer service category, setting up a pattern much like the individual categories in the back office converging into ERP suites. As evidence of this convergence Clarify purchased Metropolis software, a privately held developer of SFA, for $13.2 million in early 1996. Various analysts used various terms to describe the newly converging front office suite, but eventually *customer interaction systems* (CIS) stuck. Would this category supersede the more "local" market categories and thereby reframe all the buying decisions? Would a gorilla here "obsolete" more local gorillas?

4: Finally, the back-office-oriented ERP systems vendors were also making noises about playing in the customer service space and SFA space. For the time being, however, it appeared that Vantive, Scopus, and Clarify had a big enough lead that they would be able to weather any such onslaught. A reasonable worst-case scenario might be that ERP vendors acquired one or more of your gorilla-game investments at little or no premium over current prices, while one or more other companies in your portfolio would be left out in the cold.

At that point the gorilla-game investor had a number of choices, but before we discuss them, we need to look further into the impact of sales force automation applications on the front office market.

SALES FORCE AUTOMATION MEETS CLIENT/SERVER COMPUTING

The history of sales force automation prior to client/server computing has followed a split path. One side has gone after the field sales force, focusing on a consultative sales cycle for big-ticket purchases. The other has pursued a telesales force, selling over the phone based on inbound or outbound calling programs. At the outset of the market, it was the field-oriented SFA that was getting the most visibility. Its initial wave of deployment accompanied the first generation of laptop computers and was driven by the following value proposition:

1: Put information at the fingertips of the salesperson for use on site with customers and en route in airplanes and hotel rooms.

2: Structure the sales process for improved salesperson productivity.

3: Provide more timely and more reliable sales reports and fore-casts to upper management.

Although there were local successes with this first generation of systems, the overall market penetration was not impressive. First of all, in the absence of a mature client/server infrastructure, there were enough systems problems that many end users never really got comfortable with the new application. Second, it turned out that having the system running during a face-to-face meeting with a prospect was not in the cards, so the promised win for the sales force was not as great as originally conceived. Third, many highly successful sales people have personalities that resist structured processes, and these folks rebelled against the system and put peer pressure on their colleagues to reject it as well. Finally, in light of all the foregoing, overall end-user adoption was spotty and compliance was mediocre, which in turn made it impossible to deliver on the promise of timely, reliable sales forecasts.

This led some SFA vendors to retrench back into niche markets, a notable success being Sales Technologies, which focused intensely on the pharmaceutical marketplace. By so doing they targeted a specific sales cycle where having a huge amount of technical information on a laptop was actually useful during the sales call. Moreover, field teams were able to target sales programs more effectively with additional data about who was writing what prescriptions. But when the SFA industry tried to generalize this model to the computer industry, which also has a knowledge-intensive sales cycle, it fizzled. It turned out that the person carrying the knowledge in the laptop was not the sales executive, but the systems engineer. This outcome was fine for the laptop companies—they still sold their computers—but not for the SFA software companies.

The increasing maturity of client/server computing, however, has changed this equation. Now every salesperson carries a laptop, if for no other reason than to do e-mail. And today the infrastructure for logging into the enterprise to get that e-mail has become increasingly reliable, straightforward, and speedy. Also, today's laptops have CD-ROM capability for carrying large data files and presentation images, and the Internet allows for downloading more of same. So the barriers to end-user adoption are much lower.

Also, the pressure on sales forces to forecast more accurately has grown much higher. Part of this is in support of "just-in-time" supply-chain strategies. In addition, in the computer industry, there is huge pressure to forecast accurately when a company's products are inside the tornado. Under such conditions, it is not salesperson productivity but rather resource management and supply-chain management that are the critical success factors, and both depend heavily on accurate, timely forecasts. Taken together, these two developments have resuscitated interest in SFA for mobile, consultative sales forces.

At the same time, developments along the other dimension of SFA—telesales—have given even a bigger boost to this interest. Here the groundbreaking work was done in the telephone industry around the deployment of call centers for customer service. As these centers matured, companies became increasingly aware that a customer service call wasn't just a service opportunity, it was a sales opportunity as well. The whole notion of *cross-selling* came into prominence. And more recently, as interest in *one-on-one marketing* and *database marketing* has grown, telesales has become an increasingly important sales channel for making these targeted offers to one's database of customers. So what used to be a bowling alley marketplace is rapidly becoming a broad horizontal zone of opportunity. Tornado conditions, in other words, are forming.

These developments, in turn, have attracted the customer service vendors, including Scopus, Vantive, and Clarify, to expand their offers into the SFA space. At the same time, demand for telesales systems has also driven growth for companies already in the SFA space, including Siebel and Aurum. That has led to their growing interest in adding customer service functionality to their products. This is genuine convergence, and it means that these two categories at some point are highly likely to collide.

Buying the First Basket

By summer of 1996 two vendors, Aurum Software and Siebel Systems, had emerged as the momentum leaders in the enterprise client/server SFA category. But it appeared that the category was still in the early market. Two key pieces of evidence for this were the quarterly reports for Brock Systems and Siebel Systems.

- The largest independent SFA company in the space, Brock, had generated six-month revenues of $13 million, and was losing money. This from a company that had introduced its first product thirteen years earlier in 1983.

- Siebel, the new kid on the block, was going gangbusters, as it had just posted a $7.5 million profit *for the quarter.* However, although this news was very exciting, it was not clear whether this result augured early-market success or mainstream-market acceptance.

At this point the gorilla-game investor had several choices:

1: Play a gorilla game in the customer service category as a distinct category and invest in the basket of gorilla candidates comprising Vantive, Clarify, and Scopus.

2: Play a gorilla game in the sales force automation category as a distinct category and invest in the basket of gorilla candidates composed of Siebel and Aurum.

3: Play a gorilla game in the integrated CIS suite as a category and invest in the basket of gorilla candidates who have a shot at becoming the gorilla of the integrated CIS suite. This might cause the investor to include one or more SFA vendors in the basket, and/or exclude one or more of the three leading customer service vendors.

4: Don't play any game at all, fearing that the ERP vendors will move in and spoil the party.

Here's how a gorilla-game investor might think through these choices:

Game 4—don't play. This strategy has no risk but also no reward. Not playing is always a possibility in any category, and an investor has to use a certain amount of judgment to know when to invoke this option. The reward for playing the front office space, however, outweighs the future threat of ERP entrance for the following reasons:

- The entrance may never happen.

- If it does, it may be too late, such that these vendors' market power cannot be overthrown.

- If it is not too late, an ERP vendor may pay some premium over their current price of the holding and thus give a good return on the investment.

None of these is a sure bet, but they offer some protection against the downside risks involved, in our view enough to warrant going forward.

Game 2, investing in the SFA basket, is a risky game, even for professional investors. Because there is no evidence that the category is across the chasm, it still has the possibility of getting delayed, blocked, or even deep-sixed. The correct gorilla-game response is to monitor the category, looking for evidence that it has crossed the chasm, and then see what game is there to play.

Game 3, the integrated CIS suite basket, is an even more speculative game, incorporating not only the uncertainties of Game 2, but a compound uncertainty of a second level of consolidation predicated on Game 2 playing out as well. There just is not enough evidence yet that this is happening to warrant playing this game.

Game 1, by contrast, is a genuine gorilla-game opportunity, as of the summer of 1996.

Here is the stock chart for the customer service applications representing relative performance on a $1,000 investment:

Figure 10.2 Client/Server Customer Service Applications—1996

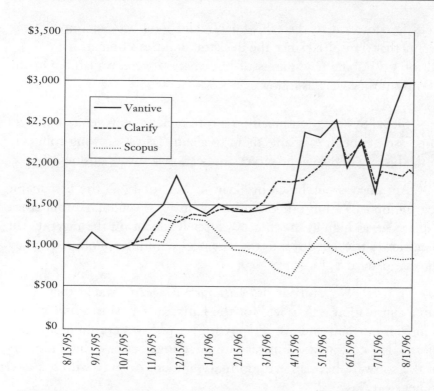

This is what "buying in the bowling alley" charts tend to look like. There are no dramatic spikes in growth because the tornado has not yet started. Moreover, there is no one company that has clearly distanced itself from the pack as yet, although Scopus looks like it is lagging.

Based on this chart you "buy the basket" as follows:

Table 10.1 Customer Service Applications Bought—1996

ACTION	DATE	ADJ. PRICE	SPLIT ADJ.	PRICE	SHARES	AMOUNT
BOT CLFY	7/1/96	24¾	2.000x	$49.50	202	$10,000
BOT SCOP	7/1/96	10⁵³⁄₆₄	1.500x	$16.24	616	$10,000
BOT VNTV	7/1/96	18⅛	2.000x	$36.25	276	$10,000

Updating the Game in the Fall of 1997 _____

Let's fast-forward to the fall of 1997 and look back at some of the events that transpired since the decision point in summer of 1996. By fall of 1997 some new pieces of information were available. On the SFA front they were as follows:

- Siebel Systems continued on a roll, racking up revenue numbers impressive enough to enable them to claim "fastest growing company in the history of the client/server application software business."

- Aurum was purchased by Baan in May of 1997, the first major acquisition of a front office vendor by an ERP vendor. Aurum stock had traded as high as the mid-30s after its debut on the market, but then slowly trickled down to the mid-teens, until Baan offered to buy the company at $21 a share.

- A June 1997 story in *VAR Business Magazine* stated that "sales force automation isn't a field for the fainthearted. Most implementations fail outright and are scrapped. SFA projects are different than most other customized software undertakings because the end users of the software have an extraordinary amount of sway within a customer's site."

- An August 1997 story in *Software Magazine* stated, "Despite the financial resources being thrown into SFA software, studies reveal that about 60% of corporate attempts to automate sales processes have not been successful."

As this news was playing out in the press and elsewhere, here is what the stock market was doing with a $1,000 investment over the period from the summer of 1996 to late 1997:

Figure 10.3 Client/Server SFA Applications

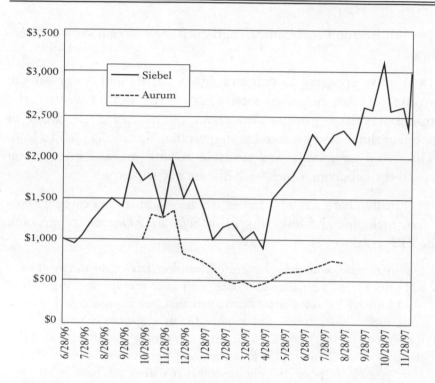

Siebel is looking like an attractive bowling alley candidate. It has almost tripled in value since the June 1996 benchmarking point. You should be torn now between wishing you had invested last summer and still being nervous about the inability of SFA applications to secure solid mainstream industry support.

Turning to the customer service market, here were some of the key developments in that space:

▪ Clarify and Scopus both had some disappointing quarters, which are not in and of themselves troubling to the gorilla-game investor, but if there are underlying problems that led to the poor performance, the information is useful. In Scopus's case the company reported two flat quarters and then the departure (resignation or firing) of four key people.

- Vantive and PeopleSoft strengthened their already cozy partnership.

- Vantive appeared to pull away from Clarify and Scopus as the favorite in the customer service category. Vantive posted the strongest revenue growth throughout the year, and the word of mouth in the industry seemed to suggest that Vantive had built a lead. (This word of mouth was available to the average investor on www.techstocks.com, which we'll discuss in Chapter 9.)

- Finally, there was additional discussion of pending category collision, including the following from *Software Magazine* referencing the ERP vendors:

> For some time, enterprise application vendors have seen the need to add sales force automation and other customer management capabilities to their ERP solutions. "Companies that buy Baan and SAP have large mobile sales forces and require highly scaleable systems using mobile computing," says Duncan Brown, a senior consultant with IT research firm Ovum. "[These companies] know about getting data from point A to point B." He expects that within the next 18 to 24 months all the ERP application players will have an SFA offering comparable to existing solutions provided by leading SFA vendors.

Meanwhile, while all this was transpiring in the press, the stock market was treating your initial basket of stocks as follows:

Figure 10.4 Client/Server Customer Service Applications—1997

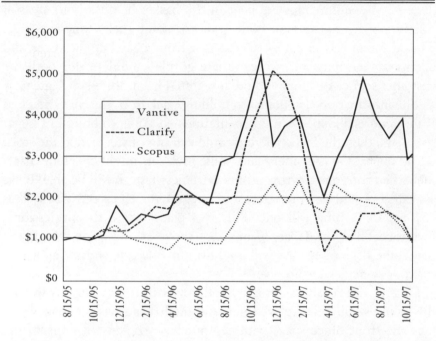

You have had a year of "excitement" with your basket (excitement is not a good thing with investing, we find). The end of 1997 finds you better off with your Vantive, worse off with your Clarify, and about the same with your Scopus. There is nothing here to write home about, but there is also nothing here to cause you to act in any dramatic way. We are still in a pre-tornado state, where stocks tend to jump around quite a bit, and although Vantive is emerging as a probable market leader, it is still too early to call the game.

So, given all this new information, what's a gorilla-game investor to do?

The information points to holding the basket of Vantive, Clarify, and Scopus, with one modification—add to the position in Vantive. Although the customer service category has not yet entered a tornado, Vantive appears to be moving into the position of leading gorilla candidate. Clarify and Scopus are kept in the basket because both are still rolling along, even though both have had some rocky times in 1997. The customer service category is still far from locked up, however, and Clarify and Scopus are still legitimate gorilla candidates for both the customer service category and the integrated front office suite category.

The information also points to holding back from the SFA category. If the reports about SFA implementations continue to be full of negative news, then the Siebel engine could run out of steam, and the stock would follow. On the other hand, some investors might conclude that if Siebel can continue to grow profits extremely fast, they'll be able to use assets (stock and cash) to attack the integrated CIS category as well as anyone. Only time will tell. This is a place where the professional investor is likely to depart from conservative gorilla-game theory and play some riskier bets. We will hold firm to our "safe course" approach for consistency's sake, however.

Finally, with regard to category collision with ERP, as of this writing the game is still being played out. Although Baan has made its move into the front office space with the purchase of Aurum, none of the other big ERP vendors (SAP, Oracle, and PeopleSoft) has as yet made a significant move. The expectation by most that follow this category is that all of them will. Bottom line: We won't know the outcome of this gorilla game for some time to come.

Table 10.2 Customer Service Applications Held-1997

ACTION	DATE	ADJ. PRICE	SPLIT ADJ.	SHARES	AMOUNT	RETURN
CLFY	8/29/97	15¾	1.000x	404	$6,364	-36%
SCOP	8/29/97	24¾	1.000x	924	$22,857	129%
VNTV	8/29/97	30½	1.000x	552	$16,828	68%
					$46,049	53%

Lessons Learned

The key lessons of the enterprise client/server application case history are as follows:

- There were three tornadoes in three separate back office categories—financials, HR, and manufacturing. Those tornadoes led to the rise of SAP, Oracle applications, Baan, and PeopleSoft. As of this writing, a fourth back office tornado is looming on the horizon in the supply chain management space. In addition to offerings from the vendors in the already established back office categories, two companies, Manugistics and I2, look like legitimate gorilla candidates.

- The back office was originally served by point vendors with point solutions, but evolved into a game of offering integrated suites called enterprise resource planning (ERP) systems.

- As of this writing the front office space has not seen a tornado. The customer service category is growing fast, but is still in the bowling alley. The SFA category, despite the hypergrowth of high flyer Siebel, is likely still in the early market. One possible exception is the telesales component of SFA (as opposed to the field sales component), which is arguably in the bowling alley.

- The SFA and customer service categories are converging into an integrated suite called customer interaction systems (CIS), in much the way the individual categories in the back office converged into ERP suites.

- Perhaps the single greatest lesson from this chapter is that the looming fight between SFA vendors, customer service vendors, and ERP vendors will test investors to make thorough assessments of company *and* category CAP before they place their bets.

Leaving Case Studies Behind _____

This brings to an end our series of case studies illustrating the principles of the gorilla game. By this point we have had more than ample opportunity to make our case. Now we would like to pass the baton over to you, our readers. By way of parting, we turn now to a pair of final chapters that we hope will get you off to a great start.

Part 4

PASSING THE
BATON

11

Tools and Processes for the Gorilla-Game Investor

As we reach this final part of the book, where our goal is to turn over the reins to you, our reader, we have come full circle to the question that drove the Introduction to the book: Just who do we think *you* are? All along, we have been hoping to carry with us a variety of audiences on a spectrum of sophistication, both in their relationship to high tech and to investing. And for the purposes of telling our story to this point, that hasn't imposed unworkable demands. But now, going forward, when it comes to suggesting investment process, we are sensitive to the notion that one size does not fit all.

In the sections that follow, therefore, we are going to follow a unified general process model for investment management, something we call SHARES, but we are going to divide up our recommended tools and sources on information into three tiers, each corresponding to a representative level of commitment and sophistication relative to gorilla-game investing, as follows:

THE SERIOUS AMATEUR

This is someone who is serious about investing but who has only two, perhaps three hours a week on average to dedicate to investing. While this may seem like a lot of time to our novice investor readers, we believe it is the minimum acceptable to seriously play the gorilla game. In addition, the serious amateur investor does not have a lot of money to invest in information, perhaps $200 or $300 a year in addition to the cost of subscribing to *The Wall Street Journal* as well as an Internet service provider.

We should also say that we are expecting this investor to play the gorilla game strictly by the book.

THE SEMIPRO

This person is somewhere between the serious amateur and the professional. Semipro investors can dedicate two or three times as many hours as serious amateurs to investments—perhaps five to seven hours a week or more. However, they still cannot dedicate anything close to the amount of attention that a full-time professional can. Moreover, while the semipro has considerably more budget compared to a serious amateur, perhaps $1,000 to $2,000 a year for information, this too is much less than professionals have at their disposal.

This investor we expect to absorb the philosophy of the gorilla game and implement it with personal variations, which will probably include some forays into non-gorilla territory.

THE PROFESSIONAL

Professionals are those with a career in investing, who can therefore dedicate their entire workweek to investing activities. Typically they might have a five-figure budget or more available for information and information-gathering activities. Portfolio managers, fund managers, asset managers, industry analysts, and the like all fit this profile.

We do not expect any of these investors to play a pure gorilla game unless they specifically create and market a fund to that end. Instead, we anticipate they will integrate insights from here into a more comprehensive investment philosophy and act off of that larger base.

THE HIGH-TECH INSIDER

There is a fourth category that to some degree cuts across all three of the above levels, and that is the *high-tech insider*. These investors may have the bulk of their investment in "sweat equity"—stock options at the high-tech company where they work—but are also likely to have a portfolio of their own. Unfortunately, they normally have little time to spend on formal investment processes, and we do not recommend a separate set of tools for them. But because they work in the industry and are exposed to lots of detailed information about their own product category as well as many other product categories, they often have very good investment ideas, so we do have a process suggestion.

If you are one of these investors, the material to follow on *scanning*, the first step in the SHARES methodology, is probably less valuable to you than it is for the others, and you may wish to skip over to the following section on hypothesizing. This would in effect make insiders HARES, which we think is fair because of the head start you have on everyone else. But like the hare, you should be careful. While tortoises make slow but steady progress toward the goal of financial independence, you may have a tendency to veer off the course and fall into all kinds of briar patches.

SHARES

In discussions about high-tech investing, whenever the question arises, How do I start? we say, "Think SHARES."

Now, SHARES for some will suggest the shares of the stocks they will go out and buy, and for others, it will suggest the power of market share and the role it plays in company valuation, and for others

still it may suggest some sharing of risks or information or investment insights. But for our purposes here, SHARES is meant to suggest the sequential process behind gorilla-game investing, which is to:

- **S**can
- **H**ypothesize
- **A**nalyze
- **R**espond
- **E**valuate
- **S**trengthen

These are the verbs that make up the actual conduct of the gorilla
game. Each stands for a process step, and at each step there are tools
and resources that can aid the investor in making successful, informed
decisions. Indeed, there are so many of these aids that the problem is
less one of finding them than of pruning them back to a useful set.

SCANNING

Scanning, literally, is a hyper-rapid form of reading, looking, or lis-
tening designed to survey a broad area of experience to detect anom-
alies worth further attention. As such, it is really just a form of *exploration*, and like most other forms of exploration, the objective is to
discover. In the gorilla game what we are trying to discover are new
market trends, emerging product categories, and stand-out companies in those categories.

All the investors whom we talked to in preparation for this book
are masters at scanning, and believe it is a key to their success. This is
because all investment theses begin with noticing something that others have not. Such "investable exceptions" are not common, needless
to say, and one must process a whole lot of ore to get a gram or two
of gold. Scanning, in this sense, is a mining process.

When you are taking up a new field, however, the most important
thing to remember about scanning is that it hurts—a lot—as in,
gives-me-a-headache, no-fun, very-discouraging, I-want-to-quit hurt.

The problem is that you are trying to run your mind swiftly and lightly over material that is causing you to stop and stumble repeatedly. You just do not understand it well enough to go through it at the necessary pace. But anything less than a fast pace yields such paltry results that you feel compelled to speed up regardless of how often you fall down. It's like learning to play chess and speed chess at the same time.

Unfortunately, there really is no substitute for going through this pain. Think of it as a barrier that will keep a whole lot of other investors out but that will let you, the persistent one, in. And the good news is that the barrier does fall. The more you scan, the better you get at it. The better you get at it, the more you get out of it. That's why successful investors put so much importance on their skill in this arena: It really does lie at the heart of their competitive advantage over the average investor.

As you get good at scanning, you will begin to sort everything you scan into one of three categories, which we like to think of as tossing items into one of three buckets:

- Confirmations
- Exceptions
- Irrelevancies

Going forward, you will find that the buckets for confirmations and irrelevancies fill up faster and faster, and there is less and less material in the exceptions bucket. This shows that your theories of the world are becoming more and more robust—hence the piling up of confirmations—and that you yourself are gaining more and more confidence in your theories—hence your increasing willingness to declare something irrelevant. That being said, however, the only valuable bucket is the *exceptions bucket*. It is only from this bucket that you can learn, and it is only from new learning that you can change your actions. By contrast, confirmations do not spur new actions—*being right again* buys you nothing. But *being right the first time*—now, that buys you a lot. So success is actually all about *being wrong and learning from it*.

More particularly, investment success most typically builds up from:

1: Being wrong, in the main because you have unwittingly absorbed some piece of conventional wisdom that is wrong.

2: Discovering that you are wrong, and doing so as an individual working on your own.

3: Acting on that discovery before the rest of the herd catches on.

Scanning is thus a casting about for places where you might be wrong. That's what the exceptions bring to your attention.

For the gorilla game, scanning focuses specifically on the technology sector. As you begin to take up scanning this sector, your first goal should be to identify the categories of products that are in hypergrowth markets or have the potential to be there soon (product categories that have, or will soon have, big CAPs) and the companies that have offerings in those categories (the gorilla candidates). This is initially more a process of subtraction than addition. Remember, as a pure gorilla-game player, your bucket for *irrelevancies* is huge. It includes all categories of any kind in the service sector—Year 2000 services, Internet service providers, systems integrators, and any form of merchant or merchandiser—as well as all vertical market categories—biomedical equipment, avionics systems, and the like. Only products that can play in broad horizontal markets are candidates for the pure gorilla game. Moreover, any product category that is already well established on Main Street—PCs, printers, mainframes, relational databases—also is out of contention. So it is only categories that are at or nearing hypergrowth that need your attention.

As you begin to ferret out these categories, your attention should shift to the companies that have product offerings in them. At this point you want to capture every tidbit possible about any one of these companies. You want to be building up a picture of the pecking order in the category, the current competitive dynamics, what differentiates each company's offerings from the others—all to feed the next stage of the SHARES process, *hypothesizing*.

Sources for Scanning

We are going to present these sources in a buildup sequence, beginning with the minimum set, and moving up to advanced. For the serious amateur investor, we recommend five scanning sources—two in the domain of general business information, three specific to technology business.

General Business Information

1: *The Wall Street Journal*

This is a basic read for anyone in the business world, and needs no introduction. However, it is worth pointing out the pages that we find most useful. We think it is important to scan four areas on the front page for technology stories: the "Business and Finance" column, the "Today's Contents" box, column one, and column six. Any story that covers high tech should be scanned, and any with gorilla game implications should be read thoroughly. Finally, the "Technology" page, which is usually somewhere between page 4 and 12 of Section B, should also be scanned for high-tech articles.

What we would encourage you *not* to do is turn immediately to Section C and scan for the latest price changes in the stocks you hold. We are not sanguine about our ability to prevent you—or ourselves, for that matter—from doing this, but it adds no value to the gorilla game and potentially could stimulate an inappropriate, fearful response.

2: Select one—*Forbes, Fortune,* or *Business Week*

All three of these magazines continue to increase their coverage of the high-tech industries. We suggest scanning the table of contents for technology-specific articles and then quickly scanning each article.

We also encourage you to read this same magazine cover to cover just to stay abreast of business trends overall. This is useful background when it comes to estimating the hypergrowth potential in a proposed tornado market.

Technology Business Scanning Sources

1: Select one—*InformationWeek, PCWeek, InfoWorld,* or *Computerworld*
All four of these are weekly trade magazines that cover the breadth of the computer systems industry. Our favorite here for investors is *InformationWeek.* Although it is a technology magazine, it is written with business issues in mind, as evidenced by the motto proudly displayed on the cover of each issue: "For Business And Technology Managers." *InformationWeek* contains a nice combination of weekly high-tech news with features and trend stories. Alternatively, *PCWeek, InfoWorld,* and *Computerworld* cover more or less the same ground but from a more product- and industry-centric point of view. If you work in the industry, you might well prefer one of these.

Whichever one you choose, we suggest moving through the entire magazine very rapidly, just scanning the headlines on each page, and stopping only when articles mention a category of interest. Warning: This is where the uninitiated gorilla-game investor is likely to experience vertigo and nausea. Until the meaning of these headlines comes to you by second nature, the bulk of them will be bizarrely uninformative, and the entire exercise will seem both painful and pointless. Press on.

2: *Upside*
Published monthly, *Upside* touts itself as "the business magazine for the technology elite." It is packed with useful feature articles, trend stories, and statistics. In addition it does some of the best interviewing of executives in high tech. As with the gorilla game, its primary focus is on changes of power in the high-tech marketplace, and as such it is a cornerstone for any high-tech investor's magazine list.

3: *The Red Herring*
In 1993 the founder and publisher of *Upside* left to become founder, publisher and editor-in chief of *The Red Herring*, a monthly magazine that, according to the cover, focuses on "the business of technology." Like *Upside*, the *Herring* is read by many high-tech executives and is also packed with useful features, trend stories, statistics, and interviews. But its differentiating feature is its "Industry Briefings."

Half of each issue is dedicated to in-depth coverage of a particular sector of high-tech. For instance, one month's issue might cover the wireless data sector, while the next will cover Internet commerce software. These briefings contain articles from noted sector analysts, industry executives, and venture capitalists, among others. They also include dozens of short write-ups of all the significant companies that participate in the featured sector—both public and private companies—and each company write-up includes company history, company strategy, financial performance, and stock market performance.

The Red Herring is arguably *the* most focused magazine for high-tech investors. It is significantly more quantitative than *Upside*, however, and most industry people we know read both regularly. Indeed, if we were stuck on an island and could have access to only two monthly publications for scanning the high-tech business landscape, these are the two we would choose.

ADDITIONAL SOURCES FOR THE SEMIPRO INVESTOR

For the semiprofessional investor we recommend all of the sources we've suggested thus far plus three more:

1: *Investor's Business Daily*

Four days a week *Investor's Business Daily* runs the "Computers & Technology Page," an excellent source of information and worth the price of the subscription all by itself. Every day the page has one interview with an industry executive, a number of charts that summarize specific industry trends, and two or three high-tech articles. We suggest scanning the entire page.

2: *ComputerLetter*

ComputerLetter is a high-tech industry newsletter that is published forty times a year by Technology Partners. Its founder and editor was once the science and technology editor for *The Wall Street Journal*. *ComputerLetter* does a very good job of dissecting trends and issues in the high-tech industry, with a primary focus more on venture capital investors than Wall Street. Not only is it well written and very efficient to read, it is the best source we know of long-range tornado forecasts. It is also the most expensive information source that we will recommend to the semipro (about $600 per year), but we think it is worth the price.

3: *The Upside News*

At the time of this writing *The Upside News* Web page (www.upside.com/news) on the *Upside* Web site appears to be one of the very best sites for scanning high-tech news and information. It is a daily publication that typically carries about ten summarized high-tech stories, most of which are also available in full-length versions at the touch of a button. What is equally useful are its links to the following three very valuable scanning sources, each of which also has about ten summarized high-tech news stories along with the corresponding full-length stories.

A. *Good Morning Silicon Valley*, a Web page published daily by *The San Jose Mercury News*, Silicon Valley's daily newspaper. Although the *Mercury* is known particularly for its excellent coverage of Silicon Valley news, this page provides good coverage of the entire high-tech industry.

B. *TechWeb*, a Web site published daily by CMP Publications, one of the three publishing firms that dominate the high-tech trade magazine business. This page is a compilation of technology stories drawn from writers from the dozens of magazines in its portfolio.

C. *Wired Online*, a Web site published by *Wired* magazine. In addition to daily news stories, the site also publishes two or three in-depth feature stories on a daily basis.

The Upside News page (including the linked pages) could keep even the most avid scanner busy beyond the time we have allocated for the semiprofessional.

ADDITIONAL SOURCES FOR THE PROFESSIONAL INVESTOR

The professional investor has access to two scanning sources that are not as easily accessible to many other investors: conferences and people.

CONFERENCES

- *Technology conferences*

There are numerous technology conferences available for investors to scan for information. Trade shows like Comdex, Interop, Internet World, and others are huge gatherings with hundreds of vendors, each with lots of information to give away. These more general venues are optimized for scanning. By contrast, conferences that focus on a particular sector of technology are more optimized for category analysis and tracking. *Upside* magazine's Web site (www.upside.com) has a searchable database of hundreds of both types.

- *Investment banking conferences*

Those investment banks with significant high-tech investment banking businesses hold annual conferences to bring together high-tech companies with the high-tech investment community. Usually these are three- to five-day conferences, and each day as many as one hundred company presentations are delivered to small audiences. Typically the presentations are twenty-five minutes long, and are delivered by the CEO, CFO, or both. Because the conferences usually have numerous presentations running simultaneously, the investor can attend as many as sixteen in a day.

- *Technologic Partners conferences*

Technologic Partners (www.tpsite.com), the publishers of *ComputerLetter* (among other publications), produces four conferences a year—one on networking technology, one on Internet technology, one on enterprise business technology, and one on personal technology. These are all two-day conferences. The first day is run like an investment banking conference, with perhaps one hundred company presentations of twenty-five minutes each. Day two of each conference is a mix of panel discussions as well as presentations from industry heavyweights.

PEOPLE

Last, but perhaps most important, the professional investor has access to people who work in, or are somehow connected to, the high-tech industry. This includes the web of service providers who work within the industry—venture capitalists, consultants, investment bankers, and analysts—end users at the major corporations, and perhaps most important, the executives of the high-tech companies themselves. All these people have insights that simply do not get published anywhere. In one sense they can be the most valuable resource for the professional investor. At the same time, however, their enthusiasm for a technology often leads them, and those who listen to them, to think a technology is just about to enter the tornado when in fact it has yet to cross the chasm.

HYPOTHESIZING

Hypothesizing just means coming up with ideas. We all do it all the time. But when it comes to investing, it is important to add on a layer of structure to focus our thinking on the issues that matter. In the gorilla game, our first set of concerns centers on detecting the onset of a tornado:

1: Where are tornado markets emerging?

2: What product categories are going to be affected?

3: Will any new categories of product be brought into prominence?

The good news here is that product vendors never make a secret of this information. Indeed, to catch the attention of the early-market visionary customer, they trumpet their tornado ambitions loudly. Many of these trumpetings, to be sure, are false, but they are not subtle nor shyly expressed. As a result, the gorilla game investor is constantly being made aware of hypotheses about emerging tornado markets; and the problem is not to come up with a new one, but to pare down the existing pile.

Our favorite test vehicle for this work, as we outlined in Chapter 4, is the *value-chain model*. Whenever we think there might be a new tornado market emerging, we get out our set of blocks and try lining up all the pieces needed to make an end-to-end working value chain. This forces us to name the product or service categories needed and to determine if any new category can be expected to arise. New categories, in particular, are the natural sites for gorilla games because their open spaces offer room for hypergrowth, presuming the market demand is there to stimulate it.

This early stage of hypothesizing is completed only when gorilla-game investors can name and crisply define the product category that has captured their attention. From then on, all subsequent ideas will be structured by focusing on this category. Choosing it wisely, therefore, and committing to it reluctantly are key.

The easiest way to eliminate poor choices is to find some improbability in the proposed value chain that, in your view, makes its success unlikely. Then you tag the proposition with that problem and say, until I hear a very good answer to this question, I am not putting any more time and energy into this area. Conversely, when you find a value-chain model that is plausible end to end—perhaps one that earlier you had put on probation and now has gotten around to addressing your earlier objections—you move on to the next series of questions, which we put under the name *analysis*.

ANALYZING

Analysis questions all begin with the phrase "Within the value-chain model for the emerging tornado market . . ." and continue as follows:

1: What product category, if any, might support a proprietary architecture with high switching costs?

2: What are the companies within that category?

3: Is there a hierarchy forming as yet?

The first of these questions is by far the most challenging, and it is where great investors distinguish themselves from good ones. Value chains assemble chaotically, meaning you cannot predict outcomes in particular, only changes of states that may or may not happen. Moreover, the vendors who come together to create these chains are hypersensitive to the possibility of any other vendor gaining proprietary architectural control. They do whatever they can to block such an outcome. This means most markets default to royalty (king/prince/serf) games—nothing wrong with that, it's where the bulk of money is made on the planet. It's just that they are not gorilla games and thus are not our immediate focus.

Whenever you are investigating a market for the first time, the gorilla game/royalty game issue is likely to be indeterminate. All you can do is ask yourself, could a gorilla game form in this space, and if so, around what kind of proprietary interface? If the answer is no, it could not happen, then move on to look at another category. If it could happen, then continue on to the next two questions.

These questions, by contrast, are relatively easy to answer, in large part due to the superb sources now available to investors because of the Internet.

SOURCES FOR ANALYZING

The Web offers such a wealth of analysis resources that, going forward, it's hard to imagine anyone ever performing product category analysis without it. We've selected seven Web sites as the cornerstone for investors to use in analyzing a product category. All seven sites have archives that can be searched with built-in search engines.

The first three are the most comprehensive: www.cmp.com (mentioned earlier as a scanning resource), www.idg.com, and www.zdnet.com. They are offered by the three largest and most powerful publishers of high-tech trade magazines: CMP Publications, IDG, and Ziff-Davis Publications, respectively. All three Web sites contain archives of dozens of high-tech trade magazines, and all enable visitors to search a specific magazine, a combination of magazines, or all of the magazines in the archive. Type a product category name in one of these search engines, and you're likely to get dozens of useful articles with detailed information about the product category you want to analyze.

We also suggest the archives at www.upside.com (*Upside*), www. herring.com (*Red Herring*), www.sentrytech.com (*Software* magazine), and www.ibd.com (*Investor's Business Daily*). Unlike the first three megasites mentioned above, these four cover the high-tech sector with a greater emphasis on analysis and commentary than on reporting. This makes them both more and less useful, so it is important to use them as a complement and not a substitute for the first three.

All seven sites in one way or another categorize the high-tech sector in order to simply get organized. Some go much further, breaking it down into subcategories and even sub-subcategories. The boundary conditions they impose are in some ways more important than the information they contain, because they trace out lines of marketplace power. Categorization, that is, always implies spheres of influence, alignments of competition and cooperation, and comparable valuations. A categorical scheme, then, is in itself a hypothesis, and testing it against your own views, especially when they contradict rather than confirm each other, can result in extremely fruitful investment insights.

Finally, once you have a short list of companies you want to pursue further, their company-specific Web sites should also be included in any product category analysis. Many companies now post their annual reports on their Web sites.

In addition to all the information on the Web, the other important sources of analysis for the serious amateur investor are prospecti for upcoming initial public offerings. These are available upon request from the investment bankers underwriting the offer. In many cases, the markets that these companies operate in have yet to reach tornado stage, and therefore your primary immediate interest in the prospectus is not to invest but rather to learn. And learn you shall.

These beauties are brimful of just the kind of ideas you are working with—who are the competitors, what is the current market share, what are the risk factors, what other categories might impinge on the future of this one. Thus in one place, for a given category, you can get the names of all the likely players and a sense right from the beginning of the probable hierarchy in place.

ADDITIONAL SOURCES FOR THE SEMIPRO INVESTOR

For the semiprofessional who has the time, browsing the Web sites of the various technology industry analyst firms can be extremely rewarding. These firms make their living selling information, but they do give a portion away for free on their Web sites to generate awareness of their services. It is harder to find free category articles or reports on these Web sites than on the sites listed previously, but when one is found, it is usually very good. The Web sites to browse are www.gartnergroup.com, www.aberdeengroup.com, www.yankee group.com, www.metagroup.com, www.idc.com, and www.forrester.com.

Similarly, investment banks with high-tech practices often have free information on their Web sites, but as with the industry analyst sites, you'll have to invest time visiting all of them to improve your odds of finding a free report on the category you're analyzing. We recommend visiting the *Herring* site for a comprehensive listing of investment bank Web sites at www.herring.com.

For people whose time is more limited, www.investools.com is a great place to visit. This site offers hundreds of industry and company research reports for a fee. Typical reports run anywhere from $5 to $20 apiece. For semipro and even pro investors who want quick access to in-depth product category research, www.investools.com is a great place to look first.

Finally, the Silicon Investor Web site at www.techstocks.com is an information-rich site that covers the computer industry, the telecommunications industry, and the biotech industry. In addition to news and information about the industries it covers, Silicon Investor also contains company profiles and stock charts. Finally, the site has some very active discussion groups, most of which are focused on particular high-tech companies.

Users of the site can write in their observations and comments for everyone else to see. The group of investors who participate appears to be a mix of serious amateurs and semipros, with some less sophisticated investors as well. We find the discussion groups to have some interesting information in them, but we also think many of the discussions are too focused on short-term results, like quarterly earnings. So, although we suggest viewing the discussion groups for good company and product category information, we also suggest that you be cautious about relying too much on the short-term bias of much of the information. Finally, although this site could have been suggested to the serious amateur investor, we find that once you're on the site you get so hooked on browsing through the discussions that before you know it, two hours have gone by. While the time spent performing this activity is valuable, we don't think the serious amateur has that much time available, while the semipro does.

Additional Sources for the Professional Investor

Because of their position in the financial industry, professional investors have ready access to a number of additional sources for category analysis, of which the following are the most important:

- Investment bank research reports on a routine basis.

- Industry analyst syndicated research reports—the full library, plus access to the authors of these reports for further query and discussion.

- In-person briefings and Q&A sessions with executives managing the companies in their portfolio.

- Daily dialogue with consultants, customers, and other investors.

The focus of all these interactions should be on refining the model of the marketplace, drawing the maps of power, understanding the sources of competitive advantage, and anticipating how competitive dynamics might change, occasionally within categories, but more commonly because of categories colliding.

Some professional investors might wince at our exclusion of the many financial on-line services as well as technical research reports. We simply don't think they are central to gorilla-game investing in its purest form. They are much more useful to investors who use other types of investing strategies (technical analysis and value investing in particular). By contrast, gorilla-game investing is more about under-standing the qualitative dynamics of a product category than getting close to the details of its financial ratios and technical charts. To be sure, the conclusions of both disciplines should at some point con-verge. We just think that the effects we are tracking to are so blatant, it doesn't take sophisticated algorithms to track them down.

RESPONDING

If as an investor you are not to fall victim to analysis paralysis, sooner or later you must buy something. You have to pull the trigger. You have to *respond*.

It's harder than you might think.

The problem starts with there never being enough data. You never *know* anything. Then there is the inevitable second-guessing, first by your inner voices, then from whatever outer voices you have shared your ideas with. Then there are the inherent procrastinating behav-iors that encumber all risk-based decisions.

So here's what we suggest. Remember why you are doing this: You need to build wealth for your family, and you are already behind in this effort, which is why you are doing the extra work it takes to invest in high tech. You must get started. Given that, here's how we recommend you go about doing it.

1: Set aside a certain amount of money to invest at the outset, and then supplement it with a certain amount of new money every quarter. Windfalls that supply additional investment capital go into the next quarter's allocation.

2: Buy any given stock on the results published in its most recent quarterly report. That is, restrict your buying times to four times per year for any given stock; and use the quarterly report as your trigger because, for what it covers, it is the most reliable source of information available. This is intended to keep you from falling prey to the spikes of fear and exuberance that drive most bad investment decisions.

3: Buy a basket of stocks in a category you have determined qualifies for gorilla-game investment now. If you have not yet discovered a new category on your own, consider some of the already known categories that still have plenty of tornado life left in them.

4: If the current market share data has not changed dramatically in the past year, you can use it to weight the amount of money you invest in each of the stocks in your basket. But be careful here. Don't defeat the risk-reduction effect of buying a basket. This is the time in the gorilla game when *diversification* reduces risk.

5: Invest the entire sum of money you have set aside. If you accumulate too big a backlog of investment funds, you put too much pressure on the next quarter's investment decisions.

Then get on with your life. What is the point in providing for your family if you do not build the kind of family connections that make a long life together enjoyable?

TOOLS FOR RESPONDING

All of the information needed to implement this process is available through the basic analysis sources recommended to the serious amateur gorilla-game investor.

If you would like a full quarterly report for a given stock, as filed with the Securities and Exchange Commission, these can be downloaded from Edgar at www.edgar-online.com.

To place your orders, we recommend using an online broker. For a comprehensive listing of online brokers go to Yahoo's list at—now, this is a long one—www.yahoo.com/Business/Companies/Financial_Services/Investment_Services/Brokerages/Online_Trading/.

To track your portfolio going forward, we recommend using one of the many Web sites that offer this service for free. Check out the Herring site's list at www.herring.com/direct.

EVALUATING

Okay. Now you are into the gorilla game. Maybe at the outset you have invested in a single category. Maybe you are further along and have investments in several categories. This kind of diversification is good, as long as each category represents a legitimate gorilla game. Too many categories, on the other hand, may create more work than you can actually do. It is important to find a limit, because when you buy a stock in the gorilla game, you have an ongoing responsibility to *evaluate* it.

The most important process issue with evaluation is *frequency*. We have argued repeatedly that nothing in the gorilla game requires a rapid response. We have hinted, in fact, that rapid responses are more likely to do damage than good. Do we really mean that? *You bet we do!*

The biggest risk you face as a gorilla-game investor, in our view, is fouling up the game by trying to micro-manage it. This is *not* a game of micro effects. If you must micro-manage, you should not play this game. Conversely, if you honestly do intend to play this game, you must *not* micro-manage. It really is that simple.

So getting back to frequency, the correct frequency for making gorilla-game decisions is four times a year. If you use a broker, then schedule four meetings a year, either by phone or in person. If you don't have a broker or similar form of counsel, just mark your calendar. But in either case, do this in advance so that you can stay on discipline.

In the context of these sessions, here's how we recommend you proceed:

1: *Use quarterly results as your fundamental scorecard.* Not all your companies will report on the same fiscal year, but that doesn't matter. You pick your own personal fiscal year and then use the most current quarterly information available.

As we have been saying—and it's worth repeating—nothing in the gorilla game happens so fast that waiting for the next quarter will penalize you. Conversely, many things happen in high tech that look earth-shaking the day they are announced, only to be seen as non-events or minor changes even a few weeks later. It is critical that you not knee-jerk react, so waiting for the quarter is a good discipline.

2: *Build a simple spreadsheet for each basket of stocks.* It should contain the following information for each stock in the basket:

A. Revenue and earnings history going back at least six quarters if available

B. Stock price chart

C. Current market capitalization

D. Price/sales ratio

E. Price/earnings ratio

F. Estimated market share in the category

All but the last piece of information is readily available from the Web sites we have already cited. Unfortunately, the last piece of information is critical, and you need to hunt for it. Indeed, like a reporter, you need to find several confirming sources because it, more than any other number, is the key to the gorilla game.

3: *Isolate the performance within market category* from the overall performance of the companies in all their markets.

This too is a genuinely difficult task. For "pure play" companies, there is no problem, but for mature companies who report revenues in many categories, isolating their performance in any one can be a challenge. Companies do not want to tell their competitors exactly where they are strong or weak. Sometimes, indeed, they wouldn't mind keeping this information from their shareholders, at least for a quarter or two, when they see themselves as skating on thin ice. Therefore, they rarely break out all their numbers in the way you would like to see them.

This is where Wall Street financial analysts earn their money. They do their best to wrest this information from the line executives and financial officers of the companies involved. This is why their reports can be so valuable to investors. It is also another reason a stockbroker, who typically has broad access to these reports, can add value to your portfolio management. It is also why the Internet is going to change the role of the private investor, because many bits of knowledge individually obtained are now getting shared in chat rooms and can aid in building up the big picture.

One way or another, however, you simply must build this performance model. It will, no doubt, be rife with fudge factors. All you have to be able to do with it is make the judgment whether the stock price is sufficiently connected to performance in this one category to be worth including in your gorilla-game portfolio. Recall, for example, that we excluded investing in 3COM for the LAN switching, because the category was such a small proportion of the company's total revenues that we did not think it would move its stock price.

For gorilla-game investing, you need to have baskets of comparables, or else you introduce a huge number of additional variables. If the bulk of the companies that are winning do not meet this criterion, it is often best to forgo the category.

4: *Use the quarterly data to evaluate the following key concerns:*

A. *Is the market (still) in hypergrowth?*

Use quarter-to-quarter and year-to-year revenue growth for the basket as your primary indicator. Two quarters in a row of change in the same direction is significant—three is a trend.

One way you will use this indicator is to signal the post-hypergrowth period—a time to sell your entire basket of stocks in a royalty game and to consolidate your holdings back into the gorilla in a gorilla game.

Another way you will use it is to signal that hypergrowth has not yet begun. Except in the case of application software, this indicates that any action on behalf of your portfolio is premature.

B. *Do earnings performances signal any shifts in power?*

Earnings in and of themselves are not the key performance metric during a hypergrowth market. Market share is. But if one company is achieving hypergrowth *and* throwing off much higher earnings than its competitors at the same time, that is a strong gorilla signal. Conversely, a string of poor earnings in comparison to competitors signals a chimp that is struggling to keep up with market growth, and paying a price to do so.

Nonetheless, we would not normally act strictly on an earnings basis during the hypergrowth stage of a gorilla or royalty market. There are simply too many situations where sacrificing earnings represents the right strategy. Instead, we would use it as a confirming indicator.

C. *Has the total market capitalization of the entire category changed over the last quarter?*

Rapid growth in the market capitalization of the entire basket of stocks in a category is the strongest indication of a tornado market. It is a confirmation of your investment strategy, which requires no action on your part, but will help you sleep much better at night.

Conversely, flat growth or a diminishing capitalization of the category is the single most important signal in the gorilla game. If it comes on Main Street, it is normally a "must consolidate" signal for the gorilla game and frequently a "sell out now" signal for a royalty game—ideally, you might have done both a bit sooner.

If growth flattens or diminishes at the beginning of what was looking to be hypergrowth, or strikes in what you were expecting to be the middle of a multiyear hypergrowth market, and it cannot be accounted for by a general slowdown in the economy and stock market overall, it signals a fundamental shift in power in the marketplace. This was unexpected, and demands an "all hands on deck" response. You must get to the bottom of why this is happening as fast as possible, and change your investment strategy accordingly.

D. *Has any company's share of the category's market capitalization changed over the last quarter?*

Share of the category's total market capitalization is the single best indicator of marketplace status within a competitive set. That is, market capitalization is fundamentally a measure of competitive advantage, and the more one company's market cap exceeds that of a competitor's, the more advantage it is perceived to have. This is really just the essential observation that drives the gorilla game.

When you see that the leader's share of the basket's market cap is beginning to outstrip the rest of the pack, that is the gorilla consolidation signal. Conversely, when you see relative market capitalization slide around a category, it is an indicator that no gorilla is emerging. In the application software arena, this can signal a "field of chimps" sector, where everyone will get something, and no one will get everything. In an enabling technology, it signals a royalty game. In either case, it suggests that you will migrate your capital out of the sector sooner or later.

E. *Has any company's market share changed over the last quarter?*

As we noted above in our discussion of performance models, market share data is the hardest to get and the least reliable once you do have it. Nonetheless, it is the leading indicator of company status in any gorilla game, and you should do your best to get whatever data you can about it.

Two quarters of trending in the same direction in market share suggests action, while three simply demands it.

To sum all this up, there is quite a bit of work reflected in the outline above. This is where gorilla-game investors should focus their time. It will take you a quarter to prepare for the next quarter's decisions. You do not have time, in other words, to get caught up in the latest flurry of rumors around the latest dip or spike in stock price.

SOURCES FOR EVALUATING

Most of the same sources that are used for analysis are also used for tracking and evaluating ongoing investments in a product category. What we would add at this point are any sector- or product-specific publications, newsletters, or conferences.

Typically, when a category first makes itself felt in the early market, it will generate one or two publications dedicated exclusively to it. These tend to be heat-seeking missiles that track technology vapors—they are not useful to the gorilla-game investor. But once the category enters the tornado, it will generate a second wave of coverage, initially getting pages in publications and break-out sessions at conferences, but eventually getting stand-alone treatment in both venues. These publications and conferences attract knowledgeable people for the life of the tornado (and a whole lot of lower-level types thereafter) and are a good source for information and opinion.

STRENGTHENING

Over time, the gorilla-game portfolio will accumulate investments in multiple categories. New capital coming in will be less and less likely to be directed toward funding new games and more and more likely to go into existing games. This gives gorilla-game investors the opportunity to *strengthen* their portfolios.

The two sources of strength are diversification and concentration. Both play a key role in portfolio management. In the gorilla game, the rules are to:

1: *Diversify* into multiple hypergrowth markets.

2: *Concentrate* into the gorilla stock wherever possible.

Weighting your diversification is simply a matter of putting new money into categories that are underfunded. To meet this goal, we do not recommend a lot of selling and buying, but simply a directing of quarterly buys to balance out the portfolio over time. There is no rush here. Simply make it part of your standard operating procedure.

By contrast, there is cause for concern on the consolidation side. Selling, by definition, is the primary way to strengthen through consolidation. The one area that is extremely time-dependent is that of selling off chimp stocks in an enabling hardware or software category, before they get hit. (In application software, as we have said repeatedly, the game allows much more freedom because the stock cannot get hit as directly.) If you miss this window, you stand to lose a significant chunk of change, so do not linger on this decision. The other selling act that demands timely execution is exiting a royalty game as the category moves out of hypergrowth.

And that's pretty much it.

As we have said repeatedly, the gorilla game is not a particularly subtle approach to investing. Nor is it intended for all investors. Nor is it intended to slight any of the thousands of investments that do not meet its hyperselective criteria. All it is intended to do is to give private investors who have determined they must generate above-average returns an opportunity to use high-tech hypergrowth markets as at least a partial vehicle for meeting their goals.

Like all investment philosophies, it is easy to justify this one in hindsight. So, to bring this book to a close, we thought we would set ourselves the much tougher challenge of looking ahead.

12

Investing in the Internet—The Mother of All Tornadoes?

To close this book, we want to take you on a test drive of gorilla-game methodology, and given that we are entering the fourth quarter of 1997 at the time of this writing, as we look out to the technology stock market, we see, like Michael Jordan, "nothing but Net."

The Internet itself is not so much in or out of the tornado as it is a tornado alley, a place of recurring tornadoes, and therefore a great place for staking out a tornado watch. In this chapter we will identify a series of actual and potential tornado opportunities—some early, some late, some ripe for the moment—and suggest how the gorilla game looks to be playing out within each case.

We will, in a word, *go on record*.

The thought is chilling. What is more unpredictable than the stock market? And what in the stock market is more unpredictable than high tech? So why would any sane person put predictions in a *book?* What, then, would the *National Enquirer* be for?

Indeed, we have inquired of the publisher if this chapter could be published on perforated paper, or possibly if there could just be a folder in the back of the book, and we could slide in an update, say, a year from now (and another the year after that). The publisher was not amused, and said we ought to just get on with it, and so we will.

THE INTERNET IN 1997

We spend a fair amount of our collective time working with clients in the Internet space, and as a result we have built up a general view of what applications will drive the coming waves of technology adoption, as laid out in the following chart. This is the same High-Tech Market Development Chart we presented in detail in Chapter 2. The frame of reference for this particular chart is the U.S. marketplace, with the bulk of the emphasis on the corporate market.

Figure 12.1 Applications on the Internet: 1997

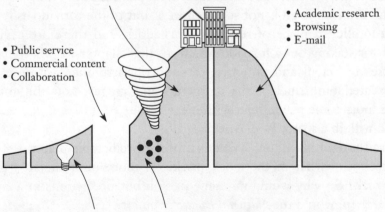

- Market research
- Competitive analysis
- Document management
- Marketing communications
- Public relations
- Personal education and entertainment

- Academic research
- Browsing
- E-mail

- Public service
- Commercial content
- Collaboration

- Self-service technical support
- Supply chain commerce
- Consumer commerce
- K–8 classroom education
- Consumer programming
- Consumer telephony

- Software distribution
- Supply chain commerce
- HR queries
- Supply chain partner support
- Industry association communications
- Virtual community communications

The easiest way to read this diagram is to start with the right-hand side and work your way to the left.

MAIN STREET

The diagram asserts that, for the U.S. market, three Internet applications—academic research, browsing, and e-mail—have already passed through the Technology Adoption Life Cycle and are firmly positioned on Main Street. Thus they offer no tornado-based gorilla-game opportunities. Moreover, since all three gained their adoption by virtue of being given away for free, there is not even a post-tornado game to contemplate, where one might invest in a gorilla later than optimally but still with a lot of future ahead (such as buying stock in IBM today, for example).

THE TORNADO

There are, however, plenty of applications inside the tornado in the fourth quarter of 1997, based on both business and consumer usage (even if the latter often takes place at work). Let's begin with market research and competitive analysis. It is hard to imagine anyone conducting this type of research these days trying to say, "We don't bother to look at the Internet." It has been designed into the very process of looking at markets and competitors. There is just too much information out there to ignore.

A second tornado application has been the Web site, both internally for document distribution, and externally for marketing communications and public relations. Again, it is hard to imagine a major corporation—or even a minor one—saying, "We don't have a Web site and don't intend to have one either." Yet, if you challenged businesses as to whether the expense of such a decision is justified, they might be hard-pressed to answer. Indeed, that is a prime signal for a tornado market—when customers adopt not because it is cost-effective but because everybody else is—they can't afford not to.

Finally, there are the people armed with browsers who are coming to those Web sites. Business usage represents part of this traffic, to be sure, but we do not think that it has reached tornado proportions.

Instead, we think the bulk of the traffic is personal and largely explorational, as when new cell phone subscribers call you from their cars—because they can. The motivation for the most part is personal, be it for education, entertainment, social interaction, or the like—and it is all based on charging no fees beyond access charges.

Nonetheless, there is gold in these hills. These personal users, or "eyeballs," as the industry has come to call them, are driving the first serious economic returns from the Web, as Web site owners convert them to cash by selling advertising space. It is not yet clear how effective this advertising is, or even how to measure its reach and results, but it is close enough to existing marketing models to attract at least pilot marketing programs.

The activity, thus, is commerce-oriented but not yet transaction-driven. That is, buying on the Web is still in its infancy, but companies are actively investing to create and develop relationships with customers and prospects in this new forum. Many of these relationships are post-sales, and with customer retention being such a major theme in business strategy today, we continue to expect lots of additional investment in this relationship-building domain. At the same time, early returns from the automobile, package delivery, and travel and hospitality industries suggest that the Web is also having a pre-sales impact, as prospective customers use it to browse, query, and seek buying assistance. As these patterns become increasingly well understood, we think they will stampede the entire pragmatist herd onto the Web. Few things are more motivating for change than the fear businesses have that some competitor is somewhere stealing a prospective customer that should have been theirs.

THE BOWLING ALLEY

Turning to niche markets, where customers adopt new technologies before the mass market in general, we are seeing a number of them forming. Perhaps the most robust is software distribution, both intra- and inter-company. As Internet speeds increase, it is becoming increasingly practical to distribute updates to existing software as well as whole programs, particularly in a client/server architecture where hosts of PCs and their users are being managed from a central site. In commercial transactions, buying software over the Internet with a credit card is becoming increasingly straightforward for the home user, and this is one area where e-commerce, if it hasn't crossed the chasm yet, will shortly.

Another bowling alley niche is self-service support for common human resources (HR) queries and simple transactions, such as selecting a health plan option, updating a personnel file to change the number of income tax deductions, or looking up the status of one's 401K plan. As companies have downsized, phone support for these transactions has become increasingly hard to justify, and frankly, like bank tellers cashing checks, adds little value. It is a perfect match for companies where most people use PCs or have access to an Internet kiosk. We're not sure just how many of these applications have actually entered the bowling alley, but we believe they are part of the general migration to the Intranet in corporate America.

Finally, the beginnings of what everyone expects to be a tornado market in the not-too-distant future are being seen in early "virtual communities." One thing that America Online's experience to date has taught everyone is that consumers love to chat. In business, a comparable phenomenon occurs on the Web sites of industry associations or narrowly defined vertical markets, where the people coming to the site have interests and needs not broadly shared (as in www.solidwaste.com—a real site, honest!). In the past, such micro-marketing has been impractical because vertically segmented communities are typically so geographically dispersed that one could not cost-effectively maintain a focus on them. But on the Internet there is no distance. Long-term, therefore, the opportunity to move to a world of pervasive one-on-one marketing is huge.

THE CHASM

Still moving from right to left in the Adoption Life Cycle, we are now at the chasm, where we see a number of compelling applications that are, at present, caught betwixt and between. As taxpayers, we put Internet-enabled public services highest on our list, since we believe they would provide greater satisfaction at lower cost. State and local governments in aggregate, however, tend to be late adopters, so we think these will be a while in coming.

Software to facilitate project collaboration and information content for sale, on the other hand, have been actively championed by early adopters for some time now. The former, however, is running aground for lack of a social context—the world is still struggling to develop good models for conducting collaboration in a leveraged way. The value of database content, on the other hand, is well understood but has been set back by the flood of free information on the Web. For the time being, it is not clear to people what, if anything, they should have to pay for, and that is blocking the commercialization of databases.

THE EARLY MARKET

Bringing our survey to a close, at the very front end of the life cycle are a number of world-changing opportunities that we expect will drive massive investment in a whole host of Internet-focused enterprises—but not yet.

One of the most promising ideas here is self-service technical support, which is gaining strong adoption within the high-tech sector and may well be across the chasm in that niche by the time you read this. Service-seeking customers and supply-chain partners who are Internet-comfortable welcome the opportunity to get information on their own. Not only does this lower the cost of support, it keeps people from having to endure lengthy periods of being on hold on the telephone. And we are seeing some sites let their customers talk directly to each other to further supplement the technical-support experience. Finally, the traffic of self-service lends itself eventually to cross-selling and then self-service sales, which is the experience that Cisco Systems has had with its Web site.

That leads us to a truly killer app in this space—supply-chain commerce. The promise here is to go after the kinds of cost-reduction gains that traditional EDI (electronic data interchange) has amply demonstrated are possible and make them available to a much broader range of industries via an Internet-enabled EDI. This would eliminate a huge amount of low-value, high-cost paperwork that currently taxes most business transactions. If one could take, say, just one-quarter of 1% of the total cost of distribution for the gross national product, such savings could drive a round of purchases that would provide provender for more than a few gorillas.

A second potential mega-market is one that has been in the press from day one; namely, the restructuring of some portion of consumer buying to take place over the Web. TV shopping networks have already demonstrated that people will adopt alternatives to going to the store, and early successes from Amazon.com in books, 1-800-FLOWERS in the florist trade, Auto-by-Tel in automobile reselling, and Dell and Gateway in PC distribution are encouraging indeed. But in most industries for now, buying-transaction volumes, as opposed to information requests, are relatively minuscule.

Third, as the network computer opportunity comes into focus, it appears that it, along with the Internet, has the potential to reengineer the classroom. At some price per seat, it becomes not only possible but economically desirable for every student and teacher to interact with a classroom- or school-based server which, in turn, will be hooked into a universe of supplementary resources. There is a Gutenberg-sized impact in this paradigm shift, but the ratio of returns to costs has to improve some in order to be compelling.

Finally, as bandwidth on the Internet continues to increase, the idea that consumers could receive interactive live programming and conduct conversations by voice and video points to increasingly feasible markets. At present, however, this market, like the others just surveyed, is still very much in the early stages of development, where a single major new customer or product announcement constitutes a news story. They are a long way from being gorilla-game investment candidates.

That brings to a close our survey of market drivers for the Internet as we see them. Now the question is, how can we leverage these drivers via the gorilla game?

THE GORILLA GAME AND THE INTERNET INVESTOR

Before we turn to our specific recommendations, we need to make clear that most typical Internet investments are *not* gorilla-game investments. As a result, the portfolio that follows really is not an "Internet portfolio" as much as it is a gorilla-game portfolio that leverages Internet-related market demands. Here's what's going on.

The bulk of investment interest in the Internet has shifted from the first wave of deployment to a second wave. The first, which drove the gorilla game chronicled in our chapter on Cisco Systems and networking hardware, focused on the deployment enabling technologies. The second wave is focused on the applications that the Internet enables. A great number of these applications fall into the category we call *transaction services*. We discussed this category in Chapter 5, and noted that, exciting though it may be, it does not participate in gorilla-game dynamics because it is not based on the deployment of proprietary architectures with high switching costs. We need to take up that issue again here.

Some of our early readers who are Internet investors have pushed back strongly on this thesis, in two areas. First, if an investment rule keeps you out of a lot of hot investments, what good is it? And second, there are lots of switching costs on the Internet that do create gorilla-like effects, and we are simply being too conservative in our approach.

In responding to the first of these issues, we will fall back on the needs of the private investors seeking to create financial independence for themselves and their families. These investors do not need to get into a lot of hot investments. They need to build their nest egg and be darned sure they don't lose it. So, while we have no quarrel with more aggressive strategies for other folks, we'll stick by our guns for our target reader.

More interesting is the challenge that maybe gorilla-game dynamics really are at work on the Internet and that we can therefore broaden our field of investment without violating our charter. The case for this comes from analyzing the growing power of the "strong sites" on the Internet. Sites with strong brands are proving they, like TV shows, can attract visitors with desirable demographic profiles. This is not being lost on the advertising community.

In the case of the search sites, moreover, vendors are paying increasingly high premiums to get privileged positions in order to intercept requests for information related to their product such that their ads can be attached to the responding Web page. Indeed, it used to be that sites had to buy content from vendors; now people beg to be listed. And as Internet users return to search sites over and over, some sites are creating "personal Web pages" for these frequent guests, which in turn leads to real switching costs. All of these elements are giving the market-share leader in this category, Yahoo, a significant source of power. Brand loyalty, network effects, switching costs—isn't this gorilla power?

We don't think it is. We do think it is power, and we do think it is investable; but no, it is not gorilla power. There simply is not the level of security in these investments that there is in a gorilla game. Therefore the rules of the gorilla game—in particular, that you not only can, but should, consolidate your investments into a single company per category—are not good rules for this sector.

In sum, then, there is an overlap of the two communities of gorilla-game investors and Internet investors, but it is smaller than one might think, as the portfolio we are about to unfold will demonstrate.

GORILLA-GAME OPPORTUNITIES INSIDE THE TORNADO

The rules of the gorilla game tell the investor to seek out enabling software and hardware opportunities inside the tornado and application software opportunities in the bowling alley. So let us look again at the applications in just these two phases of the life cycle. In each case, we will consider the opportunities created for the various categories of products within the computer systems sector. (For those who need a quick refresher on these categories, the material is covered in Chapter 5.) Here are our views.

Market research and *competitive analysis* are pretty much identical in terms of the demands they put on Internet products and services. In our view they will not create demand for any new application software. Researchers will make do instead with browsing and printing—no new markets there—and then do their analysis and summaries off-line on a PC—again, using software they already have. On the hardware side we do expect these researchers will upgrade their modems, which should add fuel to a U.S. Robotics gorilla play in 56 Kbps modems, particularly if the company can get its standard adopted over Rockwell's. (The alternative is for this market to revert to a nonproprietary standard, as has every previous modem market, transforming U.S. Robotics back into a king rather than a gorilla.)

Web-focused research and analysis will also drive demand for better search engines—something of interest to mass market consumers as well. Web search engines are a combination of enabling software and Web directories, a tornado play in which Yahoo, Excite, Lycos, Infoseek, and Alta Vista are all visible, with Yahoo the dominating player. But as we have repeatedly noted, these engines control no proprietary interface, so switching costs are low. It is just barely possible someone could come up with a radically new proprietary set of search algorithms—the problem certainly could use some more horsepower applied to it—but we do not know of any. So we see this as a king/prince/serf market based largely on branding, and not a gorilla game.

Document distribution and management are at the heart of a huge deployment of Internet-enabled infrastructure inside major corporations. These intranets have been the focus of the enabling software competition between Netscape and Microsoft, and that gorilla game will continue for some time to come. The fight is over both the browser and the server software, which we would categorize collectively as communications applications. The reason Microsoft seems so well positioned against Netscape is that it has a strong position in a second underlying battle between two operating systems, Unix and Windows NT. Because it was able to displace Novell Netware, NT is perceived as the de facto standard OS for workgroups. Most corporations, therefore, are inclined to expand NT's role to incorporate the Web-server as well, in the hopes of keeping the overall network administration task down to a minimum. To the degree Microsoft wins the OS war for the workgroup Web-server, it can use its control over the underlying standard to maneuver Netscape out of position in the browser battle. Meanwhile, the computer hardware vendors— Sun with Unix, Compaq and Digital with NT, and HP and IBM with offers in both camps—all are experiencing tornado demand for their server products. But no server hardware has a gorilla-game position: They are all playing the royalty game of king vs. prince.

Moving from intranets to "extranets," the outward-facing applications on the Internet, and specifically looking at *marketing communications* and *public relations*, much of the underlying infrastructure is similar to that of intranets, except that here the OS advantage leans more to Unix than NT. This is because the Internet was initially a Unix phenomenon, and all its core routing technologies have grown out of those standards. Sun is particularly strong here, and despite the fact that it is playing a royalty game, it still has to be considered as a tornado investment.

But the genuine gorilla game in this space is being played over the router-dominated networking hardware infrastructure. The demand to generate more and more bandwidth is insatiable, as the number of Web sites and the amount of network traffic continues to escalate exponentially. Here Cisco has an extremely strong gorilla position based on its dominant market share and proprietary routing protocols.

Another hypergrowth category at present is tools for creating and maintaining Web sites and Web content. As far as software development is concerned, the Java language is inside the tornado, and there is a tensely balanced effort within the Unix community to keep the standard open even as each vendor, and particularly Sun, seeks to bend it to proprietary advantage. The irony is that the Unix community could compete against Microsoft better if Java were under a single vendor's control, but such a capitulation seems far-fetched indeed. The closest approach might come from a software vendor gaining dominant market share of the Java application development tools marketplace, a long-shot possibility for SunSoft, Symantec, or even Microsoft.

At the same time, while Java is inside the tornado in the development community, it's important to note that *Java-based applications* are still in the early market, a distinction that may ultimately spell the difference between Sun's success or failure with Java. Microsoft, in particular, seeks to bring to bear its huge library of existing applications against the intrusion of this new threat, while at the same time seeking to coopt the Java language into its proprietary infrastructure. It makes for a very exciting competition, and to the degree that Sun's stock price is tied to Java, a possible gorilla game in the making.

Finally, exposing so many corporations' information to such public access has created a burgeoning demand for security systems, at the hardware level with the firewall, where Checkpoint has had great success, and at the middleware level with antivirus utilities from McAfee and encryption software from Security Dynamics. None of these three markets has become a gorilla-game play as yet, although RSA encryption from Security Dynamics is approaching that status; but they bear watching, as does an additional level of middleware focused on certification and authentication, which is opening up the game to new players like Cylink.

On the other end of all these systems are John and Jane Q. Public, who are coming to the Internet in increasing numbers for *personal education and entertainment*. This is driving up the number of subscribers for Internet service providers and for on-line services like America Online. These are transaction services plays that are of great interest but are not, as we have argued already, gorilla games.

To sum up, the opportunities currently inside the tornado include:

1: Browser and Web-server software, where the key rivals are Netscape and Microsoft.

2: 56 kbps modems, where the key rivals are U.S. Robotics vs. Rockwell.

3: Web-server hardware, where there is a royalty game on the Unix side that Sun is winning.

4: Java application development tools, with interesting opportunities for Sun, Symantec, and Microsoft.

5: A security systems game with opportunities for McAfee, Checkpoint, Security Dynamics, and Cylink, among others.

In all of these cases there is tornado-class market growth in the fourth quarter of 1997, so we will process each one through our gorilla-game rule set. But before we do, let's see if we can add any other candidates to our list by looking into the bowling alley.

Gorilla-Game Opportunities in the Bowling Alley

As you will recall, while the gorilla game calls for waiting until the tornado when it comes to investing in enabling software and hardware, it advocates getting an earlier start when it comes to application software. With this in mind, let us go back and take a look at our bowling alley markets for such opportunities.

Software distribution is not an application. It is instead a market driver for enabling software. We think there will be a tornado in this space, driving up demand for significant extensions to existing systems management infrastructure, and we would start an immediate tornado watch on this sector. But until it actually goes inside the tornado, we would counsel patience.

Human resources, by contrast, most definitely is an application software market. However, it just went through a client/server tornado, with PeopleSoft coming out as the gorilla. Our guess is that the incumbent vendors will be able to meet the new market demands by "Web-enabling" their current client/server applications and thus leave no opening for starting a new gorilla game.

Supply-chain partner support, however, is just different enough that we think there is a genuinely new opportunity that has not as yet been claimed by anyone. There are several approaches in play at present. The enterprise resource planning (ERP) vendors—SAP, Oracle, Baan, and the like—will try to go intercompany by Web-enabling their current intracompany offers. But these applications do not yet lend themselves easily to intercompany business processes. This, in turn, creates a window of opportunity for a second set of supply-chain application vendors whose software complements ERP—including Manugistics, I2, and Red Pepper (purchased by PeopleSoft) and Datalogix (purchased by Oracle). They may be able to get a jump on their bigger siblings because they are designed from the ground floor up as intercompany applications. A similar category of application software vendors offers a different kind of complementary support to ERP, this time for complex order configuration. Trilogy and Calico are leaders here, and like the supply chain vendors, they have intercompany structure built in to their software and therefore have interesting chances in a new Web-centric game.

There is a caveat with both these games, although it does not pose an investment hazard. A highly possible outcome to either or both is for a deep-pocketed ERP vendor to buy up one or another gorilla candidate in order to subsume it into a larger back office gorilla game. The earlier in the game this happens, the lower the return to the shareholders of the acquired company. But fighting off acquisition may lead to a competitor being acquired, and the combined forces of that competitor with a new deep-pocketed owner may overthrow what was before a winning position. Such are the challenges of the gorilla game, for management and shareholders alike.

Industry associations and *virtual communities*, to date, have made do entirely with the existing World Wide Web as their application software. Going forward, as these communities build databases and seek to interact in more structured ways, we can expect a new market category to emerge. For now, however, there are no application vendors addressing this need. Moreover, because many associations have limited resources for technical initiatives, and because communities of interest have to rely primarily on volunteers, it is likely that Internet service providers will take over this category with pay-by-the-click outsourcing offers, thereby blocking development of an application software market.

To sum up, we think the only viable sector for a bowling alley entrance into an Internet gorilla game in the last quarter of 1997 is supply-chain partner support. Here we see two gorilla games, as follows:

1: Supply-chain management, where the leading candidates are Manugistics and I2 (PeopleSoft purchased Red Pepper).

2: Order configuration, where the leading candidates are Trilogy and Calico.

The order configuration companies, however, are still private, so we will confine ourselves to the supply-chain management category.

ANSWERING THE TORNADO WATCH QUESTIONS

Most of the categories we have chosen to look at more closely are already inside the tornado, but supply-chain management is not. So let us use it to illustrate how to work with the tornado-watch question set.

1: *What emerging value chains are nearing the tornado stage of adoption?*

A. Which ones are too early or too late?

B. Which one should be the focus for the rest of this exercise?

We looked at a number of different value chains and have decided that supply-chain management is neither too early nor too late. That will be our focus.

2: *Can this value chain develop into a tornado mass market?*

A. If so, what conditions are currently holding it back?

B. Are these constraining conditions likely to be removed?

C. If so, when is the *last remaining constraint* likely to be removed, and by whom?

Much of the business strategy taught in the leading graduate schools today is drawing attention to supply chains as a source of competitive advantage, so we believe that supply-chain management will get a generous share of buying attention from major corporations. All manufacturing organizations participate in supply chains, as do many service organizations, so there is ample scope for a mass market. And as the EDI market has already shown, the opportunity to extract costs without decreasing value is demonstrably present. For all these reasons, we think a tornado will occur.

What is holding back the market is complexity on both fronts.

A. On the adoption front, supply-chain management requires adopting a new frame of reference, where each business in the chain must focus on the entire chain's operations rather than just its own.

B. On the implementation front, it requires a chain of multiple independent companies to converge on a single set of standards, protocols, and interfaces.

Both these sources of complexity are daunting. However, efforts to reduce them are under way, and in two sectors there appear to be winds swirling. Manugistics has achieved a dominant position in the consumer packaged goods arena, and I2 has achieved equally dramatic success in the high-tech sector. With a single vendor at the core of any sector, and a strong value proposition driving the market, the constraining conditions are likely to crumble.

Our best guess is that the second constraint, the need to get groups of companies interoperating on a common software base, is the last remaining constraint. If either company beats the other one to the punch by a substantial margin, it should be able to get a definitive lead. If they both succeed in roughly the same time frame, the market may well split in two, with each dominating a smaller sector for the long haul.

- *Is the tornado happening?*

    A. Rapid adoption
    B. Replicatable solution delivery
    C. Scalable marketing

As we discussed above, not quite yet. But these are the criteria for our tornado watch. In the meantime, we think there are sufficiently strong niche opportunities for both companies to sustain good returns even as chimps, so we are ready to buy in now.

- *Is this a gorilla game or a royalty game?*

    A. Proprietary architectures
    B. High switching costs

As we discussed in Chapters 4 and 5, application software that is server-based is virtually unclonable. It is thus inherently proprietary and produces high switching costs. This means application software games are highly likely to be gorilla games, as would be the case here.

- *What category of technology is involved?*

    A. Applications
    B. Enabling software
    C. Enabling hardware

The category is application software, hence our willingness to engage the market in the bowling alley.

Let the games begin!

We are now going to build our gorilla-game portfolio for the Internet. The date is September 17, 1997. At the outset we will not be able to invoke all the rules definitively, but where we cannot we will speculate about possible future developments that would cause us to. Going forward, we will maintain our fund status at the following Web site: www.gorillagame.org. There we will either crow, or eat crow.

We should note right here that, when we have to eat crow, we will no doubt attempt to slather it with a sauce of explanation and self-justification. This is a time-honored activity among all serious purveyors of stock market advice. On the other hand, should we get to serve crow, we will of course dress up as if it were a Thanksgiving feast. In short, we will act shamelessly in either case, and we can only trust that you, the discriminating reader, will penetrate all our machinations and skewer us good and proper.

TEN RULES FOR PLAYING THE GORILLA GAME _____

Rule 1. If the category is application software, begin buying in the bowling alley.

Under this rule we are going to make investments in the category of supply-chain management. As a category, it is more than a decade old and has, in EDI, a prior analog to validate its market value. Second, in its mature form it is an inherently intercompany activity, making it less vulnerable to displacement by any single ERP vendor. And third, it does leverage the Internet in a way that is very much core to its strategy.

Rule 2. If the category is enabling hardware or software, begin buying after the tornado has formed.

Under this rule we are going to make investments in the following categories:

1: Browser and Web-server software.

2: Security software.

We are not investing in 56 kbps modems, server hardware, or development tools.

Our reason for holding back on 56 kbps modems is that there are no pure plays to invest in. The battle is between U.S. Robotics on the one hand and a coalition of vendors supporting Rockwell on the other. But with U.S. Robotics merging with 3COM, and with the other standard spread across multiple vendors, we see no easy way to play this game. In the server hardware world, we think the competition will revert to a royalty game, not one controlled by any proprietary architecture. And finally, we see development tools as "bowling alley forever" in their user base, albeit the applications they create may get mass market adoption.

Our reason for investing in browser and Web-server software is that it clearly is a gorilla game, with only two major candidates in play and the likelihood of a third entering now being relatively small. Security software is a much more fluid situation, and probably we should wait a quarter or two, but book deadlines being what they are, we would rather jump into than stay out of this category. It almost certainly will be a gorilla game, as every previous play in this category has been, the reason in part being perhaps that you cannot have "open" security.

Rule 3. Buy a basket comprising *all* the gorilla candidates— usually at least two, sometimes three, and normally no more than four companies.

Our initial buy orders will include the following companies trading, as of September 15, 1997, at the following stock prices:

Supply Chain Management:

I2	41
Manugistics	36.125

Browser and Web-server software:

Microsoft	136.375
Netscape	41.625

Security Software:

Checkpoint	26.0625
Cylink	15
McAfee	58.5
Security Dynamics	35.75

As you can see, our basket for security software is a bit full because we are acting a little ahead of schedule, with Cylink in particular being a bet on the come. The category as a whole is still shaking out, and in a pure game, as noted above, we would have waited a quarter or two to see how this plays out further before investing. Additionally, in the interest of full disclosure, we wish to note the following:

---

1. The Chasm Group where Geoff Moore and Tom Kippola work has had significant strategy consulting engagements with Manugistics, Microsoft, and Cylink. Moreover, several of these engagements have led to ongoing relationships with the firms involved. The group has also conducted a number of speaking engagements for Cisco and Intel (which we are about to add to our portfolio below). Although we have tried to remain unbiased in our analysis here, there is no doubt that these management teams have had a big impact on the way we view their company's prospects.

2. In light of the above, we can foresee the possibility of ethical issues arising out of making recommendations from which we or our clients might profit in some inappropriate way. Therefore we want to make clear that we are constructing the gorilla game fund *as a hypothetical construct only*, and will not in fact be creating such an investment entity. Rather, we will use it as a model portfolio to provide a test case for the ideas in this book.

3. All of the above notwithstanding, we take our ideas extremely seriously and will act as if we have in fact invested our families' financial future in these decisions.

Rule 4. Hold gorilla stocks for the long term. Sell only on proven substitution threat.

We are going to use this rule to introduce two other companies into our portfolio at the outset—Intel and Cisco. We are not going to use it to introduce Oracle.

We are holding back from investing in Oracle for several reasons. First, its gorilla game has been in play longer than the others, and the company has not renewed its markets in the way that Intel and Cisco have been able to do. Second, the company's strategy is taking it toward more complexity, not less, deriving an increasing proportion of its revenue and profit growth from consulting services that do not participate in gorilla-game dynamics. Third, the company is under attack in the low-complexity space from Microsoft and has yet to make a definitive response that will secure its gorilla position from this new form of competition. And finally, the company's most visible strategic initiative, Network Computing, has yet to cross the chasm. All in all, we still think Oracle is a very strong company and a sound investment, but it does not map as well to the gorilla-game profile at this time as it has in the past.

Intel and Cisco, by contrast, do. Both are strongly positioned in their home markets with little immediate threat, although in Cisco's case there's a need to stay very nimble as routing technologies mutate. And both are leveraging gorilla positions to aggressively attack adjacent markets, whether the new opportunities be gorilla or royalty games. We think both companies have strong gorilla futures, and we want them in our portfolio.

Our initial buy order has been supplemented therefore with the following companies trading at the following stock prices:

Grandfather gorillas:

Cisco	74.5
Intel	95.81

In addition, we are going to use this rule to "double up" our holdings in Microsoft. We think that no other company on the planet has its gorilla advantages, and therefore we are going to buy twice as much Microsoft as anything else.

Rule 5. Hold application software chimp stocks as long as they exhibit potential for further market expansion.

This is the rule we shall invoke as we watch the progress of Manugistics and I2.

Rule 6. Hold kings and princes lightly, selling individual stocks on a stumble and the category upon deceleration of hypergrowth.

It is possible that one or more of the subcategories in security software could become defined around an open systems interface, thereby transforming the market from a gorilla to a royalty game. At the moment, however, our portfolio has been created to stay clear of royalty games in general. Our reasons are that these games, while potentially lucrative, are hard to predict and require nimble exits, precisely the kind of volatility we are at pains to reduce.

Rule 7. Once it becomes clear to you that a company will never become a gorilla, sell its stock.

Many would argue that this rule applies to Netscape and that we should not have included it in our portfolio. The problem is, going forward, more and more companies will have to compete with Microsoft, and the turbulence that creates is going to be part of the gorilla game. Netscape is still positioned at or near the center of the Internet tornado, and our policy is to not to predict outcomes of marketplace competition, only to react to them after they settle out. We simply do not think the browser and Web software battle is settled.

Rule 8. Money taken out of non-gorilla stocks should immediately be reinvested in the remaining gorilla candidates.

As noted in Chapter 5, this is the key principle behind our ongoing portfolio management policy: *Reduce risk through consolidation, not diversification*. There is a vision of the future that would say, Hey, beat the rush, and put all your money in Microsoft now. We actually take that scenario quite seriously because the natural outcome of the gorilla game is to have increasingly greater holdings in increasingly fewer stocks. But we believe that there is no need to beat the rush, and that we should leverage the Darwinian selection processes of the market to ensure that we do indeed end up with a "portfolio of the fittest."

Rule 9. In a gorilla collision, hold your gorilla candidates until there has been a definitive outcome.

This is another occasion for us to second-guess the Netscape investment because there is no question it has been in a gorilla collision with Microsoft. And because Netscape is a relatively immature gorilla, and Microsoft is an established big bad gorilla (the biggest baddest ever, as far as we can see), the early returns do not look good for Netscape.

Indeed, the three of us are not of one mind on this issue. Tom is adamant that Netscape is ultimately going to lose out big to Microsoft and his arguments are highly persuasive. Paul and Geoff are holding out, but more on theoretical grounds than practical ones.

The theory is that in a marketplace as dynamic as the Internet, changes come quickly and from unanticipated directions. There is still a huge amount of unexpressed energy and opportunity in this marketplace, and extrapolating today's power positions before they have been actualized is riskier than normal. Evolution is an adaptive process, and in times of hypergrowth, no one can anticipate its outcomes. If we had to call the outcome of the game today, we would side with Tom's conclusions. But we don't think it is time to call the game. We think we should let the market do its work, let the competition for survival of the fittest actually play out, and then adjust our portfolio accordingly once a victory has been won. In other words, don't predict—respond.

But investment is more than theory. It is also based on intuition and experience, something we all respect, hence our conflicted state. What we have compromised upon is keeping Netscape in the portfolio, but giving Tom I-told-you-so privileges if it tanks, and Paul and Geoff the same if it soars.

Rule 10. Most news has nothing to do with the gorilla game. Learn to ignore it.

On September 17, 1997, the local business press for the San Francisco Bay Area reported the following headlines. Here's how we reacted to them in terms of our gorilla-game agenda:

- *Jobs takes interim CEO title at Apple.*
Ignore. Apple is not part of any gorilla game in play.

- *Intel announces multi-level cell flash memory (the 4-state bit).*
Ignore. Flash memory is not inside a tornado at present, and this development is very early-market.

- *Microsoft slips launch of Windows 98.*
File away. This could significantly reduce Microsoft's earnings in some future quarter, causing its stock to take a hit. We want to buy Microsoft on any downturn for the foreseeable future because we think it is the archetypal gorilla.

- *Consumer prices modest despite gas price hike.*
Ignore.

- *Industrial output soars.*
Ignore.

- *Personal bankruptcies recede.*

Ignore.

- *Inventories up slightly.*

Ignore.

- *Netscape fixes the flaw on redesigned Web site.*

Ignore. This is not about anything that will affect the balance of power in Netscape's market.

- *Oracle profits off sharply.*

Read on to discover that this was an accounting charge and that the company made the Wall Street estimates. File away as another gorilla quarter for Oracle.

- *Pointcast to upgrade "push."*

Read and file away. Push technologies may create a tornado opportunity in the future, although the current received wisdom is that they will be absorbed by Netscape and Microsoft.

- *PC shipments in U.S. show surprising surge.*

Ignore. PCs have long since moved onto Main Street. The surge is relative to forecast, not a tornado surprise.

- *E*Trade outperforms its stats.*

Read and file away. E*Trade is a transaction services company so will never be a gorilla-game investment. But e-commerce is going to be a tornado that may create gorilla-game opportunities for software companies, and E*Trade may be a leading indicator of tornado activity.

- *Dow climbs 175, bonds soar.*

Ignore. No market index is of any importance to the gorilla game.

WRAP-UP

We have illustrated how we have picked our specific companies. All that remains is to allocate our funds across this set of investment candidates. Our approach is to weight by category first and then make adjustments as needed. Going in, we favor weighting all the categories equally, and allocating funds equally within categories. Going forward, we will use gorilla-game rules to move funds within and between categories.

Assuming a $10,000 capital base, here is our test portfolio:

Table 12.1 The Gorilla Game Test Portfolio—September 15, 1997

Supply Chain Management		**$2500**			
I2	$1250	@	41	30 shares	$1230
Manugistics	$1250	@	36.125	34 shares	$1228
Browser and web server		**$2500**			
Microsoft	$1250	@	136.375	9 shares	$1227
Netscape	$1250	@	41.625	30 shares	$1249
Security		**$2500**			
Checkpoint	$625	@	26.0625	23 shares	$599
Cylink	$625	@	15	41 shares	$615
McAfee	$625	@	58.5	10 shares	$585
Security Dynamics	$625	@	35.75	17 shares	$608
Grandfather gorillas		**$2500**			
Cisco	$833	@	74.5	11 shares	$820
Intel	$833	@	95.81	8 shares	$766
Microsoft	$834	@	136.375	6 shares	$818
Total					**$9745**

This is what we will track.

Epilogue

That's it from our end.

Just to recap the journey, we began by "Setting the Context," which took on the challenge of explaining what makes high-tech markets and the high-tech stock market so volatile. The short answer to that question, as we saw, is *tornadoes*. What we learned at the same time is that, in the eye of these tornadoes, a *gorilla* is often born. That gorilla is destined to enjoy competitive advantages unlike any others in the marketplace. And those marketplace advantages, in turn, generate stock market returns that are also unparalleled.

With that context in place, we turned to "The Rules of the Game," which translated these ideas into a practical investment model. After laying out a map of the high-tech sector, we explained how to stalk tornadoes and, once found, how to capture the gorillas within them. In the process we laid out our *Ten Rules for Playing the Gorilla Game*.

In Part Three, "Case Studies," we "played out" the gorilla game in three situations, one from the past (relational databases), one in the present (networking hardware), and one in the future (customer support software). In each chapter we sought to validate the principles of the gorilla game while at the same time being true to the uncertainties of the moment. A key takeaway from this section is that you do not have to have perfect timing or perfect judgment to be successful with this investment approach.

Finally, in "Passing the Baton," we have sought to point gorilla-game investors to the information sources and to offer a sample gorilla-game portfolio, all just to help you get started with your own private gorilla fund.

From now on it is up to you and the market.

In parting we might all reflect upon how blessed we are, especially in the United States, with capital markets that lend themselves to private investors. In one of our early chapters, we noted that for gorilla-game theory to work, you need equity markets which have low costs of transactions, broad dissemination of information, and high legal integrity. In each of these areas, there have been strong initiatives in the last decade to improve what already were excellent systems:

- Today, with entities like E-Schwab and E*Trade, private investors enjoy the lowest trading costs in the history of the market. And with NASDAQ restructuring its pricing mechanisms, the spread between bid and asked has been narrowed to the further benefit of the private investor.
- In the realm of information dissemination, with the meteoric rise of the Internet, there is almost nothing that the professional investor can learn that the private investor can't ferret out almost as quickly. The bank of tools we advocated in Chapter 11 is just the tip of a gargantuan iceberg, and there is no way that anyone can restrict anyone else from getting at that information.
- Finally, in the realm of ethics and legal integrity, U.S. markets lead the world in policing their own ranks, and the consent decree that set up the new watchdog functions at NASDAQ simply puts in place the next generation of this surveillance. This is a critical domain for us all to protect because as long as U.S. markets enjoy the trust of the world, they will operate to the benefit of us all.

Now is also a good time to reflect upon how much all of high tech, for sure all of the computer industry, owes to the semiconductor industry, and specifically to its ongoing ability to meet Moore's Law of doubling the price/performance of its chips every eighteen months. It is this continued influx of "free" price/performance gains that generates the fountain of discontinuous innovations that spawn the tornadoes that create the gorillas that generate the funds for all our portfolios. We should remember in all humility that Moore's Law is not, in fact, a law at all, but rather a testimony to the creativity and drive of these scientists and engineers.

And finally, we should acknowledge that at the core of all this wealth creation is not a set of financial instruments but rather a vast network of teams, each working to bring some new value chain into existence, to ramp it up to global market capability, to bring the next generation of products and services to customers and consumers. The high-tech sector represents a new manifestation of the human spirit in business activity, one that crosses boundaries both organizationally and geographically in unprecedented ways. Like CNN broadcasts, high-tech businesses are breaking down barriers that have held back the full expression of talent and resources around the globe. We all know that technology as technology has the power to change the quality of human life dramatically. But maybe now it is time to acknowledge that the practice of high-tech business does too.

In parting, we would like to wish each of our readers good fortune in your particular investments, regardless of what path you follow, and to invite those of you who go forward with the gorilla game to come visit us from time to time at our web site at www.gorillagame.org.

Happy hunting from

Geoffrey Moore, Paul Johnson, and Tom Kippola

Index